This book examines fiction and ethnography as related forms for analyzing and exhibiting social life. Focusing on the novels of Nathaniel Hawthorne, Henry James, and Edith Wharton, the study argues that novels and ethnographies collaborated to produce an unstable but powerful master discourse of "culture," a discourse that allowed writers to turn new social energies and fears into particular kinds of authorial expertise. Crossing a range of institutions (anthropology, literature, museums, law) and texts (novels, ethnographies, travel books, social theory), this study allows fiction to take its place in a web of social practices that categorize, display, and regulate what Wharton calls "the customs of the country."

For the functional identity of literature – an identity always hotly contested – the implications are far-reaching. Although belonging to the sphere of high culture, the work of Hawthorne, James, and Wharton was neither a sealed-off aestheticism nor a nostalgic retreat from modern life. Their fiction, Bentley concludes, was part of a broad effort, across the nation and throughout literate American society, to negotiate issues of social control and cohesion through new representations of culture.

CAMBRIDGE STUDIES IN AMERICAN LITERATURE AND CULTURE

THE ETHNOGRAPHY
OF MANNERS

Books in the series

Continued on pages following the Index

THE ETHNOGRAPHY
OF MANNERS

Hawthorne, James, Wharton

NANCY BENTLEY
University of Pennsylvania

CAMBRIDGE
UNIVERSITY PRESS

Published by the Press Syndicate of the University of Cambridge
The Pitt Building, Trumpington Street, Cambridge CB2 IRP
40 West 20th Street, New York, NY 10011-4211, USA
10 Stamford Road, Oakleigh, Melbourne 3166, Australia

First published 1995

Printed in the United States of America

Library of Congress Cataloging-in-Publication Data
Bentley, Nancy, 1961–
The Ethnography of Manners : Hawthorne, James, Wharton / Nancy Bentley.
p. cm. – (Cambridge studies in American literature and culture ; 90)
Includes index.
ISBN 0-521-46190-1 (hardback)
1. American fiction – History and criticism. 2. Hawthorne, Nathaniel, 1804–
1864 – Knowledge – Manners and customs. 3. Wharton, Edith, 1862–1937–
Knowledge – Manners and customs. 4. James, Henry, 1843–1916 – Knowedge
– Manners and customs. 5. Literature and anthropology – United States. 6.
Literature and society – United States. 7. Manners and customs in literature.
8. Ethnology in literature. I. Title. II. Series
PS374.M33B46 1995
813'.409 – dc20 94-3355
CIP

A catalog record for this book is available from the British Library.

ISBN 0-521-46190-1 hardback

For my parents,
Joseph and Barbara

Contents

Acknowledgments

I am indebted to many people for assistance in writing this book. Sacvan Bercovitch offered guidance and support in innumerable ways. His generosity as a teacher, advisor, and reader made the book possible. Philip Fisher provided clarity and encouragement at important junctures. The suggestions and friendship of Susan Mizruchi have left their mark on the book, as has her own exemplary work.

Amy Kaplan's insightful comments helped to shape a number of chapters. I also want to thank Donald Pease and the members of the 1993 Dartmouth Humanities Institute for their heartening responses. I am grateful for the financial support provided by Dartmouth College, the National Endowment for the Humanities, and the Mellon Foundation.

Eric Sundquist and Susan Chang at Cambridge University Press were extraordinarily helpful. The excellent suggestions of an anonymous reader at the press improved this book in important ways. I also want to thank others who read portions of the work and offered assistance of various kinds: Millicent Bell, Lawrence Buell, Eric Cheyfitz, Richard Fox, Leland Monk, Cyrus Patell, Laurel Thatcher Ulrich, Lynn Wardley, and Sue Sun Yom. For a friend in need, Amy Boesky, Lee Monk, and David Suchoff were friends indeed.

My deepest gratitude is for the sustaining help I received from my family. Joseph and Barbara Bentley were ideal supporters. Amy Bentley's comments on Chapter 5 and my conversations with Linda Johnson supplied buoying relief. I want to thank Carol and John Armstrong for their assistance in preparing the index. Jamie Bentley Ulrich arrived in time to turn tedious manuscript preparations into the work of a joyful season. I owe the most to Karl Ulrich, whose support was unfailing.

A different version of Chapter 2 first appeared as "Slaves and Fauns: Hawthorne and the Uses of Primitivism," in *ELH* 57 (1990). I am grateful for permission to reprint.

THE ETHNOGRAPHY
OF MANNERS

CHAPTER I

The equivocation of culture

Of all learned discourse, the ethnological seems to come closest
to a fiction.

–Roland Barthes

After his arrival in London, where he would establish his career as
a novelist, Henry James wrote, "I take possession of the Old World.
I inhale it – I appropriate it." Beginning his fieldwork in the
Trobriand Islands, Bronislaw Malinowski wrote in his diary of
"feelings of ownership": "This island, though not 'discovered' by
me, is for the first time experienced artistically and mastered intel-
lectually."[1] James's life in London, of course, was dramatically different from Malinowski's in the Trobriands, but coupled together,
the quotations point to a striking similarity. In these two ventures –
an American crossing the Atlantic to repossess the Old World, and
an anthropologist mastering a "primitive" world – the language of
colonial discovery is cast in new terms: these travelers come not to
seize lands and people but to write them. Despite their differences,
James's innovations in realist fiction and Malinowski's in ethnography are part of a new way of seeing and writing about social
life that developed in the later nineteenth century. Each writer
refashions an earlier, more provincial genre of manners – the novel
of manners, in one case, and the traveler's customs-and-manners
survey, in the other – to produce a complex professional and international discourse. Each discourse, in turn, fosters for the writer an
enhanced authority over a bounded sphere of culture, an aesthetic
and intellectual "ownership" of manners intended to surpass coars-
er forms of cultural possession. Virtually unknown at the time of
their respective arrivals, James and Malinowski each would become, by way of his books and essays, a new kind of liberal hero,
each becoming an acknowledged expert, a recognized "Master" of

culture. In these two exemplary careers, writing about manners becomes the genesis of a modern liberal authority.[2]

Edith Wharton, who knew both writers personally and read them carefully, would bring to the surface their common strategies by describing her New York "tribes" of the rich, aligning drawing-room culture and ethnographic culture – we might say table manners and tribal manners – as interchangeable idioms. In this way, Wharton reads both James and Malinowski as practitioners of what she would call "a backward glance," a vision of inherited manners as the true site of social origins and transformations, enabling her to telescope the old world of tribal primitivism with the Old World of Europe and the New World's Old World that she calls Old New York, all in opposition to the sphere of modern America but containing the keys to its future as a civilization. Through these permutations, Wharton revises and exhibits manners as the essential, sometimes disguised, rites of social cohesion and punishment rather than as inherent standards of propriety, giving her a new purchase on a particular social body and its powers, transitions, and supposed signs of decline or extinction. This backward glance, then, is anything but glancing. As the remarks by James and Malinowski suggest, it is a vision that "takes possession," that takes up and explains seemingly marginal practices by deciphering a cultural logic hidden in what Wharton calls the "nether side" of the social scene. It is a form of expert observation, realized in writing, that gives the observer mastery over a cultural territory. "Do New York!" As famously prompted by James, Wharton would "do" New York, as he had done cosmopolitan Europe and as Malinowski was simultaneously doing the Trobriand Islands.

But what does it mean for a novelist to master manners in this way, as a venture comparable to the enterprise of writing an ethnography? In the simplest sense, it reminds us that novel writing is a social practice. James's advice to Wharton expressly casts fiction as an activity or process, something one can do to aesthetically "appropriate" a social scene. In its phrasing, James's injunction to "do" New York anticipates Clifford Geertz's emphasis on anthropology as the work of "doing ethnography."[3] In my study, understanding fiction – primarily novels by Hawthorne, James, and Wharton – means understanding what it is to do fiction, what kind of social and aesthetic office it performs. To analyze fiction as a practice, as a way of mastering manners on the page, I explore conver-

gences between novels and ethnographic texts and their collaboration in helping to produce our modern discourse of culture. In turn,
the collaboration opens for us new historical and critical perspectives on the particular mastery of manners that is fiction writing.

In my use of it, however, the domain of "culture" has neither the
intellectual coherence nor the historical sovereignty that my claim
of collaboration might seem to suggest. For Malinowski and James,
writing about manners seemed to promise a formal mastery of
culture, but of late the discourse of culture has been discussed as
presenting us with a "predicament" far more than a secure possession. Even as culture has become a ruling category of thought, it
has exemplified with unsettling clarity the "crisis in representation" that Edward Said notes is symptomatic, even normative, for
the human sciences in our time. "Culture is a deeply compromised
idea I cannot yet do without": this declaration in James Clifford's
study of a constellation of twentieth-century ethnography, literature, and art, entitled *The Predicament of Culture*, points to a rather
remarkable state of affairs. It suggests that the culture concept has
both an enduring analytic centrality and a new instability – that it
is at once foundational and equivocal.[4]

A century ago, few would have predicted a "deeply compromised" status for the idea of culture. Wharton's smooth suturing of
the imagery of tribal rituals and bourgeois manners implies a new
compatibility between what had been historically antagonistic
strains of the culture idea. By splicing together the roles of novelist
and ethnographer to create a figure she calls "the drawing-room
naturalist," Wharton appears to transcend blithely the distinction
between a humanist tradition, in which culture signifies a set of
prized Western values that advance human perfectibility, and a
sociological sense of culture as the web of institutions and lived
relations that structure any human community, what E. B. Tylor
announced in 1871 as "culture in its wide ethnographic sense."
Within this expanded sense of culture, savage and civilized worlds
can share, at long last, a common language of interpretation. Raymond Williams, for instance, asserts just such a historical merging
of these disparate notions of culture in his groundbreaking work,
Culture and Society (1958), where he argues that Tylor's anthropological understanding of culture as an organic "whole way of life" has
its roots in a rich literary tradition and is "continuous from Cole-
ridge and Carlyle," but that "what was a personal assertion of

value has become a general intellectual method."[5] Like Williams's study, my argument in this book assumes that ethnographic culture shares a kinship with the more belletristic lineage of Arnoldian culture, but the intellectual history narrated by Williams, in which the "culture" of social scientists is the undisturbed outgrowth of the "culture" articulated by poets and critics, offers little to account for the current perplexities in cultural and literary studies.

It does not account for the contradictions, for instance, in the way notions of culture are now deployed in arguments of virtually all political stripes. How it is that culture is invoked as a signature of authenticity (every genuine folk or people has its own pattern of culture) at the same time that it can serve as the mark of the inauthentic (the merely "culturally constructed" inferiority of women)? Why is culture a category of both the local (Balinese or Appalachian lifeways) and the global (the culture of consumption)? What of the fact that the idea of culture can be shown to carry a vestigial imprint of the imperialism it supposedly was designed to combat? More pertinent here than these blurry semantic boundaries is the broader "crisis" of representation that the word brings to the fore. Just what is the class of objects to which the language of culture gives intelligible verbal form? As many scholars have observed, the discourse of culture shows with sometimes embarrassing ease that the invisible thing called culture is a "serious fiction" that must exist before there can be constituted any concrete object for cultural analysis to address. Such circularity is by no means unique to the study of culture, but it is especially striking when it surfaces there.[6] In this study, recognizing the self-referential language of culture prompts new questions about just what writers like James and Malinowski had "discovered" and mastered when they portrayed the social manners of their respective fields. We leave off asking whether they adequately captured what Malinowski called a "true picture" of Trobriand tribal life or what James called a "fundamental statement" of Old World society and, with a sometimes disorienting slippage to a different level of inquiry, we are led to questions about the conditions of representation that make tribal life and Old World society visible as coherent objects to be described in the first place.[7] Once such questions come into view, the fictive status of culture persistently shadows the interpretation of fiction, and novels never quite rid themselves of this background riddle of representation.

In the span of time reaching from Hawthorne's era to our own, then, fields of discourse organized around the culture idea offer us both the resources of an authorial mastery and the vexations of an authorial crisis. How did we get from one to the other, from the magisterial force of, say, Arnold's *Culture and Anarchy* and Tylor's *Primitive Culture* to the "conceptual free-for-all" muddying the term "culture" today, or the politically conflicted connotations of a phrase like "cultural relativism"?[8] To put the question that way presupposes a story of entropy, a falling off from a once-coherent fullness of meaning. But it is one of the aims of this study to rearrange that entropic tale of a modern predicament of culture. Instead of suggesting a lapse from an earlier coherence, I will argue that definitive authorial powers *and* dilemmas are present from the first in the nineteenth-century production of a discourse of culture in fiction, and that the resulting mastery and anxiety together mutually constitute both the social authority of novelists and the fictions of society they bring to life. In this study, the very predicaments inherent in representing culture provide a window on the formation of a high literary authorship for American novelists, a new select status organized around a specialized practice of writing about manners. By the same token, culture is treated here as a problematic but enabling myth, a literal pretext for the work of writing manners and the site at which fiction both feeds and is nourished by other nonfictional genres. It is not the concept of culture that is at issue here, then, but its particular services as a serious fiction in the later nineteenth and early twentieth centuries. Viewed in this way, the troubling circularity in texts about culture is also a productive circularity; New York exists as a culture in part because authors like Wharton had "done" it, no less than New York had "done" or produced Edith Wharton and her fiction.

What I describe is not a closed system, however. The relations between fiction and culture are in some sense circular, but they are not tautological. My analysis is concerned with preserving the real uncertainty and mutability in fiction's relation to the social world it represents. Literary scholars run the risk of lodging a tautology in our own critical practice when interpretations are determined in advance by an assumption that novels either irresistibly uphold or inherently critique the political force fields of the society they depict. This tautological trap is something I want not merely to avoid but to analyze. Debates about the political disposition of fiction have a special weight for the particular body of literature I will examine, a literature in which the portrait of manners has been seen as either a genteel armor designed to fend off the approach of a chaotic modernity or, conversely, as a subtle destabilizing of the social restrictions that everyday manners necessarily enforce. The later nineteenth and early twentieth centuries saw a flourishing literature of manners by writers from the United States. The three I examine most closely, Hawthorne, James, and Wharton, together produced what would amount to a small library of manners – innumerable volumes of travel writing, "international" novels and short stories, notebooks of social observation, and critical essays on American life. This library is central to what historians have shown was the formation of a sphere of high literary art in the United States during this era. We can identify a national institution of letters that took shape around Hawthorne's career, became professionalized through the monumental figure of James, and was claimed for women writers by Wharton.[9]

But if the "school of Hawthorne," as it has been called, was the core of an institutionalization of American letters, there is no simple way to gauge the politics of its sanctified authority. The familiar provinces of this fiction – the secure spaces of homes, drawing rooms, and European galleries – might suggest that these writers were in retreat from what appeared to be the anarchic tendencies of the new kind of market society taking root in these decades. And the literature I examine can indeed seem sealed away from other literary trends of this period – from the popular adventure novels, for instance, which made visible the far reaches of commercial and political empires, or the biological fables of naturalist fiction with their revised wilderness territories of the marketplace, laboratory, and battlefield, or the postbellum race melodramas by both African American and white writers that displaced Civil War conflicts onto literary landscapes. Yet it is easy to point to textual clues indicating that some of the political themes and energies from these subgenres had crossed the threshold into the indoor narratives of manners and high culture as well. In Hawthorne's *Marble Faun*, for instance, Praxiteles' statue of a faun is made a figure of the "tribes below us," and fine art mediates questions of a "savageness" that figures forth modern immigration, racial conflict, and urban unrest. In Wharton's New York, Washington Square is a "reservation" for elite "Aborigines" who are "vanishing" with the advance of new-money invaders, as emergent class tensions are coded ethnographically. James's refined heroines emit silent "primitive wails" behind the walls of country-house settings, one of the hints of the severity and eeriness that mark James's revision of an earlier body of domestic fiction. These metaphors are more than a stylistic gloss. Through them the novels display traces of the social contests and worldly dislocations that were addressed more openly in other kinds of contemporary fiction. With the estranging stare that defines Victorian anthropology, the parlors and museums of polite society were refashioned into conspicuous exhibits of a new and often ominous-seeming social reality. In this fiction, the civility of the drawing room – and the sovereign sign of Civilization itself – are subjected to disfiguring narrative pressures. When we pay close attention to these defamiliarizations, it becomes harder to assume an inherent social conservatism in this American literature of manners.

But neither is it certain that these kinds of exotic formal features – either the estranging "latitude" of reference in Hawthorne's romance or the extravagant metaphors in the realism of James and Wharton – are in themselves evidence of the authors' desire to resist the sway of inherited institutions and powers. In fact, by laying claim to manners, to the details of custom, dress, body carriage, and verbal style, the novelists become authorities over the most subtle and intimate (and therefore most powerful) kinds of institutional regulation. Manners, the personalized, bodily absorption of social habits and decorum, are deeply political. As Pierre Bourdieu notes, manners are the "symbolic taxes" by which a society fashions individuals for its own survival, extracting a tribute unknowingly paid by our own reflexive gestures and physical bearing.

> The principles em-bodied in this way are placed beyond the grasp of consciousness, and hence cannot be touched by voluntary, deliberate transformation, cannot even be made explicit; nothing seems more ineffable, more incommunicable than . . . the transubstantiation achieved by the hidden persuasion of an implicit pedagogy, capable of instilling a whole cosmology, an ethic, a metaphysic, a political philosophy, through injunctions as insignificant as "stand up straight" or "don't hold your knife in your left hand" . . . . The concessions of *politeness* always contain *political* concessions.[10]

Viewed in this way, manners are a form of active regulation, the installation of a social order deep within the body and personality of the subject. Similarly, the activity of writing about manners is a contingent – though not identical – process of supervision, providing as it does a natural-seeming account of the fashioning of the self as a rounded, social character. To recognize as much, though, still leaves open the question of the nature of that supervision, whether the portrait of manners in a novel is intended either to reinforce or to subvert the internalized "cosmology" that is the matrix for the controlling laws of decorum. Does writing about manners defend or undermine the hierarchies they serve?

These opposed alternatives, I suggest, constitute a false dilemma. By recasting narratives of manners as a kind of practice, I seek to offer a more dynamic model of novelists' authority over manners, and over the potent social powers that manners implant in the subject. Fiction is not a static judgment on the society it depicts; it does not merely endorse or condemn a preexisting reality. Rather, fiction constitutes one of the activities through which writers order and circulate the authority to write about society in the first place. Novel writing is itself one of the finite ways in which a society goes about inventing, testing, and altering its claims to legitimacy. At the same time, writing fiction is one of the ways in which manners become intelligible as the stuff of a larger totality, the web of invisible social relations – a perceived culture – that endows the minutiae of social manners with their meaning. Novels are a way of creating, not just reporting, the real, governing fictions of culture. At the same time, though, the writers' mastery of culture is inseparable from a profound uneasiness about the individual in society, or about what we might call here the *subject of manners*: that is, the subject or self understood as wholly constructed and controlled by the ruling powers of manners, the identity wholly composed – and therefore potentially de-composed – by external social forces. If deciphering the power of manners held the promise of social control, it also threatened cherished myths of individual agency. This study tracks the productive play of these interlocking energies of cultural mastery and anxiety by exploring ethnographic tropes informing fiction. Reading the traces of an imagined primitivism in a literature of manners, I analyze scenarios in which a civilization's power to cultivate the self converts all too easily to a savage loss of civilized composure, an unraveling of identity that motivates an even greater vigilance over manners.

A return to my starting examples of James and Malinowski can illustrate these conditions. Recent criticism has significantly reoriented James's accomplishment as a novelist. Whereas his mastery of form once signified James's supreme aesthetic detachment, in many current interpretations that same trait reveals his social engagement; critics have explored the way James's sophisticated narrative strategies, even at their most experimental and arcane, are continuous with social practices of the turn-of-the-century era.[11] Yet this common interest in the cultural grounding of James's vision has not ushered in any clear consensus. Is James through this mastery a master spy, an invisible agent of power exercising the pleasure of "seeing without being seen," as one reader has suggested, or, at the other end of the spectrum, is he a hero of subversion, a figure whose powers of sight are used to unsettle imposed social and sexual identities?[12] Is he a plainclothes policeman or a disguised double agent, a Mata Hari for the Resistance, in a top hat and waistcoat? James's narrative practice can be cast still differently and, I think, more profitably, in a historical context that includes the rise of professional ethnography and a new scientific interest in customs and manners. So situated, James's role as novelist is neither one of surveillance nor of a decentering subversion but, like the ethnographer's, a role always ambiguously partaking of both – both the pleasures of spying and the unsettling energies of relativism. It is this ambiguity that makes James a figure of a particular liberal authority, whose office it is to communicate between a civilization and the forms of otherness that the civilization's own powers have "discovered" and aspired to master.

By calling James's fiction "ethnographic," I mean that James practices what Michel de Certeau calls an operational schema of "ethnological isolation" and inversion: a "recipe," as Certeau labels it, of "cutting out and turning over" that produces the intellectual control expressed in the remarks by James and Malinowski quoted at the beginning of this chapter. It is a technique in which the writer "cuts out certain practices" from a broader social fabric, "in such a way as to treat them as a separate population, forming a coherent whole but foreign to the place in which the theory is produced." This group of practices, "at first obscure, silent, and remote . . . is inverted to become the element that illuminates theory and sustains discourse."[13] The strategy, which, as Certeau suggests, is rooted in nineteenth-century ethnology, provided perhaps the most powerful analytic fulcrum for the emergent social sciences.

The remote totem markings of Emile Durkheim's Australian tribes, "cut out and turned over," hold the key to the cohesion of modern society. The intricacies that Lewis Morgan discovered in the Iroquois kinship system contain the secret to understanding the nature of property. Maori magic lies behind the neurosis of Freud's Vienna patient and her casual decision to walk past the shop where her husband's razors are sharpened, revealing in that city stroll "the pleasurably accented idea that her husband might cut his throat."[14] These kinds of startling inversions often made scholars themselves conspicuous (and occasionally notorious), even as they were installed as cultural authorities. The public display of expertise, of skills possessed by the few and held up before mere spectators, was one of the ways that the hierarchical space of expert authority was ordered in the later nineteenth century.[15]

James's own formal expertise is nowhere more on display than in his 1901 novel *The Sacred Fount*, a work that he said was "calculated to minister to curiosity."[16] The curiosities of the novel are obvious: the narrator describes an astonishing weekend party at an English country villa where one woman looks decades younger than she appeared when he last saw her. Similarly, a man once exquisitely stupid now is discovered to be witty and learned. But in pointing to these occult elements of the curious, James includes the more distancing or clinical term "to minister," suggesting an intention to cultivate or manage, even to administer the curious. Within the novel, the ministering is done by the unnamed narrator, a character armed with extraordinary powers of observation and an elegant but outrageous theory. The narrator is convinced that the miraculous new youthfulness of Mrs. Brissenden has come at the expense of the preternatural aging of her husband, and that the new intelligence of Gilbert Long must be drawn from some other, unidentified woman now slipping quickly into imbecility. These linked transferences, he deduces, contain the secret to an underlying social arrangement of alliances and love affairs among the small social circle ("intimacy of course had to be postulated"). The novel is James's most explicit romance of science, with the central narrative energy devoted to a search for "a law governing delicate phenomena." Like Certeau's recipe, the narrator's method promises what he calls "the joy of the intellectual mastery of things unamenable." By isolating particular gestures, words, and images from among "the pleasant give and take of society," the novel defines a cultural totality, a discrete condition the narrator calls "our civilized state." But in an inversion as dazzling as any of Frazer's or Freud's, the give and take of polite manners are traced to a logic of barbaric sacrifice: "Mrs. Briss had to get her blood," and "Mr. Briss . . . can only die."[17]

There is more here than a rhetorical inversion between noble savages and savage nobles. As curious as James's premise is, the novel's portrait of decline and renewal gives narrative form to one of the era's pervasive obsessions. A 1900 article in the *Atlantic Monthly* warned of a "softening of manners," a "sort of satiety of civilization" or enervation that threatened literally to erode the health and nervous condition of those in the higher social strata.[18] Critics like Dr. James Weir described an ungoverned slippage whereby the weakening of the elite fed a dangerous strength in the underclasses: "The rich become effeminate, weak, and immoral, and the lower classes . . . led on by their savage inclinations, undertake strikes, mobs, boycotts and riots."[19] Everywhere were published warnings about the "decay of personality" and loss of "nerve force" among the wealthy bourgeoisie, a class disease that was the result of "being civilized too much."[20]

Reading James's tale of the "civilized state," however, contemporary readers tended to locate the idea of decay in James himself. The signs of a "morbid" and "decadent" strain in James's recent fiction, one reviewer wrote, had emerged in *The Sacred Fount* in a full-blown "chronic state of periphrastic perversity." James, to be sure, invites this identification when he has the narrator's search for a law of scientific symmetry dissolve into that character's own panic and morbid self-consciousness. Nevertheless, James defended the novel as "very close and sustained," and even his critics conceded the "scientific exactitude" of the novel's treatment. Is *The Sacred Fount* a "morbid analysis" of social manners, as one critic called it, or is it a social analysis of morbid manners?[21] James makes it impossible to tell the difference. But the ambiguity is not James's alone, for the novel condenses and frames what was a pronounced doubleness in the society at large. Alongside the era's pervasive displays of professional and technical proficiency, visible in Eakins's clinical paintings, in industrial exhibits, and highly publicized discoveries – alongside such images of specialized mastery were equally visible expressions of its antithesis, displays of what Mark Seltzer has called "melodramas of uncertain agency": spectacles of a fragmented and diminished sense of self, published accounts of "our

general looseness and slackness" of will, and a perceived erosion of
the firm lines of Victorian character.[22] Certainly, accounts of a
crisis of agency have been a conventional feature of liberal writings
since Mill. But in this period the "melodramas" appeared in highly
stylized forms that were mirror images of some of the new professional identities: self-diagnosed as a psychological pathology by
psychologist William James, for instance, or fashioned into a badge
of historical damage by historian Henry Adams, or spilled onto the
pages of a fieldwork diary by ethnographer Malinowski.

My last example carries a particular significance, because many
writers in the later part of the century thought they had found in
social customs and habits a field in which to submit to scientific
scrutiny the otherwise uncertain outlines of civilized selfhood. In an
age that feared a decay or "softening" of manners, the professional
study of primitive society – "the science of manners," as Marcel
Mauss would rename it – promised a powerful source of knowledge.[23] The force of customs, wrote Yale scholar William Graham
Sumner, is "not incidental or subordinate" but "supreme and controlling." Comparing tribal and modern societies, Sumner's book
Folkways traced the development of "manners, customs, usages and
mores" – everything from forms of marriage to fashion and styles of
female posture – in order to show that social convention is a "dominating force in history."[24] The exotic world of savages, distant in
time or space, was paradoxically the site of greatest theoretical
clarity, visible to the trained eye in a way the confusion of modern
society was not. Ethnology, Malinowski wrote, "has introduced law
and order into what seemed chaotic and freakish."[25] Confident of
the progressive laws of culture, scientists even used them to teach
the unruly. The proper arrangement of artifacts in the Pitt Rivers
ethnological museum, its founder affirmed, would be a tool of internal class control: "The law that nature makes no jumps can be
taught by the history of mechanical contrivances, in such a way as
at least to make men cautious how they listen to scatter-brained
revolutionary suggestions."[26]

The laws of culture likewise applied to the restless masses' counterpart: the too restful rich. In contrast to the widespread notes of
alarm, for instance, Thorstein Veblen brought scientific composure
to the notion of leisure-class decline. Like James's novel, Veblen
supplies a precise theory to account for perceived symptoms of
enervation. The key is ethnological: the "traditions, usages, and

habits of thought" of the leisure class, he writes, belong to an "archaic cultural plane," a level of civilization somewhere above Eskimo society and on a par with Brahmin India. Veblen's book is an especially vivid example of Certeau's "ethnological isolation": Veblen's famous notion of conspicuous consumption identifies and links together an otherwise heterogeneous collection of practices. Inverting canons of costliness and value into canons of waste, Veblen is able to explain as versions of the same social phenomenon items as diverse as closely cropped lawns, women's corsets, and low birthrates. The smallest details of household life, "cut out and turned over," together make visible and predictable the cultural condition that critics like Weir register as an invisible but potent disease. Veblen's own term for this method is "ethnological generalization," a comparative analysis that produces an ideal legibility for new and disturbing social features. With this ethnological method, Veblen checks society's panic at decline through the sure laws of progressive culture, converting its alarm into his brand of bemused contempt. He reproduces a narrative of overcivilization but arrests it by brilliantly embodying the idea of decline in the customs and manners of the rich, thereby preserving for liberal society the natural "instinct for workmanship" that ensures continuing cultural progress.[27]

Perhaps it is for that reason that William Dean Howells recommended Veblen's book as an "aid to literature," for certain kinds of art – modern novels in particular – were assailed by many as damning evidence of overcivilization. Sumner, Tylor, and James Frazer all catalogued current works of "pernicious literature" as ethnological data (full of "gloom and savagery," such works "relax the inhibitions" and erode "an independence of character," Sumner writes in *Folkways*).[28] As readers of Malinowski's diary learned, when it was posthumously published in 1967, novels were Malinowski's own fetish symbol for the panicked "loss of subjectivism" he frequently suffered during fieldwork (33): bingeing on Conrad, Thackeray, as well as "trashy novels" brought on what he called "my Dostoevskian state" (144, 122). When paired with the genre of ethnography, the modern novel was an antitype that embodied the uncertain status of individual agency and the equivocal advances of civilization. "Reading myself to death," Malinowski writes, and vows "I [won't] touch another novel in N[ew] G[uinea]," only later to report, "Dissipation: I take up novel reading" (63, 195).

Novel reading, then, could be charged with eroding the regulation of manners. But what of a novel like *The Sacred Fount*, which,
while one of the most Dostoevskian of James's very self-reflexive
novels, is also the novel that reaches most nearly the idea of perfect
social observation, of expert vision and supervision? Comparing the
villa to a "museum" (22), the novel presents the characters as
carefully exhibited artifacts; one woman is figured as an "old dead
pastel under glass" (51). The secret to this enclosed social world is
located in what Malinowski called the living "documents" of culture: that is, the behavior, words, gestures, and the very bodies of
the inhabitants. The invisible "softening" of manners is now perfectly embodied in what the narrator calls his "little gallery" of
human examples (22). But the amorphous decay that alarmed contemporary observers is here in the novel an enclosed and regulated
economy: two people are in rapid decline, while two others are
strengthened in perfect proportion. The case of the Brissendens,
then, might appear to follow the model that Patrick Geddes set
forth in his influential 1889 volume *The Evolution of Sex*, which argued that male cell metabolism burns at a fierce and virile rate,
whereas women's "anabolic" cells are conservative: "males live at a
loss . . . females, on the other hand, live at a profit."[29] James's
system, though, is finally neither a biological nor a gender economy
but, like the theories of anthropology, an interlocking social economy. The determining principle in this world lies in invisible social
relations – veiled love affairs, secret exchanges, and unacknowledged collaborations. A submerged code of social and sexual kinship, foreign and even shocking to the narrator and to the
reader, is the key to understanding the "civilized state." The code is
not biological but cultural: bodies, gestures, and words can be
understood only through the "inextricable web of affinities" that is
culture. As recent histories of anthropology have suggested, the
idea of a holistic web of culture is a cognitive structure that makes
the social perfectly legible, with invisible relations and forces un-
veiled through expert observation. In the crucial work of Marcel
Mauss, Lévi-Strauss claimed, "the social . . . becomes a system,
among whose parts connections, equivalences, and interdependent
aspects can be discovered." The same organic relations are the
obsession of James's narrator, driven as he is by "that special beauty in my scheme through which the whole depended so on each part
and each part so guaranteed the whole" (223).[30]

In *The Sacred Fount*, though, this abstract web of culture *is* most fully realized in bodies, just as anthropology realized the origins of culture in the body of primitive man, the savage. In fact, James's narrator is able to distill the whole system into a single body part: the back. Human backs seem to hold the deepest evidence for the narrator's theory:

> As I stood there watching [Mrs. Briss] recede and fairly studying, in my preoccupation, her handsome affirmative back and that special sweep of her long dress – it was indisputable . . . that my consciousness was aware of having performed a full revolution. . . . Poor [Mr.] Briss' back. . . . had hitherto seemed the most eloquent of his aspects, [especially] the stoop of his shoulders. . . . I seemed perpetually, at Newmarch, to be taking his measure from behind. (192, 197, 227)

A passage from Malinowski's fieldwork diary reveals that Malinowski shared the same propensity for observing backs:

> At 5 went to Kaulaka. A pretty, finely built girl walked ahead of me. I watched the muscles of her back, her figure, her legs, and the beauty of the body so hidden to us, whites, fascinated me. Probably even with my own wife I'll never have the opportunity to observe the play of back muscles for as long as with this little animal. At this moment I was sorry I was not a savage and could not possess this pretty girl. At Kaulaka, looked around, noting things to photograph. (255–6)

Here the "backward glance" of ethnography proves to be corporeal as well as temporal. Both passages reveal what Seltzer has called the realist fantasy of surveillance: perfect vision, on one hand, and a perfect embodiment of the social, on the other.[31] As observers, the narrator and Malinowski have a camera-like power to see and display the real; as cultural objects, the Brissendens and the Trobriand girl embody social meaning in their very torsos and limbs. Through the power of the narrator's theory, for instance, the "stoop" of Mr. Briss's shoulders yields a graphic "measure" of his decline. Similarly, the body of the Trobriand girl is fixed in Malinowski's sight as a previously "hidden" object of evidence, placing it among the "things to photograph" that will produce knowledge of culture. Moreover, the diary passage signifies graphically the way such ethnological sight is a way of looking *behind the back* of the native culture, that it approaches the body of the native without hailing that body as a subject that requires a direct address. The double structure of vision and embodiment has tremendous efficiency. Just as Malinowski's fieldwork observation establishes a new and definitive representation of what he calls "savage society," so the narrator's vision reveals "our civilized state": gazing at Mrs. Briss's back, the narrator's "full revolution in consciousness" allows him to see in total "the beauty and the terror of conditions so highly organized" (167).

But although the narrator finds in these conditions much of the sublimated "terror" or barbarism that Veblen found, the "beauty" that he finds there points as well to an important difference. *The Sacred Fount* also acknowledges that the narrator's surveillance, his "indiscreet observations," include desire as well as mastery. Malinowski's description of watching the Trobriand girl exposes the same thing. The objective mastery of his gaze is inseparable from a subjective desire that was, according to the diary, the source of Malinowski's personal undoing. Upon publication, the diary produced a tremendous scandal (Clifford Geertz called it "The Double Helix" of his discipline), not only because of the pages of sexual fantasies and the eruptions of racist disgust ("my feelings are decidedly tending to 'Exterminate the brutes'" (69), he writes in one display of his novel reading), but because of the damage it finally inflicted on the authority of the anthropologist as hero. For the ethnographic authority Malinowski helped to enshrine was founded not so much on elevated empathy and respect as on an intellectual mastery of what others had managed only to crudely conquer or convert, and it is this erosion of mastery and self-possession that the diary dissects and anatomizes. In it, Malinowski records a "loss of subjectivism and deprivation of the will ([is] blood flowing away from [the] brain?)" (33). His complaints include bouts of "point-ophobia – a nervous aversion for pointed objects" (87). Perhaps most striking for some academics is his nihilism at contemplating his future as a husband and a professor: "Mate with her, beget children, write books, die" (219).

The imperious backward glance in *The Sacred Fount* similarly contains the seeds of its own dissolution. Just after the narrator's "revolution in consciousness" while staring at Mrs. Briss's back, he confesses a disturbing "chill to my curiosity." This numbness may be, like Malinowski's, a chilling effect that comes from desire, for as the plot develops, a theory story threatens to become a love story: to his shock the narrator confronts the prospect that he has fallen in love with one of his subjects. An even more provocative possibility: he could be the missing "woman" (as he had symmetrically figured it) in the quartet of leading couples.[32] These possibilities set off an unraveling of the "tangle of hypothesis I had for convenience called my theory" (174). But this collapse of mastery does not abolish the notion of social laws. In fact, the narrator's bouts of panic at what seemed to be the ebbing of his own powers ("I feel drained – I feel dry!") could be further evidence of those laws: *he* could be a weakening source – a sacred fount – for someone else's proportional strength. The possibility of laws remain, though now invisible and unfixed, while a crisis of agency is realized in full view: like Malinowski, he describes a personal "collapse" (297), with his "palace of thought" reduced to a "heap of disfigured fragments" (311), and now personally convinced that he "should never again quite hang together" (319).

These closing words of the novel are echoed in the final sentence of Malinowski's diary: "Truly I lack character" (298). But the difference between novels and diaries is important here. Malinowski records his lack of mastery as a private confession, and the diary was suppressed even after his death in order to protect the discipline. (Its rather odd posthumous title – *A Diary in the Strict Sense of the Term* – can be read as an anxious rhetorical strategy to cordon off diary sentiments from professional norms, precisely the two categories that blur together in the actual entries.) James's novel, on the other hand, is a public work, created not by compulsion but by design. James deliberately erases the distinction between mastery and self-dissolution, the opposition upon which was erected the apparatus of expert knowledge. But does it follow that the novel is designed to subvert the disciplining of manners? I would argue rather that James's aim is to design a crisis of agency *as part of* a design to make novel writing a discipline of its own. Alongside his representation of laws, James includes a vivid representation of a subjective crisis – indeed, he makes of that crisis another spectacular embodiment. *We* watch the narrator, just as he had watched Mrs. Brissenden's back. The narrator could be his own best body of evidence for a theory of overcivilization. It raises the possibility that the fiction of a crisis is as important as the fiction of mastery – indeed that crisis is necessary to James's fictional mastery. There are rewards for James in embodying the panic of agency in his overcivilized narrator – rewards, too, we might say, for embodying it in his fiction, and even somewhat more problematically in his own name and reputation, as the word "James" came to be available as a signifier for morbid self-consciousness (of *The Sacred Fount*, one reviewer said "he outJames's James").[33] In part, the reward seems to lie in implicating himself in overcivilization, as he portrays with intimate detail an "expert observer" (28) who experiences the agonies of uncertainty; at the same time, there is further profit in externalizing and embodying the crisis outside of himself in a textual space that affords authorial control. By representing the disintegration of self so dreaded in this era, James is able to master the uncertainty even as he displays it. He does indeed outJames himself in *The Sacred Fount*, for the novel brings a representation of laws and of a crisis of agency into communication without requiring the impossible resolution that strict reason would demand and science must therefore evade. This strategy is different from *creating* ambiguity (which is what frowning critics charged); it is a matter instead of managing or ministering to it, not suppressing but fostering and bringing into a dynamic exchange the era's romancing of cultural laws and equally charged investment in the perils of uncertain agency. By converting surveillance into spectacle, by inverting the ethnographer with his "little gallery" of natives, James displays a mobility of critical energy that contrasts with Veblen's arresting but static ethnography of the rich.

But if in doing so James is less imperious, it is important to recognize that the uncertainties and acts of self-implication in James's fiction are also the source of his specialized authority. I am referring to James's achievement as the master of ambiguity and of the laws he set down for fiction writing – principles that, if not followed by other writers, were followed to the extent that other writers now assumed that fiction could and should have laws. It has been persuasively argued that James's creation of his career as the Master was patterned after the powerful new model of the professional, with a specialized domain, regulating laws, and exclusive skills; it is a mastery that comes not from aesthetic retreat but precisely from an institutionalization that intersects with other emergent disciplines.[34] *The Sacred Fount* shows that James is master both of laws and of the cultural crisis that seemed not to be subdued but rather to thrive in the era of professionalization. *The Sacred Fount* exhibits the mutual reliance between the era's crisis of cultural authority and the cultural laws that were to minister to it.

What James displays and mobilizes in a single novel, Malinowski splits into two genres, a diary and an ethnography. The significance of the diary has usually been seen as its exposure of the secret contradictions in anthropology. But the example of James suggests a different way to think about the scandal of Malinowski's diary. James could be said to show Malinowski the way to profit from overcivilization and its discontents: by embodying them. We can see the diary not as a hidden confession but as a document that chronicles the power of observing – and of writing, of materially composing – one's own uncertainty. As a record of overcivilization, the diary is a companion volume to his studies of savages and shows the ethnographer moving fluidly between inscribing cultural laws and recording a painful "loss of subjectivism." It was a mobility that, like James's, was finally productive, giving rise to a new kind of authority. Perhaps novels were, after all, a sacred fount for ethnography – that is, a fount in James's odd revisionary sense of a source that is never a sure origin but is rather a provocative site of imaginative exchange.

So, too, is ethnography a similar source for fiction, in the present study. My interest is not in securing facts that determine the historical influence of each genre upon the other, though such source studies have yielded insights important to this book. Rather my aim – not unlike that of *The Sacred Fount* – is to examine relations that are imagined, representational, even in a sense occult, relations not of logic or positive historical contact but of mutually transforming affinities between proximate narrative bodies: novels and ethnographies broadly defined. These two genres, though assigned in this period to utterly different zones of "civilized" and "savage" life, were linked through an indeterminate exchange of images, narrative energies, and structures of feeling. Such mimetic exchange is at the heart of a critical revision of representation during this time, a transformation that revealed civilization and primitivism to be repertoires of unstable signs rather than solid and discrete spheres of social reality.[35] Tracing strands of this exchange between genres, I will analyze what *The Sacred Fount* distills in novel form: a body of fiction in which manners enact a civility that is at times indistinguishable from a refined species of cannibalism; implicit theories of culture that threaten to be the fantasy of a willful observer; and a model of the highly cultivated self in which the very eloquence of voice and acuity of insight seem to heighten the danger of self-disintegration. Yet the disorder that results does not threaten an end to storytelling, as we might expect; rather, the equivocations are a motive or driving force for telling stories. The uncertain, shifting relations between language and the cultural objects that language names and calls into existence are precisely the conditions that generate the fiction I consider here. To the extent that James's novel articulates these conditions in the tale of a brilliant but hapless participant-observer, his odd book *The Sacred Fount* is not eccentric but paradigmatic. It is a template for the conflicted but finally productive revision of manners undertaken in the fiction of Hawthorne, James, and Wharton.

James's fondness for cultural incongruities, for "having the primitive jostle against the genteel," as one critic describes it, thus generates narrative conflicts as well as narrative authority, in a reciprocal influence that I trace across the boundaries of fiction.[36] Exchanges between texts, of course, would not have been possible without a real, global economy of exchange, an underwriting of both novels and ethnographies by the commercial and colonial empires of this period. In a crucial sense, the "jostling" of gentility with tribal life took place most dramatically in face-to-face encounters on the imperial frontier. When we heed what Edward Said claims is the final inseparability of culture and imperialism, the unspoken historical underpinnings for a novel like *The Sacred Fount* point to an interpretation that is almost too obvious: the real sacred fount, the body drained of energy and autonomous life to feed the culture and personal cultivation of others, was of course the body, real and political, of the native living within the intimate, insidious marriage that was colonialism.[37] That body would never be among the guests at an English country house – tellingly, the narrator cannot or will not identify the missing source when he looks only to this insular company – but the apprehension of parasitic ties yoking elite English society with some unseen alterity is inscribed for us in the language of manners. Read in this way, *The Sacred Fount* is an allegory of the novel of manners. In this species of fiction, manners are precisely the site of exchange between domestic and exotic territories, between the affairs of private homes and the politics of foreign affairs. By importing a figural primitivism from ethnography, the literature of manners serves to domesticate the forms of otherness that were increasingly difficult to shut out from view.

Arguably, this process of domestication, of bringing indoors and into the very mannerisms of polite society images of the otherness in ethnography, was a process that helped to sustain the unequal relations of force between the West and colonial territories. But there are limits to reading this importation of the exotic into novels of manners as a covert imperialism. For one thing, the domestication at work in the texts I will analyze is concerned with the perceived strangers and strangeness already at home.[38] This is especially true of novels about life in the United States, where what was foreign was not always easy to distinguish from what was domestic – hence the uncanniness of the Other in America, whether it is the immigrant, the freedman or another racial stranger, or the overcivilized citizen, Veblen's rich "barbarian" made somehow un-American through her conspicuous consumption, all figures portrayed as simultaneously inside and outside of American society. The "aliens" who were already on the metropolitan scene, along with the alien-seeming self that the city appeared to produce, are the primary referents for the ethnographic operations in this fiction. One should not lose sight of the paradox that by appropriating images of tribal life to describe metropolitan society, writers also managed to render the actual lives of men and women of the tribe invisible, and hence more easily exploited. But in important ways, the ethnographic discourse in fiction began to narrate conflicts that were changing bourgeois life from within. An ethnographic diction allowed novelists to domesticate precisely those social facts that would have been ignored discretely in private homes and institutions of high culture: an increasing immigration and racial diversity, along with the theories of race and citizenship that accompanied them (Chapter 2); new urban conditions that altered the indoor world of bourgeois social life and its presumed civility (Chapter 3); the strange, unnerving desires that seemed unleashed by commodity consumption (Chapter 4); and the specter of new and uncertain powers of agency for women (Chapter 5).

This study proposes, then, that a shared repertoire of ethnographic tropes and practices allowed a fiction of the drawing room to play host to alien features of modernity. But just how hospitable was the fiction of manners to this alien matter and to the matter of aliens? Was the domestication designed to subdue and tame any perceived threats from without? What are the implications of admitting otherness into the homes and galleries of polite society? I have called this strategy a form of domestication through manners, but it is not obvious that it was driven by the will to oppress or even by the need for sure socialization.

The widely varying critical judgments of James are a case in point. Some have seen in the imported strangeness of his fiction a critical power that breaks up the controls imposed on bourgeois subjectivity and in turn imposed by that subject on others. But still other critics find his fiction to be the terminal point – the farthest reach of efficacy as well as the limit – of those same disciplinary controls. At issue is the work of manners. As Richard Godden argues, manners as traditionally featured in the novel foster the self-possession of an integrated ego. In contrast to the traits of the dispersed, "disintegral self" necessary to an emergent consumer capitalism, "manners and taste are cumulative and integrative" in this period, and "the selfhood that they realize is its own ultimate possession." Therefore, the novel of manners, and the Jamesian novel of manners in particular, Godden claims, is fundamentally at odds with the most potent shaping (or misshaping) forces of this phase of modernity. The genre and the selfhood it represents are archaic, and James's novels amount to a fiction of evasion that attempts to displace what he cannot admit into his world of manners. The ironies of the Jamesian novel of manners, its "tissue of displacements" and dismantling of character, are for Godden the inadvertent results of a failed rearguard action. But for a critic like Ross Posnock, in contrast, the very displacements and incongruities staged in James's writings are the sources of a critical power that makes the novelist a godfather to the most advanced critiques of bourgeois identity and authority. By absorbing otherness, James's writings puncture the "complacencies and confinements of the genteel," creating "the space to improvise new forms of identity and pleasure."[39]

My reading of *The Sacred Fount* suggests that these seeming antinomies are really critical partners, that both the anxious evasion and the deliberate display of fragmented manners are obverse impulses at play in the same field of narration. It is a mistake, I think, to see the disintegration of gentility as the sole desired end of James's fiction, but neither does that staged disintegration amount to a reactionary elegy for the established authority of the genteel class. For James – as for Hawthorne and Wharton – a crisis of manners is the occasion not for mourning or reforming manners but for grasping a new societal authority reformed from within the world of genteel decorum. For the "drawing-room naturalist," manners can never again be a matter of mere propriety, but their demystification yields a critical distance from which to supervise those manners even as the demystifying process unsettles the very foundation of drawing-room society. The "house of fiction" I examine, then, is an uneasy amalgam, half parlor, half museum, and haunted by the ghosts of absent tribal inhabitants, an equivocal site that nevertheless allows writers to give rich aesthetic expression to new features of modernity. Rather than either suppressing or celebrating otherness, the novelists I examine *cultivate* it, in both senses of that word; they feed it and give it a recognizable life in literature, at the same time as they master it through an ironic assimilation. Such cultivation, as the root of the word suggests, shows us a concept of culture as a social practice in action: it shows us a dynamic, ongoing process through which a work of fiction gives polished form to otherwise disparate, conflicted features of social life. Culture, in its "wide ethnographic sense," provided a way for a literature of manners to capitalize on its own predicament.

CHAPTER 2

Nathaniel Hawthorne and the fetish of race

Arise and fly
The reeling Faun, the sensual feast;
Move upward, working out the beast.
                    −Alfred Tennyson, *In Memoriam*

In an 1862 travel essay about his trip to wartime Washington, Hawthorne compared a group of escaped slaves with mythic fauns. The men and women walking north on a Virginia road, he wrote, "were unlike the specimens of their race whom we are accustomed to see at the North":

> So rudely were they attired, – as if their garb had grown upon them spontaneously, – so picturesquely natural in manners, and wearing such a crust of primeval simplicity (which is quite polished away from the northern black man), that they seem a kind of creature by themselves, not altogether human, but perhaps quite as good, and akin to the fauns and rustic deities of olden times.

This striking fantasy appears in the middle of a narrative piece that Hawthorne wrote in the name of realism. He begins by distinguishing the essay from his fiction, telling of his reluctant turn away from the "fantasies" of romance in order to face the "dread time of civil war": "I determined to look a little more closely at matters with my own eyes." Hawthorne takes up a new role as eyewitness, tracking "signs" of war from New England to Virginia.[1]

The fanciful image of a faun, of course, had been central to Hawthorne's most recent romance novel, *The Marble Faun*, published just over a year earlier. The faun reappears here in his travel record at a moment of heightened anxiety: the sight of the slaves is introduced as "one very pregnant token of a social system thoroughly disturbed." The bondsmen become Hawthorne's emblem of the real political crisis, yet it is precisely his sense of the unreal that he emphasizes when he describes them as mythic creatures "of olden times." The image of slave as faun thus creates a link between opposed dimensions – between a contemporary "social system" and a realm of myth, between the eyewitnessing of travel observations and the reinvention of pagan fantasy, and between a battlefield realism and an ethereal sphere of romance. The result is a double image of the African American, with the rustic slave-faun distinguished from "the northern black man." Like Belinda's scissors, the image joins to divide.

The doubling of romance and realism in this passage, then, corresponds with an uncanny racial doubling. Here the "black man" is and is not like a faun, and the image contains a mix of both innocence and menace that Hawthorne attaches to the sight of the escaping slaves. What are we to make of the unstable conjunction? Distressed as Hawthorne is at the upheavals of the war, it would be a mistake to see the essay's sudden irruption of fantasy as a wish to escape a conflicted social reality. The faun does not signal the return of a repressed – or, as many critics have argued, a now-faltering – romance mode that had failed to sustain Hawthorne's creativity in the face of what he called "war matters" and wartime facts of race. Here and elsewhere in Hawthorne's writing, the slippage between realism and romance is not a sign of weakening powers but is rather the basis for a remarkable economy of expression that depends on historical ambiguities about race. Like the faun in Hawthorne's novel, race in nineteenth-century America was an entity poised "between the Real and the Fantastic," a position that offered writers certain resources of imagination – though it offered little to most escaping bondsmen.

Consider another of Hawthorne's fauns, this one inspired by the sight of Praxiteles' statue. Far from evading any scenario of race, the description in Hawthorne's Italian travel notebook of the famous sculpted faun pulls in a strange racial reference where none is called for. Gazing at the statue, Hawthorne finds that the fanciful faun reminds him of an actual and repellent figure, a "bearded woman" in an exhibition, though he no sooner makes the comparison than he insists upon a difference.

> I like these strange, sweet, playful, rustic creatures, almost entirely human as they are, yet linked so prettily, without monstrosity, to the lower tribes. . . . In my mind, they connect themselves with that ugly, bearded woman, who was lately exhibited in England, and by

> some supposed to have been engendered betwixt a human mother
> and an orang-outang; but she was a wretched monster – the faun, a
> natural and delightful link betwixt human and brute life.[2]

Once again a faun is a resonant but equivocal image for Hawthorne. He does not specify whom or what he means by the "lower
tribes" linked in his mind with the image of the faun, nor does he
indicate any racial identity for the woman he recalls exhibited in
England, though the rumor of transpecies mating between humans
and orangutans was a scurrilous and shopworn racist conceit that
had long been attached to blacks.[3] These imprecise associations
create an image of racial uncertainty. But the indeterminacy in the
description is very much to the point, for, as with virtually all
questions about race in this period, the image both raises and defers
questions about the relation of a normative human life to "lower"
creatures; with the faun, the connection is a happy one; with the
bearded woman it is "wretched" and transgressive. In this way the
faun-woman has the force of a taboo, conjoining desire and repul-
sion and articulating both an identification and a disavowal. It
might not go too far to say that the image of the faun is something
of a personal fetish for Hawthorne, a repeating form he invokes to
mark an overdetermined relation between "human and brute life."

The topic could hardly be said to be Hawthorne's fetish alone,
though, since the relation between "human and brute life" was
perhaps the defining scientific obsession of the nineteenth-century
and the focus of debates imposed on a host of postbellum preoc-
cupations, from immigration to assimilation and Reconstruction.
The question of the relation between human and "lower" forms,
including the question of just who counted as fully human, was a
problem subsumed under the idea of race – subsumed, but by no
means answered or explained by it. In a sense, the mystified and
shifting thing called "race" was the fetish for the era as a whole, a
category of thought and a motive for action that concentrated powerful, contradictory assertions in a single conceptual object.

Like a fetish, Hawthorne's faun erases the boundary between the
human and the less-than-human, the faun itself fitting neither category but standing for an identity between them. What appears to
be an antithesis – human versus brute – functions rather as a
slippery linkage that in the course of Hawthorne's notebook entry
alternatively claims and rejects an identification between kinds of
"creatures": humans, tribes, women, apes, monsters. We could say

that what the faun represents is thus thoroughly confused, or we could say that what it represents is thus endlessly flexible, that with this figure Hawthorne is able to choose when and how to acknowledge a kinship to other classes of creatures even as he is able to forgo choosing in any final, definitive sense. It is the flexibility that I find more provocative, for, despite what seems to be the compulsive nature of his memory of the orangutan woman, the illogical links that materialize around the memory give Hawthorne a rich semantic field in which to make subtle affiliations and discriminations, including distinctions that would come to carry notable consequences in the emergent postwar society. The figure of the faun allows Hawthorne to acknowledge sympathetically the people he calls elsewhere in the essay "America's dark progeny" at the same time that he newly marks them as "a kind of creature by themselves," producing rhetorical results not unlike the results of postbellum policies with their strategic vacillation between attempts to "Americanize" the freedmen and efforts to enforce a Jim Crow isolation as "a kind of creature by themselves."

While the figure of the faun in these two pieces is deliberately linked to markers of race, the "modern faun" in Hawthorne's novel appears far removed from contemporary American conflicts, racial or otherwise.[4] The distance is not only geographic but thematic: with its Italian setting, the novel presents a meditation on art and classical world history. The novel thus appears to be about what might be considered culture rather than race – that is, about an aesthetic and historical inheritance rather than inherited biological traits. The spritelike character Donatello, teasingly presented as a descendant of the fauns of ancient poetry, is a re-creation of Praxiteles' sculpted faun, and Roman statuary and paintings serve as the medium of Hawthorne's ruminative story about moral awakening. But these European materials notwithstanding, the faun of the novel is also shaped by American anxieties about a "social system thoroughly disturbed," including the prospect of America's uncertain relations with its "lower orders." Though the foreground of the novel presents the legends, ruins, and galleries of the Eternal City, *The Marble Faun* is rooted in a historical moment that, like the Virginia landscape in the "War Matters" essay, was to make newly visible the presence of unsettled and unsettling racial strangers. The Old World of Italy, and the even older one of ancient myth, provide Hawthorne with the symbolic material for an internal eth-

nographic drama, a doubling of culture and race that was also one
of the subtexts of early anthropology. The novel turns out to be
about *both* culture and race, or, more accurately, about the way the
two were deployed variously as both synonyms and antonyms, according to the changing needs of a number of nineteenth-century
plots. Just as Rousseau's Noble Savage signified Europe's past in
order to forge a weapon for its present-day politics (usurping the
title "noble" from the nobles), so too Hawthorne's fanciful faun is
part of a nineteenth-century primitivism that organized a field of
strategically shifting reference and values.[5] What Hawthorne calls
the aesthetic "laws and proprieties" (1239) of his romance both
limn and illuminate the equivocal "laws of culture" that animated
nineteenth-century primitivism.

COMPOSING THE DIVERSITY OF FOLKS

In the novel's first paragraph, "four individuals" stand in the sculpture gallery in the Capitol, linked through works of high art ("famous productions of antique sculpture, . . . still shining in the
undiminished majesty and beauty of their ideal life") to an allegory
of universal moral meaning: "the Human Soul, with its choice of
Innocence or Evil close at hand" (857). This opening annexes new
territory for the American romance, a territory of high culture and
monumental art. Hawthorne's preface expresses a certain uneasiness at "appropriating" as literary "spoils" the art and antiquity
from the museum world of Italy, but the same notes of caution are
also indirect evidence of Hawthorne's fictional conquest: the writer
who had hitherto chronicled stories of "our stalwart Republic" was
now claiming the Old World and its greatest monuments for the art
of American "romance-writers" (854).

Yet the actual unfolding of the narrative repeatedly lapses from
this idealized space of high culture. Immediately after presenting
the sculpture gallery, the narrator brings into view "a shapeless
confusion of modern edifices" set among the ancient buildings and
ruins of the Roman streets. The process of reading *The Marble Faun*
requires a series of perceptual shifts in and out of the special territory of romance (a space "artfully and airily removed from our
mundane sphere" [1239], as Hawthorne describes it in his postscript). The narrative digressions create a doubled novel in which a
number of topoi are represented in contradictory ways, sometimes

idealized, sometimes debased. The most prominent of these doubled images is the picture of Rome itself. It appears by turns as the
mythic Eternal City and as a site of urban blight. Here is the
ethereal Rome:

> [Rome brings] a vague sense of ponderous remembrances; a percep-
> tion of such weight and density in a by-gone life, of which this past
> was the centre, that the present moment is pressed down or crowded
> out. . . . Viewed through this medium, our narrative . . . may seem
> not widely different from the texture of all our lives. Side by side
> with the massiveness of the Roman Past, all matters, that we handle
> or dream of, now-a-days, look evanescent and visionary alike. (858)

The mass of history is so great that finally time itself is displaced.
Rome becomes a "visionary" space on which the narrator can write
a story of the eternal meaning transmitted through culture.

But despite the careful construction of an "airy" narrative texture from the very stones of Rome, Hawthorne goes on to disengage
this allegorical diction through scenes that return the full time-
bound density of the city:

> Rome, *as it now exists*, has grown up under the Popes, and seems like
> *nothing but* a heap of broken rubbish, thrown into the great chasm
> between our own days and the Empire, merely to fill it up; and, for
> the better part of two thousand years, its annals of obscure policies,
> and wars, and continually recurring misfortunes, seem also but bro-
> ken rubbish. (944, emphasis added)

Rome here resists any allegorical reading, offering only "annals of
obscure policies" and inglorious wars. Unlike the earlier description of a Rome that signified "the texture of all our lives," this world
cannot be allegorically represented, either: "We know not how to
characterize, in any accordant and compatible terms, the Rome
that lies before us." An impoverished, mimetic Rome ("as it now
exists") repeatedly breaks into the transparent romance discourse.
In order to return to the larger meaning of his tale, the narrator
must reengage the language of an eternal Rome: "Yet how is it
possible to say an unkind or irreverential word of Rome? – the City
of all time, and of all the world!" (945).

But the frequency and intensity of the lapses increase. In one
passage, the language of disillusion reaches its highest pitch: the
narrator builds a single page-long sentence that is a mounting
diatribe against modern Rome as a "corpse" with "indescribably

ugly" streets and a plague of "Italian trickery." Yet this onslaught still closes with a reversal to the Eternal City "drawing us thitherward again" as if it were "more intimately our home, than even the spot where we were born" (1124). Switching between narrative styles in this way, the novel presents its material in alternating aspects. At times, Catholicism serves as a figure of universal religious spirit; at other moments, the same Roman Catholic signs are dead forms behind which are "scarlet superstitions" or worse. Donatello and Miriam are descendants of legend, and Hawthorne is careful to supply a lineage linking each to mythic stories; but other human figures – Italian "ruffians," "unwashed babies," "Roman housekeepers," characters of "German ingenuity" and of "Italian superstition" – are standard national types. Works of art often function in *The Marble Faun* as resonant symbols that hold mystic meaning like the scarlet *A*; yet at times art appears as nothing more than lifeless objects, as reflected in the chapter title "The Emptiness of Picture-Galleries."

Many readers have found these passages about modern Rome distracting, annoying patches of travel writing that intrude into the "airy" territory of romance. But it is worth considering why Hawthorne might have borrowed conventions from travel writing for use in a romance novel and what the effects of such a generic mixing might be. The travel-book realism Hawthorne incorporates into his romance gives him a narrative form that affords not only the "poetic or fairy precinct" he notes in his preface but also gives him an authoritative language for writing about manners. It is a double discourse that makes for a complex romancing of race.

By the time *The Marble Faun* was published, a huge number of travel books about Italy already made the coexistence of these two divergent registers a standard, even banal, style of prose. Travelers laid before their readers the ideal beauty and transcendent meanings captured in the classical forms from antiquity. But they also included quasi-sociological descriptions that built upon a long history of customs-and-manners portraits and anticipated the writings of the emergent professional travel writer, the ethnographer. Like Hawthorne's novel, travel books combine very different narrative styles: the manners and habits of contemporary Italians are presented in a language of empirical observation whereas Italian art and landscapes are composed in a mode of visionary aesthetics. These categories were not always kept distinct from one another;

glimpses of Italian peasants or even beggars, for instance, were often blended into picturesque landscapes that were as ageless to American eyes as the Pantheon, as when Harriet Beecher Stowe described the sight of an old woman and a young girl selling oranges in the Sorrento Gorge: "the whole golden scene receded centuries back, and they saw them in a vision as they might and must have been in other days." (Melville mockingly referred to the practice of aestheticizing the poor as the "povertiresque" style.)[6] But as a rule these two subjects – the spirit or "genius" of Italy, and the behavior and appearance of present-day Romans – inhabit different, often antagonistic representational spaces. When in a travel letter Shelley distinguished "two Italies," one poetic and one debased, he was only thematizing a practice of splitting that was commonplace for Anglo-American travelers:

> There are two Italies; one composed of the green earth and transparent sea and the mighty ruins of ancient times, and aerial mountains, and the warm and radiant atmosphere which is interfused through all things. The other consists of the Italians of the present day, their works and ways. The one is the most sublime and lovely contemplation that can be conceived by the imagination of man; the other the most degrading, disgusting and odious.[7]

Not all travel accounts are as condemning as Shelley's; more than a few writers show a genuine appreciation of modern Italians. But his polarization of "two Italies" identifies a binarism that governs much of the Anglo-American travel writing about Italy, an opposition between a diminished modern society and a numinous indwelling Italian spirit associated with eternal art and antiquity. His letter also captures for us the contrasting styles of this body of travel writing – the language of spirit ("radiant atmosphere," "contemplation," "imagination") that defines the Italy of nature and the rich past, and the factual description used to represent contemporary Italians ("their works and ways".) The doubled discourse achieves a remarkable dispossession of Italians, for the Rome of American travel books is no longer the true homeland of contemporary Italian inhabitants: instead the Romans are a "poor superstitious" people, as one writer put it, "having no affinity to their heroic ancestors."[8]

In the preface Hawthorne denies any attempt at a "portraiture of Italian manners and character" (854). But the statement is really a disclaimer for the portions of the narrative that are devoted precise-

ly to describing Italians ("There are many things in the religious
customs of these people that seem good; many things, at least, that
might be both good and beautiful, if the soul of goodness and the
sense of beauty were as much alive in the Italians, now, as they
must have been when those customs were first imagined and
adopted" [1098]. The postscript makes a similar gesture of denial:
writing of his faun, Hawthorne states that he "had hoped to mystify
this anomalous creature between the Real and the Fantastic, in
such a manner that the reader's sympathies might be excited . . .
without impelling him to ask how Cuvier would have classified poor
Donatello" (1239). But Hawthorne's smiling reference to Cuvier
acknowledges more than it dismisses. By combining an allegorical
romance with the genre of the travel book, he grafted onto his novel
a language of classification that was part of the same enterprise of
racial cataloguing as Cuvier's comparative anatomy. Throughout
The Marble Faun, the narrator is repeatedly classifying and comparing national traits, with the "gothic race" and the "present Roman
character" ranked alongside traits to be found in "New England, or
in Russia, or . . . in a hut of the Esquimaux" (1166).

Like Shelley, Hawthorne does not give the "present Roman character" high praise. But what is more pertinent than the particular
way he ranks the traits of diverse collective "characters" is the fact
that the act of ranking makes such characters belong to categories
of the same order. Italians, Yankees, Russians, and Eskimos become comparable and thus equivalent kinds of human groups,
whereas writers today would be expected to distinguish between
racial, ethnic, and regional identities (though the expectation carries no guarantee that such distinctions are ever real, consistent, or
applicable). The traveler's customs-and-manners report allows
writers to designate what Mandeville called "the diversity of
folkys," and in the nineteenth century – no less than today – the
authority to nominate and define diversity carries with it a range of
complex implications. Even in a work of fiction, the discourse of
manners gives the "traveler" the ability to confer on others the
status of a coherent folk or race, at the same as it renders race a
category of remarkably malleable properties.

In fact, fiction turns out to have been necessary to the travel
writer's authority for nominating race. The link between fiction and
race in travel writing has a long history. Michel de Certeau points
to Montaigne's essay "Of Cannibals" as an *index locorum* for the

customs-and-manners report of travel writing. In this essay, as Certeau reads it, Montaigne gives a classic form to the dual articulation of a writing subject and an ethnographic object, the structure that secures the authority to represent the "diversity of folks": the travel report, Certeau writes, "combines a representation of the other" with "the fabrication and accreditation of the text as witness of the other."[9] The fabrication here rests not in a traveler's lies (Montaigne never visited the Americas, nor did he claim to) but in the making of a text. The power to designate a people or "folk" is derived not from the act of seeing but of writing, from the "text as witness": that is, a representation of manners on the page and the circulation of the page through the medium of print. In retrospect, the resulting picture of human diversity often looks suspiciously like a catalogue of preexisting stereotypes. For instance, the compendium of manners in the medieval cosmogeny, one of the earliest ethnographic genres, identified the world's peoples through condensed lists of communal virtues and vices: "The uncleanness & filthiness of the Suevians. The foolishnes of the Saxons. The hardines of the Picts. The Luxurye of the Scots. The Dronkennes and violency of the Spaniards. The anger of the Britaines. The rapacity and greediness of the Normans."[10]

As reified as these traits are, however, the cosmogeny also shows an important kind of flexibility common to most customs-and-manners writings. The representation of manners is the site where a collective character or "disposition" can be made interchangeable with physical traits – typical body size and facial features, skin shadings, the color of eyes and hair. In the cosmogeny, as in the versions of ethnographic reports that follow it, there is a mimetic transfer between what we would now distinguish as physical traits and cultural properties. The measurable "stature" of the Picts thus lends its status to an objectified "hardines" of Picts, in the very process in which Picts are themselves constituted as an object, along with Spaniards and Scots. There is a mutual infiltration of the racial and the cultural in manners writing, a porousness that is part of the discursive process that names and defines who counts – literally, who is counted – in the list of the world's peoples.

What was a centuries-old practice in travel writing found scientific expression in nineteenth-century ethnological theory. "It needs only to contrast national characters," Herbert Spencer wrote, "to see that mental peculiarities caused by habit become hereditary."

The "variety of dispositions" among nations and races "have been gradually produced in the course of generations." And if mental "habit" and social "modes of life" are the products of heredity, it is only logical – or at least symmetrical – to argue, as an American sociologist did, that inherited "physical traits" should also "reveal themselves in the temperamental differences of Chinamen, Latins, and Anglo-Saxons."[11] In travel writing, and in the racial theory that borrowed from travel writing, the representation of a people and their "character" was less a matter of observation than composition. By "composition" I mean a resourceful, flexible, tautological construction of character in printed discourse, a mutually constitutive *composure* of the national and the racial, the mental and the physical – in short, a double discourse of cultural character and racial characteristics. Whatever the influence of genes or training or climate, there was a more fundamental sense in which racial characters were transmitted on the printed page, in fiction as well as in books of travel and social theory.

In *The Marble Faun*, the same mimetic slippage between race and culture provides the very makeup of its fictional actors and determines their ultimate fate: dispossession for some, repatriation for others. Donatello and Miriam have received their personal qualities, their motives and temperament or "spirits," from inherited fables, yet they are also linked to a collection of racial types. In patterning Miriam after Beatrice Cenci, Hawthorne creates an archetypal figure of sexual transgression and tragic knowledge in the character of a sorrowful woman. Recalling a dark legend, she is a ready figure for Hawthorne's allegorical tale. But while Miriam's "hidden significance" at one level locates a "great errour" or "fatal weakness" in the human condition, it is also a hidden *racial* significance. Kenyon, the American sculptor, connects the romance "mystery" of Miriam's past life with a mystery of "breeding": "We do not even know whether she is a countrywoman of ours, or an Englishwoman, or a German. There is Anglo-Saxon blood in her veins, one would say, and a right English accent on her tongue, but much that is not English breeding, nor American (942)." Not only is Miriam's breeding unknown, but the category of breeding itself presents a notable uncertainty here. English grammar allows for a functional ambiguity about "English breeding": with this sentence structure it is possible that Kenyon means to contrast breeding with blood (she has Anglo-Saxon blood and yet a manner that is non-Anglo) but equally possible that he means to connect them as synonyms (she has Anglo-Saxon blood but a blood or breeding that seems non-Anglo as well). The grammatical uncertainty, though, is probably semantically accurate, since it corresponds nicely to an ambiguity in what is probably the most familiar usage of "breeding," namely, a tutelage by one's kin, producing a set of personal qualities that is still a family inheritance. Used in this manner, "breeding" does not exactly mean an influence of "blood," but it does not rule out that meaning either. Breeding is both nature and nurture but neither exclusively. A similarly unfixed meaning is associated with the category of national identity in this passage, as well. Neither English nor American "breeding" is identical with "Anglo-Saxon blood" in the passage, though it is equally true that neither appears in any sure opposition – either to blood or to each other.

In all likelihood, Hawthorne did not put careful thought into any of these shifting distinctions and affinities but simply grouped together a number of loosely defined rumors of origin to lend the character an aura of romance exoticism. This has been the explanation for additional rumors about Miriam that critics have identified as echoes of nineteenth-century racism. The "rich Oriental character in her face" prompts the story that she is "the heiress of a great Jewish banker." In the most charged racial reference, Miriam is whispered to be a genteel Southern mulatta whose "one burning drop of African blood in her veins so affected her with a sense of ignominy, that she relinquished all, and fled her country" (870). The novel also makes an unmistakable association between Miriam and Kenyon's Cleopatra statue, a figure to which "the sculptor had not shunned to give full Nubian lips, and other characteristics of the Egyptian physiognomy" (957–8). Clearly the point of these multiple allusions to blood and physiognomy is their indeterminacy rather than any racial determinism. Despite all the rumors – or rather, *with* all the rumors – Miriam's background cannot be fully known. The inscriptions of race are meant to heighten the rich indirection of Hawthorne's romance method. Yet it is precisely the elaborate but casual and unsystematic nature of these racial associations that is most significant, for the indeterminacy of reference produces what we might call a "romance determinism." In the romance novel, that is, the very uncertainty of Miriam's origins and past life is a sure mark of some unseen and unnamed otherness within that drives her destiny in the plot. An invisible identity, which has only outward hints in her dark coloring or in the "Oriental character in her face," determines Miriam's final position in the novel: a figure of separateness, of a "subtile quality" that places her "at a distance" (869), which is finally the insuperable distance of "the other side of a fathomless abyss" (1237).

This final image of Miriam only solidifies what we know from the first: that she is "out of the sphere of humanity," as if belonging to "a far-off region, the remoteness of which – while yet her face is so close before us – makes us shiver as at a spectre" (905). In this sense, Miriam is not a member of any particular race so much as an emblem *of* race or, what amounts to the same thing, an emblem of racial difference – of race *as* difference – a contentless, unspecified alterity from a "a far-off region" that is brought uncannily "close before us." Like the figure of the tragic mulatta she is rumored to be, Miriam embodies an invisible, undetectable identity that nevertheless determines her social fate. But she is thus an emblem of a special, if inexact, kind of racial identity that is not physical but spiritual, an ineffable identity never exhausted by any list of traits, with only a secondary manifestation in features like face, hair, or stature, if such signs are there at all. Our tag description of "romance determinism" is not without some historical accuracy, then, as it recalls the ideas of Romantic thinkers such as Herder, who conceived of race as a spiritual, supraindividual entity that is the essential "genius" of a people, a notion of race that would become the basis of the anthropological idea of culture.[12]

Hawthorne's romance, then, far from being at odds with the question of race, instead manages to spiritualize it, to make it a matter of invisible, benign, and even moral meaning. Race offers the spiritual ingredients of romance. The rumored details of Miriam's race – her variously Jewish, African, English, German, Italian origins – are enumerated only so as to be dissolved into some more refined quality of character, a romance quality that, quite logically, determines her place in the romance novel, as the tragic Other, always "at a distance."

That this spiritualizing of race is one of the aims of Hawthorne's *Marble Faun* seems clear from the novel's admiring description of what Praxiteles was able to do with his marble faun: "Praxiteles has subtly diffused, throughout his work, that mute mystery which so hopelessly perplexes us, whenever we attempt to gain an intellec-

tual or sympathetic knowledge of the lower orders of creation"
(861). Hawthorne's romance novel, though obsessed by "lower tribes"
and "lower orders," claims to have no knowledge about such orders
(as a realist work would claim) but rather aspires to "diffuse" and
aestheticize the perplexity that the question of lower orders seems
to pose. We can see both the perplexity and the strategy of romance
diffusion most clearly in the character of Donatello. But we also
discover in Donatello that Hawthorne's diffusion does not in fact
dispel social and political puzzles but rather facilitates a "mute"
and strategic mystery of race.

THE MUTE MYSTERY OF RACE

Donatello is an odd inversion of the eighteenth-century noble savage: he is a nobleman who has the romantic savage's rustic simplicity. "Betwixt man and animal," he is likened to "a creature of
the happy tribes below us" (917). Yet this happy mediation of
human and brute orders, creating "a being in whom both races
meet, on friendly ground" (861), does not achieve the stable equipoise that the picturesque mediation seems designed to produce.
For instance, Miriam glimpses in a flash of Donatello's anger a
"trait of savageness" that presages his ability to murder. "His lips
were drawn apart, so as to disclose his set teeth, thus giving him a
look of animal rage which we seldom see except in persons of the
simplest and rudest natures" (927). Apparently one of the perplexities about the "lower orders of creation" is just what it means to
have a savage nature, whether such "persons" belong to the "happy
tribes" or are creatures of angry, murderous "savageness." This is
of course a very old riddle: historically these alternatives are mutually exclusive theories about natural man. For Donatello, however,
belonging to the "tribes below" means one is a creature of both a
kindly *and* a sinister nature.

> Beautiful, strong, brave, kindly, sincere, of honest impulses, and
> endowed with simple tastes, and the love of homely pleasures, he
> was believed to possess gifts by which he could associate himself
> with the wild things of the forests. . . . On the other hand, there
> were deficiencies both of intellect and heart. . . . These defects were
> less perceptible in early youth, but showed themselves more strongly
> with advancing age, when, as the animal spirits settled down upon a
> lower level, the representative of the Monte Benis was apt to become

sensual, addicted to gross pleasures, heavy, unsympathizing, and insulated within the narrow limits of a surly selfishness. (1046)

Donatello's character is fashioned not by choosing between competing theories of primitivism but by an amalgamation of primitive types: Donatello is the noble savage *and* the savage savage *and* (at least potentially) the civilized savage, that is, the Italian sensualist "addicted to gross pleasures." As with his portrait of Miriam, Hawthorne creates this romance character by multiplying, and thus diffusing, a subtext of conflicting racial allusions. This becomes most obvious in "The Pedigree of Monte Beni," a chapter in which Donatello's "pedigree," like Miriam's "breeding," is a highly malleable category that obviates the problem of racial determinism by making race something richly indeterminate. Tracing Donatello's "wild blood" (1045), the narrator gives in excessive detail a lineage that combines an Italian "genealogy" with what are stressed as "altogether mythical" origins. The result is that genealogy itself becomes a matter of myth – though this is not to say that all that is inherited is merely mythic. The elaborate pedigree makes race a matter of every and any kind of human category: the "scattered qualities of his race" (1046) include an inherited "family character," a family history, a class identity, a nationality, a "pre-historic" tribal identity ("the Pelasgic race," men of "Asiatic birth"), and a "wild paternity" of acknowledged myth. By widening, and thus blurring, the category of "his race," Hawthorne seems to be insisting that Donatello's identity is anything but racial – if by racial we mean Cuvier's sense of race, the only sense Hawthorne expressly excludes from Donatello's pedigree.

I do not mean to suggest that the expansive use of the category of race is unique to Hawthorne; rather Hawthorne's chapter dramatizes the elasticity of the nineteenth-century usage "in a period," as one historian notes, "when almost any human group – whether linguistic, religious, or national – might be called a 'race.'"[13] However, the portrait of Donatello also suggests that the wide use of the term was not a semantic blandness but an expansive usage that was distinctly useful. It suggests, that is, that race is an overdetermined site where what "perplexes us" (Hawthorne's "Public" [854] of presumably white Americans) about worrisome "lower orders" could be aesthetically transformed into a matter of "romantic interest" (1044). Like the Virginia slaves converted in Hawthorne's imagination into fauns, Donatello and his pedigree as a modern faun transform all that engaged Cuvier about race – anatomy and mental capacity, reproduction and miscegenation – into a fiction of moral allegory. Race and any contemporary politics of race become the stuff of romance: fanciful and not material, allegorical and not political, spiritual and not determinate.

Still, certain features of Donatello's pedigree seem to be determinate. Certainly some are material features: the chapter also includes an odd focus on what Hawthorne calls a "hereditary peculiarity," those "characteristics," such as "a supernumerary finger, or an anomalous shape of feature, like the Austrian lip," that can remain latent in a number of generations and then reappear in later descendants. For a novel that aims to "mystify" (1239) the questions of Donatello's pedigree "between the Real and the Fantastic," there is a curious stress in the chapter on these quite exact hereditary features. Although the point of this survey of Donatello's origins seems to be the "qualities of his race" that are immaterial – the "gifts" and "deficiencies" of "family character" – the narrator nevertheless turns from character to inherited physical characteristics when he wants to foreshadow Donatello's fate. Kenyon sees in portraits of Monte Beni ancestors certain "physical features of the race" that "had a tendency to look grim and savage" (1047). Like the "trait of savageness" that Miriam sees when Donatello bares his "set teeth," these "savage" physical features seem to foretell Donatello's act of murder and his banishment to "the uneasy streets of Rome," where, like Miriam, he is "rendered remote and strange" (1179–80).

Does inheriting savage features make one a savage? Spencer thought so: "Hereditary transmission applies to psychical peculiarities as well as to physical peculiarities." Just as a racial physiology is a matter of permanent traits, so too, by this reasoning, would social and "psychical" traits be a racial inheritance. As a central problem in nineteenth-century racial theory, this Lamarckian question locates precisely the kind of uneasy perplexities Hawthorne meant to dispel in his romance.[14] In *The Marble Faun*, though, the problem of traits still could be said to pose an aesthetic puzzle, if not a racial one, for the early signs of "grim and savage" ancestral features in Donatello's face predict something the plot will eventually both confirm and deny. The savage features he inherits become marks of the impulsive, dramatic murder he commits; traits, it seems, can foretell acts. But rather than allowing Donatello to degenerate into the "surly animal" that his ancestors tend to resemble, the allegorical plot points us toward his redemptive transformation through a fortunate fall. (The novel's first title was *The Transformation*.) The crime and the remorse it instills create in Donatello a "thousand high capabilities" that make him tragically but fully human. Yet although the express intent of the novel is to retell "the story of the Fall of Man," it is impossible to overlook the fact that the character who is the novel's moral center, Hilda, actually decries the doctrine of a *felix culpa*. Hilda silences Kenyon's suggestion that sin can bring about a "higher and purer state": "Do you not perceive what a mockery your creed makes, not only of all religious sentiment, but of moral law?" (1236).

In this light, the revision of Hawthorne's original title *The Transformation* seems especially significant, a gesture of ambiguity about the very conversion the plot is designed to dramatize. Moreover, the actual transformation of Donatello is not in fact dramatized but remains curiously absent from the novel: "For all the times that he is said to do so, we do not see Donatello become more richly human as the novel progresses." The novel appears to harbor real doubts about its own imaginative proposition of the romance transformation from faun to man, doubts that produce what one critic calls a "fundamental disjuncture" in the work as a whole.[15] How should we read this internal resistance in the novel and the division it produces? Is the faultline in the book an artistic lapse, or has Hawthorne's romance in fact extended rather than dissolved the "mute mystery" of the divide between the human and the "lower orders" that he perceived in the faun?

Interestingly, in the imagination of the white "Public" addressed in Hawthorne's preface, the possibility of transformation was as vexed a question for those he labeled "fauns" on the Virginia road as it was for his modern faun in Italy. During Reconstruction and its aftermath, the question of whether freedmen really could become free Americans was a point of continuing debate. Frederick Douglass had declared his own transformation: "you shall see a slave become a man." It was pointedly a self-transformation, not of his inalienable human nature, but of his social status and personal self-regard.[16] Following the Civil War, though, when white authorities were to rewrite the law precisely to foster the same transformation from slaves to citizens, resistance to that enterprise turned to what both Hawthorne and Spencer called "hereditary peculiarities," the "race habits" that were said to make any true transformation impossible.

> The negro child, even when reared in a white family under the most favorable conditions, fails to take on the mental and moral characteristics of the Caucasian race. His mental attitudes toward persons and things, toward organized society, toward life, and toward religion never become quite the same as those of the white. His natural instincts, it is true, may be modified by training, and perhaps indefinitely in the course of generations; but the race habit of a thousand generations or more is not set aside by the voluntary or enforced imitation of visible models, and there is always a strong tendency to reversion. The reappearance of voodooism and fetishism among the negroes of the South, though surrounded by Christian influence, is indeed to be regarded as due not so much to the preservation of some primitive copy of such religious practices brought over from Africa as to the innate tendency of the negro mind to take such attitudes toward nature and the universe as tend to develop such religions.[17]

The notably inconsistent concept of a "race habit" is the pivotal category in this passage. By "habit," the writer means mentalistic phenomena of "attitudes" and "moral characteristics," "which make personal and social development tend to take one direction rather than another." But cast as *race* habits, such characteristics, though not immutable, and admittedly open to change in the "course of generations," ensure that "negro" development will never be "quite the same" as that of whites. The author of this passage, a scholar who later became president of the American Sociological Society, gives with one hand ("development") what he takes away with the other ("reversion"). From the perspective of present-day anthropology, the demonstrable contradictions here make this a piece of bad science. But what is bad science by today's standards is in fact a rich, complex illumination of a real and efficient social praxis. Inherited, though not inherent, the idea of a race habit keeps formally open the prospect of the freedmen's transformation but closes it in practical terms, for the simple reason that any habit deemed racial will by definition carry the mark of difference. In this way ethnological theory distills in formal terms a broader praxis of the post–Civil War era, operations by which U.S. institutions held open the prospect of social and political development for the for-

merly enslaved but in practice foreclosed the prospect by enshrin-
ing in law and custom what the landmark Plessy *v.* Ferguson case
would call "distinctions based upon color."[18]

And even where civil society did remain open to the possibility of
development for people of color, it could always shut down the
prospect for reasons of culture. Another scholar, for instance, argues that "the breaking down of the instincts and habits of servi-
tude, and the acquisition, by the masses of the Negro people, of the
instincts and habits of freedom, have proceeded slowly but steadily" since Emancipation. But at the same time it was asserted that
whites' color prejudice was "the instinctive expression of a sense of
cultural difference and social status."[19] Thus, even when racial
difference is conceded to be breaking down, cultural difference
could be elided with ineradicable racial instinct. This half of the
freedman's double bind was also expressed in the Plessy decision,
which declared that "legislation is powerless to eradicate racial
instincts" and that a state was "at liberty to act with reference to
the established usages, customs, and traditions of the people." The
Plessy case, a capstone to the legal codification of Jim Crow, derived much of its effectiveness from the slippery junctions between
culture and race in nineteenth-century racial theory: distinctions of
color are the reason for legally codifying a different cultural status,
and distinctions in cultural status are the proof of instinctive differences of color. Race and culture can never be proposed as identical,
for the elimination of all difference in meaning would eliminate the
leverage necessary for each to afford the other a strategic equivocation. But by the same token, if race and culture are entirely separ-
able, all equivocation is eliminated. What emerges, then, is an
uncanny kind of identity – a racial identity, which, as the white-
looking Homer Plessy had shown, was not even a matter of visible
color but makes race visible in the things of culture, the (legislated)
customs and manners of a segregated society.[20]

I have suggested that a similar doubling of race and culture can
help explain an aesthetic segregation in *The Marble Faun*, a "fundamental disjunction" that has led critics to go so far as to declare the
novel in effect two books between the same covers. The uncanny
romance identity of Miriam and Donatello sets them apart from the
Americans Kenyon and Hilda, creating what has been read as
"precisely opposed novels." The difference goes beyond their divergent passions and actions. By the end of the novel, the pairs

move in wholly different physical spaces and social worlds, a spatial separation that reflects their quite distinct orders of fictive status: "They seem to inhabit the same world, but in fact they are incommensurate."[21] This incommensurability has remained the central interpretive problem for the novel's critics, who look variously to biographical, historical, and ideological solutions to the aesthetic split. But what if the division is itself a solution, a novelistic version of a broader practice of *designing* the incommensurate?

By suggesting that the novel's formal disjunctions share something with the social and racial disjunctions that emerged in post–Civil War America, I am not arguing that this aesthetic divide signals a segregationist urge cloaked in fiction, even though Hilda's "involuntary repellent gesture" at the sight of Miriam and her "shrinking" recoil and "expression of horrour" at the idea of Donatello's transformation are both gestures that resemble the supposed "instinctive expression" of "a sense of cultural difference" that some cited to prop up racial segregation. I want to argue rather that Hawthorne's allegory has been shaped by a desire precisely to purify a story of human development from all troubling questions of human difference, a desire that itself makes a defining aesthetic difference in the text. When Kenyon introduces questions of cultural and racial identity, of uncertain "blood" and "accent" and "breeding," to explain Miriam's difference, Hilda reacts with distinct "displeasure" ("I love her dearly" and "trust her most entirely") (943). Questions of blood are lodged in the moral tale but are then expressly refused a determining position in the novel's meditation on the moral development from "lower orders" to the highest humanity. Hilda's reasons for recoil are emphatically reasons of "moral law" (1236). When she says she and Miriam must remain "forever strangers," it is an anguished response that is actually prompted by her sympathy for Miriam. "I would keep ever at your side," Hilda tells her, but "the pure, white atmosphere, in which I try to discern what things are good and true, would be discolored" (1025).

Hilda's aversion is thus a matter of morality, not color – though in this very speech her language superimposes moral discernments and color distinctions. That Hilda in her "white atmosphere" rejects Miriam and Donatello for fear of being "discolored" is not the product of a disguised racial code Hawthorne has implanted in the novel. It is rather the creation of history's codes, of the doubling of the moral and the racial that history has inscribed within the language to such a degree that talk about what is "good and true" is talk about whiteness, while the devil himself is (in *The Scarlet Letter*, for instance) quite simply "the Black man." Hilda's rejection in the name of "moral law" is a "white wisdom" (1236) that pulls Kenyon back from the "verge" of blasphemy and secures the final segregation in the novel, the actual removal of Kenyon and Hilda to the source of her white wisdom, Hawthorne's America.

To contextualize *The Marble Faun* in this way is to pose the possibility that the internal division in the novel is not so much the result of an artistic lapse or a failure of Hawthorne's nerve in the face of heterodoxy as it is an aesthetic faultline from a problem of social "orders," a problem Hawthorne has spiritualized in art. With its incommensurate plots, *The Marble Faun* formally keeps apart as distinctly different "orders" what Hawthorne's other textual fauns literally embody as a distressing racial disorder. The novel thus resolves through a strategy of irresolution what I believe was a sincere and, finally, a moral preoccupation for Hawthorne: the perplexing relation to "lower orders."[22] From this perspective, what Hawthorne's moral allegory explores is the nature of being "lower" – whether what is low is the product of a fixed design or whether it is possible to bring about a historical transformation of hierarchical orders. The segregation in the text is not a separation of exotic strangers from Americans (though this is in fact what the story line finally achieves). It is rather an aesthetic division that provides two ways, separate if not equal, of confronting the energies summoned by the figure of the faun, the transgressive energies evoked in the reading public by the problem of "lower orders." What the novel could be said to segregate, then, is Hawthorne's divided mind, an imagination drawn both to the safe illusion of what the Plessy case would call an immutable "nature of things," but drawn as well to the threatening yet still, I think, inspiring prospect that catastrophes, even crimes, and perhaps wars could transform the American nature of things.[23]

What these divided sentiments mean in formal terms is a double territory of romance, governed by a careful design of difference. Though the Americans share the plot with their two "Italian friends," the couples are separated by a boundary not just of cultural customs but of fictional kind. Kenyon sculpts his Cleopatra in a "repose of despair," but Miriam *is* that despairing Cleopatra – like the statue, an aesthetic object representing exotic, passionate "womanhood." The American visitors gaze upon Praxitiles' faun in the Capitol gallery, but Donatello *is* a reanimated faun, with all the ambiguities that such a creature signifies for Hawthorne. Hilda and Kenyon belong in the colony of American artists, while Donatello and Miriam belong to the order of myths that had an imaginative life in the paintings and sculptures those artists copied. Moreover, Hilda and Kenyon are not only artists but cultural observers. Like tourists or Old World ethnographers, the Americans always retain a distance – a social if not emotional distance – from the people and objects they observe. The "chasm" widens, so that by the end of the novel, Miriam and Donatello have become almost purely iconic. In the concluding scenes they appear only as silent, disguised figures that Hilda and Kenyon gaze on from a distance "as if . . . on the other side of a fathomless abyss" (1237). The two transgressive characters are in some ways the novel's most vibrant, figures not only of erotic possibility and passionate acts and beliefs but of the exciting and solemn prospect of transforming human subjectivity. But despite these attractions the two serve finally as objects of contemplation more than as subjects who contemplate, as emblems rather than agents. They have the value of the cultural relic, a stilled object that preserves and aestheticizes otherness.

Hawthorne's own title prepares this: the faun is a stylized artifact valued not only for its beauty but for its imagined resolution to historical perplexities, "a being in whom both races meet, on friendly ground." As we have seen, though, the story of Hawthorne's faun does not seamlessly mediate the problem of higher and lower orders. Instead it distributes or defers the problem by articulating incommensurate stories that share the same novel. As if to acknowledge the difficulties in this tactic, the narrator concedes in the first chapter that "the idea" of the faun "grows coarse, when we handle it, and hardens in our grasp" (861). But the aim of Hawthorne's method is clear: through a romancing of "coarse" categories of race and pedigree, Hawthorne envisions a resolution of the difference between higher and lower orders, achieved "without monstrosity." For Hawthorne, romance is a place where different orders "meet, on friendly ground," a mediation designed to offer otherness without monstrosity.

In this regard, we can say that Hawthorne's romance territory is also the nineteenth-century ethnographer's territory of culture. In

1915, Alfred Kroeber called the idea of acquired race habits "a biological and historical monstrosity." What plagued the early "study of culture," Kroeber later wrote, was "the blind and bland shuttling back and forth between an equivocal 'race' and an equivocal 'civilization.'"[24] But what came to appear theoretically grotesque was in fact a crucial element in the development of cultural anthropology. Even as it emerged as a distinct professional tool, the anthropological concept of culture was inseparable from the concept of race. E. B. Tylor famously defined culture "in its wide ethnographic sense" at the beginning of his 1871 study *Primitive Culture*: culture is "that complex whole which includes knowledge, belief, art, morals, law, custom, and any other capabilities and habits acquired by man as a member of society." Enumerating social rather than physical elements and insisting on their integration in a "complex whole," the passage has been canonized as the classic statement of the anthropological culture concept, which, through its relativism and holism, breaks away from earlier notions of both racial temperament and high civilization. Yet a closer reading of *Primitive Culture* shows that Tylor's culture consists of "different grades" that are unmistakably racial. Culture in Tylor's book is produced in part from ethnographic comparisons that structure an "order of culture" through color: "Thus, on the definite basis of compared facts, ethnographers are able to set up at least a rough scale of civilization. Few would dispute that the following races are arranged rightly in order of culture: Australian, Tahitian, Aztec, Chinese, Italian." Tylor's culture has hierarchical stages, stages that are in fact hierarchical races. Until Franz Boas made it his object to sever race from culture, the concept of culture in anthropology was articulated through a racial "scale of civilization." Historian George Stocking notes that "'culture,' in its anthropological sense, provided a functionally equivalent substitute for the older idea of 'race temperament.'" Like the field of culture in *The Marble Faun*, the culture concept of early anthropology drew upon an equivocation of race, and did so without any (as yet) perceived theoretical monstrosity.[25]

This is not to say that particular uses of ethnological theory never appeared monstrous. Frederick Douglass, for one, pointed to the travesty of Jim Crow, a political expression (if a distorted one) of the color "scale" that informed Tylor's idea of culture. Aided by racial theory, the dismantling of civil rights for blacks had made "the citizenship granted in the Fourteenth Amendment . . . practically a mockery." Douglass's antebellum narrative had stressed an envisioning of freedom: "*you shall see* a slave become a man." But in the aftermath of the war the nation had failed to realize the moral vision of civil enfranchisement, and Douglass's own American self-transformation was supplanted by a grotesque parody of American citizenship. The monstrosity of a distinct, racially marked citizenship, perhaps the most poignant example of the strategic interpolation of race and culture, is the obverse of Hawthorne's ideal of the "delightful" faun: a coarse color citizenship created by substituting sophistry for perplexity, that exploits rather than diffuses the boundaries distinguishing the "lower orders."[26]

Yet the category of race did not make all transformation unthinkable in this period. Scholar William Thomas argues that a "formation of true races" is "taking place before our eyes at the present moment." Many apparently could envision what Frederick Jackson Turner described as a process in which "immigrants were Americanized, liberated, and fused into a mixed race" or "composite nationality." But Thomas's point about the race formation achieved "before our eyes" was an assertion about "historic races," that is, emergent national characters of which presumably an American "race" was one.[27] This process of Americanization, moreover, could be set against the enfranchisement of African Americans and selected immigrant groups, for what Kroeber would call the "shuttling" between race and culture made it possible to exclude certain populations from the American "race" on the basis of their culture. Postbellum debates about immigration, for instance, featured arguments to refuse entrance to all but those "Aryanized in spirit and in genius by contact" with whites. Others argued that real Americanization was of necessity restricted to those with certain cultural traits we might best compare to Hilda's love of law, traits which turn out to have a racial base: an "ethnical affinity" with the Teutonic race, the argument went, includes a "substantial consensus of opinion concerning rights and wrongs, liberty and government, policy and interests." This strain of thought, for instance, would lead Woodrow Wilson to insist that Filipinos must accept U.S. tutelage in the "discipline of law," that they must "love order and instinctively yield to it."[28]

In this body of social thought, citizenship had become a racial capacity and immigration a matter of racial assimilation. Similarly, white emigration was also a question of assimilation, or rather the impossibility of assimilation. One prominent racial theorist declared "the almost universal opinion" that "true colonization in the tropics by the white race is impossible." Emigration was a kind of fatality: "To urge the emigration of women, children, or of any save those in the most robust health to the tropics may not be to murder in the first degree, but it should be classed, to put it mildly, as incitement to it." Speaking to the same issue, American ethnographer Daniel Brinton declared that "there is no such thing as acclimation. A race never was acclimated, and in the present condition of the world, a race never can become acclimated."[29]

In *The Marble Faun*, being American does not mean that a citizen has an American racial identity, but it does mean that there is a certain danger for citizens in emigration and that emigration may even signal the prospect of death. The penultimate paragraph in the novel announces the return of Hilda and Kenyon to America through an uneasy meditation on questions of social acclimation:

> they resolved to go back to their own land; because the years, after all, have a kind of emptiness, when we spend too many of them on a foreign shore. We defer the reality of life, in such cases, until a future moment, when we shall again breathe our native air; but by-and-by, there are no future moments; or, if we do return, we find that the native air has lost its invigorating quality, and that life has shifted its reality to the spot where we had deemed ourselves only temporary residents. Thus, between two countries, we have none at all, or only that little space of either, in which we finally lay down our discontented bones. It is wise, therefore, to come back betimes – or never. (1237)

The return to America is shadowed by the possibility of never returning. Doubled in this way, the passage offers a summation of the novel's aesthetic equivocations. With its language of shifts and deferrals, its abrupt formal reversals and elegiac tone, it seems unable to decide whether permanent emigration is an impossibility or an all too real possibility – and both prospects, anyway, are haunted by "a kind of emptiness." The resolution to Hawthorne's international romance is presented through striking hesitations: "between two countries, we have none at all." For a novel that is meant to define American identity against its Old World origins, this conclusion concedes a remarkable uncertainty about that identity and about where and how to locate "the reality of life" (by itself an unusual stated emphasis in a Hawthorne romance).

At the moment of closure the novel hesitates, something the

social documents we have been examining seem rarely to do. With their uncertain and "discontented" tone, Hawthorne's concluding ruminations about living within and without one's "native air" are a sharp contrast to the racial arguments about American emigration and immigration which, for all their inconsistencies of logic, tended to assert strict boundaries of identity: negro assimilation "fails"; races acclimate "never"; white colonization of the tropics is "impossible"; for certain immigrant groups, American "civilization has no effect." Yet the equivocation in the novel's final passage also could be said to make legible the suspensions and shifts of logic that operate within that body of racial theory and are the ground for its authoritative certainty. The speculations on culture and race that soon would harden into immigration policies are here the fluid musings of an emigration elegy. But *The Marble Faun* could be said already to contain this discrepancy itself: critics have noted that the novel's final brooding tone is at odds with its own plot resolution in the absolutist creed of Hilda, the "Anglo-Saxon girl." The narrator's wistfulness might well reflect the personal melancholy of a writer who was nearing his death. But the resulting ambiguity – Hilda's strict certainty about law and emigration, and the narrator's sense of "emptiness" about reality and emigration – relies on an open margin for maneuvering that resembles the space of equivocation in the contemporary discourse of race. Hawthorne's famous ambiguity, here an ambiguous account of what happens to Americans abroad, marks for us an enabling ambiguity in the era's social thought, a capacity for shifting and doubling that informed arguments about who belongs where in American society and world geography. Moreover, it marks rather more concretely a formal ambiguity in *The Marble Faun* that allows for the sorting of people into "their own land." Hawthorne's romance enacts journeys of reverse emigration of which the final return of Hilda and Kenyon to America is only the most visible instance. Central to this narrative sorting are principles of cultural law and meditations on racial death, two imaginative structures that informed nineteenth-century primitivism and placed race on a continuum of time.

MAPPING THE PRIMITIVE

Prompted by a sense of "human promise" and the dictates of "moral law," Hilda and Kenyon return to America. Yet for Hawthorne at the time he was completing *The Marble Faun* in England, America appeared to pose the danger of lawlessness. Abolitionists and other agitators seemed to him like "terrorists of France," eager to rend the country into "distracted fragments." As war approached and then broke out, Hawthorne repeatedly referred to it in images of the violent tearing apart of order – a society "overturned from its foundations," convulsed in "death throes," and facing "utter ruin."[30] When a British friend gave him a "shaded map of negrodom" that indicated proportions of the black and white populations in the South, Hawthorne wrote "what a terrible amount of trouble and expense in washing that sheet white, and after all I am afraid we shall only variegate it with blood and dirt." For Hawthorne, moreover, the prospect of war seemed to distill a more general threat to social order. Henry James saw in Hawthorne's campaign biography, *The Life of Franklin Pierce*, an attempt to quiet "the many-headed monster of universal suffrage." Living in England, Hawthorne was attuned to the sounds from across the Atlantic of a "miserable confusion" he believed endemic in American society, hearing "the most piercing shriek, the wildest yell, and all the ugly sounds of popular turmoil, inseparable from the life of a republic."[31] Yet in *The Marble Faun* itself, an America never directly portrayed is nonetheless the repository and "home" of the highest wisdom and moral low. In the novel, it is Italy that seems to hold the threat of political and popular turmoil, whereas the America described in the novel's preface is a "stalwart" nation of "commonplace prosperity" (854).

Why this apparent transposition of Old and New Worlds? There is no incongruity, if we recognize that Italy in *The Marble Faun* is the site of what Tylor called "primitive culture," the place of origins whose very errors hold the keys to the laws of culture and the promise of continuing progress. In Tylor's work, the anthropological imagination represents the power of making sense out of the riddles and "strife" of contemporary social life. Tylor staked out primitive culture "not merely as a matter of curious research, but as an important practical guide to the understanding of the present." His "scale of civilization" promised a powerful genealogy of modernity, a narrative of origins that could account for the social difference or "unevenness" perceived at home and abroad. Rather than study directly the "seething problems of our own day, the ferment and sharp strife," Tylor writes, the anthropologist goes to the source and seeks "to gain insight into general laws of culture, in study among antiquarian relics."[32]

In *The Marble Faun*, Italy offers the "antiquarian relics" for a modern America, and the novel's imagined excavations of pagan art and ancient icons are the source of general laws of culture, laws that can confirm "prosperity" and progress for an unrepresented America. *The Marble Faun* is as much about time as about geography (as space is made a function of time in the concept of the Old World), and Hilda and Kenyon's travel to Italy is a journey back into the earlier social forms that preceded American institutions. While Donatello represents what Kenyon calls "the childhood of the race," a simpler man that existed before the complexities of civilized life, Italy and the Italians represent survivals of "early" institutions: the Catholicism superseded by Protestant Christianity, the jumble of class ranks eliminated in American republicanism, the "petty industry" of household economies and village market days erased in rational modern economies. "To the eyes of an observer from the Western world," as the narrator puts it, these sights are sometimes charming, sometimes wretched, but always backward (1093). Tylor introduced his *Primitive Culture* with a similar transposition of time and space. The "early stages" of our evolution "lie distant from us in time as the stars lie distant from us in space."[33] This temporal lens is the key to the resources of imagination created from a primitive Italy.

In nineteenth-century primitivism, the operative traits are not physical but moral and temporal: to be primitive was to belong to a particular place in time, though that same temporal identity might well determine one's proper homeland. Conceived in this way, the concept of primitive culture could be transferred from colonized peoples to European societies as an instrument to gauge the advancement of a given nation or social class. As George Stocking demonstrates, in his history of Victorian anthropology, Anglo-American theories of the development of civilization out of savagery were strongly conditioned by a middle-class consciousness that emerged at the beginning of the century. The social values of the industrialized middle classes became the evolutionary principles of all human progress. Self-discipline and sexual restraint, rational control over instinct and superstition, the ability to delay economic gratifications and physical pleasures – these bourgeois virtues were writ large as universal forces in human history. The savage had failed to progress, in short, because he lacked the key ingredients in Weber's Protestant work ethic. Herbert Spencer's 1871 descriptions of "Primitive Man – Emotional" and "Primitive Man – Intellec-

tual" distilled two decades of evolutionary theory about the traits of
the "inferior races." The emotional life of the uncivilized man was
dominated by "impulsiveness," the "sudden, or approximately-
reflex, passing of single passion into the conduct it prompts." Given
to "childish mirthfulness," he is unable to conceive future consequences or needs; "desire goes at once to gratification." Primitive
man had no "moral nature." His intellectual nature was marked by
"acute senses and quick perceptions." But although "mental energies go out in restless perception, they cannot go out in deliberate
thought." The savage had "the mind of a child with the passions of
a man."[34]

The phrase serves equally well as a description of Hawthorne's
fictional faun. Donatello gave "the idea of being not precisely man,
nor yet a child, but, in a high and beautiful sense, an animal" (916).
As in the current theories of primitive man, Donatello's life is determined by his impulsiveness: his sudden flaring of anger against the
model leads him to murder in a "breathless instant." Aside from his
bursts of passion, however, he is "mirthful," a "thing of sportive,
animal nature," and his face shows a "simple expression and sensuous beauty" (984). In this sense Donatello is primitive not by way
of his pedigree but because of his character, or rather what he lacks
in character: he has "no principle of virtue, and would be incapable
of comprehending such"; there is a "lack of moral severity" (860).

But as an overtly mythic character, Donatello owes less to Spencer than to a strain of "soft" primitivism drawn to mythologies and
folk legends. This branch of evolutionist thinking nostalgically
looked back to a vanished preindustrial world. Nineteenth-century
antiquarians studied and often idealized prehistoric European societies and disappearing rural communities. Folk cultures were perceived as "survivals" of Europe's earliest societies. But where
eighteenth-century antiquarians had included didactic "reflections" on the primitive customs they catalogued, "shewing which
may be retain'd and which ought to be laid aside," the later folk
movement tended to celebrate what were assumed to be organically
rooted customs of premodern Europe. Admiration from these
nineteenth-century scholars was less qualified, because the folkways now seemed so utterly to belong to the past. Antiquarians
devoted special attention to native mythologies: ballads, superstitions, legends – "folk-lore," in a pointedly literary sense.[35] Hawthorne's "modern faun," then, created by superimposing myth on

modernity, was not a unique trope. Donatello reflects in part a historical self-consciousness that placed idealized lore against the backdrop of urban societies. "The belief in Fairies is by no means extinct in England," wrote one scholar. "Where steam engines, cotton mills, mail coaches, and similar exorcists have not yet penetrated, numerous legends might be collected." Moreover, Hawthorne was not the only writer to set the classical faun in high relief against industrial civilization. Tylor pointed to dryads and fauns as "perfect types" of a vanished animistic world. Explorer Alfred Russel Wallace, later a leading Darwinist, used the figure of the faun in a passage from his 1853 *Narrative of Travels on the Amazon and Rio Negro*. Although he saw the Brazilian tribes as free from the "annoyances of civilization," Wallace never lost faith in the "struggle for existence" in the civilized world that drew out "the highest powers and energies of the race." But if the "struggle resulted in a society where millions suffered "dread miseries . . . while but a few enjoy the grateful fruits," then Wallace declared he would rather live as an Indian native and watch his children grow "like wild fauns" – "rich without wealth, happy without gold."[36]

Like Donatello, Wallace's faun signifies a nostalgic primitivism, an ideal form of the very lack of bourgeois strictures that in other contexts would be sure to evoke disgust. But as Stocking points out, the *bon sauvage* of the eighteenth-century philosophers was the "fantasy of a precapitalist mentality that saw labor as the curse of a fallen man exiled from the Garden." In contrast, the faun that Hawthorne and Wallace invoke is a fantasy of an industrialized world. To middle-class observers, modern civilization certainly produced troubling effects (such as the "dread miseries" Wallace saw among the poor masses), but it was nevertheless an ascension over nature rather than a corrupted decline from the natural state. The primitive faun, therefore, is a joyous but decidedly mythic creature, the "poet's imagining" of a simpler time that never existed. It represents a social alternative that is self-consciously an imaginary legend and therefore, finally, no alternative at all. The "moral" of Donatello's story, as Kenyon expounds it, is "that human beings, of Donatello's character, compounded especially for happiness, have no longer any business on earth, or elsewhere. Life has grown so sadly serious, that such men must change their nature, or else perish, like the antediluvian creatures that required, as the condition of their existence, a more summer-like atmosphere than ours"

(1235–6). The faun articulates discontent with modernity but contains and distances it as poetry. Where Rousseau's polemic held up the New World savage as an example of a superior human existence, Hawthorne's faun represents a wistful and purely imaginary "memory" of a lower one. The only possible "earthly paradise" Wallace envisions in Brazil, in fact, is the future civilization that could be built there through the "energy of Saxon races."[37]

"Soft" primitivism follows the logic of elegy, in which language can both praise and bury in the same gesture. It is a romance logic with a central place in the history of American race politics. This elegiac mode, for instance, governed the way many American authors represented North American tribes, once natives no longer were a threat to white removal policies. Writers spoke with the same mournful inevitability that we can hear in Kenyon's declaration that certain human beings who enjoy a natural "happiness . . . have no longer any business on earth": "Like all the tribes," wrote one observer, "this also dwindles away at the approach of the whites. A melancholy fact. The Indians' bones must enrich the soil, before the plough of civilized man can open it." However noble and inspirational, Indian culture ontologically belonged to an anterior, almost mythic world, admired and mourned precisely as it was disempowered. Remarking on the whites' treatment of Indians, Washington Irving cannily acknowledged the elegiac strategy of replacing racial conflict with a more pleasing poetic myth, including the myth of the faun: "If, perchance, some dubious memorial of them should survive, it may be in the romantic dreams of the poet, to people in imagination his glades and groves, like the fauns and satyrs and sylvan deities of antiquity."[38]

Irving here recognizes what we might describe as the danger of becoming a faun, a romantic spiritualizing of "lower tribes" that is earned at the cost of their extinction. The mythic primitive might signify a "delightful link between human and brute life," but his power to signify was founded upon his removal as a living inhabitant. Moreover, when the same primitive traits were seen in "civilized" people, the white men and women of slums and rural enclaves, they earned a far harsher judgment. Since the forces which advanced the middle classes in America and Europe were assumed to be the forces of progress for all eras and races, the "inequalities of development" between social strata recapitulated the uneven development of racial groups. Victorian England and America perceived an "internal primitivism" of rural laborers and urban poor. "In a progressive community all the sections do not advance *pari passu*," wrote John F. McLennan, "so that we may see in the lower some of the phases through which the more advanced have passed."[39] The primitivism of the surviving lower "phases" was rarely celebrated, especially when it came to the "savagery" to be found in urban slums. Even for sympathetic observers like Friedrich Engels and Henry Mayhew, the coarse behavior of the poor in Manchester and London made them seem alien, undeveloped creatures. Slum dwellers were routinely compared to non-European savages – most frequently to African tribes, but also to Indians of North and South America, South Sea Islanders, Eskimos, and Australian aborigines. (Some writers went so far as to argue that "native populations" in manufacturing districts were literally of a different race; one influential study reported that factory workers in England were developing the physical characteristics of Africans.)[40] In the United States, populations of freed American slaves would be only one of several classes of primitives enclosed within the borders of white American civilization.

Nineteenth-century primitivism, then, appeared in discordant forms, as nostalgic retrospection (civilization's childhood) and as debased behavior (civilization's other), a dual manifestation that supplied a powerful ordering principle. Its power came from its versatility, for the category of the primitive was able to underwrite physical as well as temporal boundaries. In the case of Indian resettlement, this dual segregation was an explicit policy: for peoples "belonging" to the past, legal spaces of primitivism were located (and relocated) on the national map. The limits of cultural development could be redrawn as cartographic boundaries. What is more, the American Indian ceased to be an adversarial contemporary and became an artifact from the past. Whereas observers in the Jacksonian period had spoken of a confrontation between two incompatible cultures, writers now described a single line of cultural development between red and white America, making Indian culture oddly continuous with U.S. expansion. Lewis Henry Morgan wrote of the Indians as proto-democrats whose destiny was not terminated but rather fulfilled in an Anglo-American civilization. In the reservations of North American Indians, we can see an almost perfect reciprocity between temporary and spatial distancing.[41]

Segregation in nineteenth-century cities, on the other hand, was less a matter of overt social policy than the ad hoc boundaries of the urban landscape. White "primitives" found themselves in the rather more spontaneously formed reservations of ghettos and work slums. The effect was much the same: a social topography that located an undeveloped stage of culture in a bounded space. Perceiving the new urban spaces as a dark terra incognita, visitors became self-styled travelers, who explored and recorded the details of an alien world just as did the famed Victorian explorers of Africa. A review of Mayhew's book on the London poor stated that "he has travelled through the unknown regions of our metropolis, and returned with full reports concerning the strange tribes of men which he may be said to have discovered."[42] The same idea of a dark space of savagery shaped descriptions of Jewish ghettos in Italy and eastern Europe, as well as the "Celtic fringes" and other enclaves of "undeveloped" peasant communities. As American Bayard Taylor described his frightened passage through the "Jew's City" in Prague, its borders enclose a distinct and dangerous foreign world he passes through as if running history's gauntlet:

> We came first into a dark, narrow street whose sides were lined with booths of old clothes and second-hand articles. A sharp-faced old woman thrust a coat before my face. Instantly a man assailed me on the other side: "Here are vests!" I broke loose from them and ran on. One seized me by the arm, crying, "Lieber Herr, buy some stockings!" I rushed desperately on and finally got safe through.[43]

Under the category of the primitive, these widely differing social groups – the new manufacturing poor, the inhabitants of segregated ghettos and rural clans, and the savages of America and colonial outposts – could all be correlated as surviving fossils of civilization's origins. They existed, in Tylor's word, "as proofs and examples of an older condition of culture out of which a new has been evolved."[44] The past, as measured by middle-class advancement, could be distributed in space and provide a visible map of progress.

It was a map that also could be color coded: the "shaded map of negrodom" given to Hawthorne was a graphic instance. Primitivism could be expressed in terms of three modes: time, color, and place. Johann Bachofen, whose treatise *Das Mutterrecht* was published a year after *The Marble Faun*, described his work to Lewis Morgan as an attempt to place "the phenomena of the so-called classical antiquity in parallel with other corresponding phenomena, whether of decayed peoples of civilization or of still existing barbarian races."[45] This three-sided primitivism is the same constellation that shapes Hawthorne's narrative. In *The Marble Faun* the antiquity of the classical world is set alongside the "decayed" modern Italians, with antebellum conflicts over "barbarian races" casting a shadow from across the Atlantic. The novel conducts an imaginary journey into a varied landscape of more primitive stages of civilization, tracing a map of time that structured the nineteenth-century field of culture.

This primitivism offered an ideal synoptic vision. It therefore offered a species of social supervision as well. The same temporal mapping of culture allowed observers to see at a glance who was out of place in a given society. For Hawthorne in Virginia, for instance, one unsettling aspect to the sight of the fugitives is that slaves who have left the plantation no longer belong to any established place in American society. I do not mean that Hawthorne sees them as wrongfully liberated, no longer "in their place." Rather, cast as beings of "primeval simplicity," Hawthorne's fugitives are temporally displaced. Not yet citizens, they have no true dwelling space outside of a slave society: "For the sake of the manhood which is latent in them, I would not have turned them back; but I should have felt almost as reluctant, on their own account, to hasten them forward to the stranger's land."[46] Hawthorne was far from being alone in his belief that escaped bondsmen and "the specimens of their race" in the North were fundamentally homeless in America. He was in the company of such champions of "the negro" as Stowe and Lincoln, who could imagine African Americans restored to full social life only on the African continent. True liberty for the slave was a separate *place*, Liberia. The freedman, according to Hawthorne, did not belong in the free North, where the "primeval simplicity" is "quite polished away from the northern black man." The "polish" of modern society, in other words, makes the primitive into a "colored" citizen, a person polished "black." Entering modernity, the primitive exchanges romance for mere race, becoming one of the "specimens of their race we are accustomed to see at the North." But as Africans – that is, as inhabitants of Africa – the escaped bondsmen would find their true temporal home. The logic of this politics of black emigration mirrors the logic of Hilda and Kenyon's return home from expatriation, which is a journey back to their proper national time as much as to their national home.

Similarly, the excursions of the Americans in the Italian countryside mirror the journey of the black fugitives across America: both are travels in the wrong cultural time. Modern critics have read these somewhat aimless wanderings as signs of the unraveling of the narrative plot, Hawthorne's further indulgence in travelogue recollections. But the excursions in fact serve to map out the territories of the Old World and focus them through the alternating lenses of antipathy and empathy, the "soft" and savage versions of primitivism. Hilda's walk through the alleys of Rome makes visible spaces of modern savagery that are explicitly contrasted with the "familiar street of her New England": "Hilda's present expedition led her into what was – physically, at least – the foulest and ugliest part of Rome. In that vicinity lies the Ghetto, where thousands of Jews are crowded within a narrow compass, and lead a close, unclean, and multitudinous life." Describing a second neighborhood, "on the borders of this region," the narrator stresses that the place has been virtually untouched by the centuries of civilization since the "old Romans." He speculates "whether the ancient Romans were as unclean a people as we everywhere find those who have succeeded them." The inhabitants are literally autochthonous: "Dirt was everywhere, strewing the narrow streets, and incrusting the tall shabbiness of the edifices, from the foundations to the roofs; it lay upon the thresholds, and looked out of windows, and assumed the guise of human life in the children, that seemed to be engendered out of it. Their father was the Sun, and their mother – a heap of Roman mud!" (1176).

Hilda's "expedition," described in the same terms used by urban explorers, revisits a "condition of culture" that has survived centuries of progress. A temporal idea – that Italian culture is exhausted – is located and displayed in a concentrated space. These alien and vaguely threatening populations are defined, and *con*fined, through interdependent dimensions of time and geography. Significantly, Hilda passes through this space. Her physical act expresses the evolutionary frame that ensures that her New England world has surpassed this stage of primitive development. The logical extension of this act is her return to America, when, after having passed through the layers of time concentrated in Rome, she finds that there are "no future moments" in Italy and returns to the forward-moving current of time in America as if through natural law.

But it would be a distortion to ignore the powerful attractions that the novel discovers in Rome. Repellent tracts of urban life are matched by spaces of ideal cultural origins. The past also can be traversed with pleasure, as Kenyon does in his "nomadic" journey through the countryside with Donatello, which provides "a very little taste of [a] primitive mode of existence" (1093). In the "enchanted ground" of the Villa Borghese, a Golden Age has "come back again" (925), and the restrictions that have advanced Western civilization are magically suspended: within the grounds of the villa, Miriam and Donatello feel "as if they had strayed across the limits of Arcadia . . . and come under a civil polity" requiring "little restraint" (917). In the Roman ghettos the lack of civilized restraints is a disturbing reality, but relocated in a world of acknowledged myth it evokes all the poignant pleasures of elegy: the gardens are a "glimpse far backward into Arcadian life," and "the result of all is a scene, pensive, lovely, dreamlike, enjoyable, and sad" (912). Like the enclosure of the slums, the attractions of a primitive life of "little restraint" are safely cordoned, preserved in a romance territory of vanished time. Traveling the landscape of Italy, observing the lives of Miriam and Donatello, Hilda and Kenyon experience a life of license and impulse and erotic energy, but these taboos are safely enclosed in a flexible rhetoric of temporal and spatial distance. Even as he gives dramatic life to energies of desire, Hawthorne will finally insist that these energies belong to the Old World and are therefore the native elements of an irrevocable time or an alien place. Italy serves as America's space of primitivism, just as America had served that role for Europe.

CULTURE AND THE AESTHETICS OF PRIMITIVISM

By turning to Europe for the setting of *The Marble Faun*, Hawthorne found a new site for his old obsession: human transgression and law as the operative riddles of modern liberalism. The world of Rome, like the New England of *The Scarlet Letter*, is the ground for a narrative excavation of the origins of American democracy. If the Puritan scaffold is the ironic ancestor of the nineteenth-century Customs House (a space where Hawthorne brilliantly converges different meanings of the term "custom" – commercial, political, and social), then the churches and paintings of Catholic Rome and the much older pagan myths and idols of a vanished Etruscan world are artifacts lodged even more deeply in the texture of American culture. As Sacvan Bercovitch has shown, Hawthorne's examina-

tion of the past in *The Scarlet Letter* supplies an ironic, sweeping arc
of national development joining vital yet irrational beliefs and
harsh practices with the tempering reason of modern consensual
law. The novel enacts the aesthetics of American liberalism and its
ability to transmute diverse historical materials and explosive social conflicts into a vehicle of continuity. Hester's story distills a
multilayered drama of the organic movement from transgressive
desire and dissent to a self-legitimating law, as her remarkable but
heretical defiance and the Puritans' severe penalty are transformed
into the operative tensions that foster the liberal order yet to be
born.[47] A decade later, *The Marble Faun* transplants the same dramatic pattern onto the stage of world history. By enlarging a national history into a global one, Hawthorne was participating in the
early formation of a symbolics of ethnographic culture. In 1861, the
same year that *The Marble Faun* appeared, Henry Maine published
his *Ancient Law*, one the first studies to juxtapose modern society
with primitive precedents ("the early forms of jural conceptions . . .
are to the jurist what the primary crusts of the earth are to the
geologist. They contain, potentially, all the forms in which law has
subsequently exhibited itself"). It is significant that a book considered a starting point for modern anthropology was a legal study
tracing twin concerns of modernity – contract and crime – to their
origins in "archaic" forms of savage practices and punishments.
For, like so much of Victorian fiction, early anthropology sought to
substantiate a liberal vision of natural law by working through a
fascination with the prospect of unchained human desire and will.
In 1871, Lewis Henry Morgan (like Maine, a lawyer) began his
Ancient Society, which turned more than two decades of research
among the Iroquois into an ethnological mirror of modern government, family, and property, thereby unearthing strange, sometimes
violent sources for the liberal social order. Like Hawthorne, both
Maine and Morgan passed backward through imperial Rome to a
primitive world in order to discover the keys to modern life in
ancient societies. In these books, two central artifacts of liberalism,
English law and American democracy, are authenticated through
an archaeology of their primitive roots. What Morgan calls "ethnical periods," Tylor describes as stages of "primitive culture," giving
the lasting name of culture to the discourse that would supply
liberalism and its consensual law with what researchers called a
"deep history." The ethnological approach makes law the product

not of a divine lawgiver or of a sovereign human reason but of a history of deeply rooted customs and rites – the sphere of culture. But it also binds modern law to what the idea of culture seems on its face to deny: a state of potentially limitless, barely restrained human desire, the submerged specter of which becomes the continuing incitement to the constraints of law. Freud would make this ironic lineage clear when he argued that the fears and desires of the savage, his seemingly indecipherable taboos, are "the root of our customs and law" and the "dark origin of our own 'categorical imperative.' "[48]

The same structure of ethnographic irony can help explain why Hawthorne's fears of popular turmoil were transferred to a primitive Italy in the process of writing America as the land of law. To borrow Tylor's words, the "sharp strife" of modern America can be explained, perhaps explained away, as the "unevenness" of cultural development among groups. The incommensurate plots in the novel are not incoherent; they tell of an American past (Italy) that confirms the American future. The story places America on time's side, but does so by claiming a temporal affiliation with dark energies that belong to the past, though they can never be safely confined there. Through the drama of Miriam and Donatello, who are claimed as well as cast off, the novel reconstructs America as a place of law and defines those who belong in America as not only law-abiding but lovers of law, Woodrow Wilson's true Americans who "love order and instinctively yield to it." Far from being slavish, this is a condition of passionate, internal, *native* love for a land of law. Hilda's renunciation is meant to carry all of the empathy and profound compassion she feels for Miriam and Donatello. But such feelings are precisely what animates her instinct to cleave to the law. To be American is to belong to the future and to embody the law in one's very passions and instincts.

But if Hawthorne's novel is designed to reign in potentially disruptive energies, if the preface's famous description of America as a place of placid, "common-place prosperity" is closer to a wish than a complaint, we must recognize that the novel's transgressions are in many ways more attractive, more potentially *compelling*, than its censures. This raises the possibility that transgressive desires have their place in America after all. And perhaps primitives have their proper place in the American landscape, too. Certainly many critics have found the stories of Miriam and Donatello more compel-

ling than those of Hilda and Kenyon: for such readers the transgressive couple are on the side of "redemption" rather than Hilda's
"condemnation," on the side of "freedom" as opposed to "restriction." Such readers in essence *bring back* Miriam and Donatello
from the murky punishment the novel imposes: that is, readers
bring them back from the margins to the center, finding in the
couple's deeply felt transgressions and penance a "moral complexity" that outstrips Hilda's "moral absolutism."[49] In a sense critics
even bring them back to America when they nominate the Italians,
with their creative and transforming desire, as the true subjects for
Hawthorne's last American romance (thereby performing a kind of
critical immigration in the Hawthorne corpus by making Miriam
and Donatello, as is said of immigrants, the "real" Americans).

But in an important sense, Hilda and Kenyon themselves never
entirely leave behind the transgressive energies unearthed in Italy
and embodied in Miriam and Donatello. By novel's end, the transgressive primitive remains a presence in the book, and a potentially
destabilizing one, though the dangers and attractions of primitivism are also what inform the American love of law. For Kenyon the
abiding power of what was consigned to the past confronts him at
the Roman Carnival. The Carnival is presented first as another
dead vestige: "To own the truth, the Carnival is alive, this present
year, only because it has existed through centuries gone by. It is
traditionary, not actual" (1216). As long as the narrator insists on
this temporal perspective, the riotous crowd remains an empty
spectacle. But at a certain point the scene modulates. At the sight of
military forces lining the street corners, the narrator describes not a
timeworn repetition of custom but a potential scene of modern-day
mob revolt.

> Yet the government seemed to imagine that there might be excite-
> ment enough (wild mirth, perchance, following its antics beyond
> law, and frisking from frolic into earnest,) to render it expedient to
> guard the Corso with an imposing show of military power. . . . Had
> that chained tiger-cat, the Roman populace, shown only so much as
> the tips of his claws, the sabres would have been flashing and the
> bullets whistling, in right earnest, among the combatants who now
> pelted one another with mock sugar-plums and wilted flowers.
> (1220)

No longer simply "traditionary," the scene threatens to become
"actual," a disorder no longer contained by time. Beneath "the

merriment of this famous festival" we glimpse the possibility of rebellion and a confrontation with "military power." Even more telling, the possibility of a riot may become the prospect of an American riot. While the narrator reminds himself that the Roman Carnival is a "hereditary festival" and therefore merely an illusion of anarchy ("in the end, he would see that all this apparently unbounded license is kept strictly within a limit of its own"), his anxieties gravitate to the "popular rudeness" that he feels would be sure to break out "in any Anglo-Saxon city" under the same mob conditions (1220–1).[50] In Kenyon's mind, the threat of disorder is actually greater in the land of Hilda the "Anglo-Saxon girl." As if to make good on the threat, the "populace" of the Carnival suddenly comes to life around Kenyon with an all too real aggression: "Hereupon, a whole host of absurd figures surrounded him. . . . Clowns and parti-coloured harlequins; orang-outangs; bear-headed, bull-headed, and dog-headed individuals; faces that would have been human but for their enormous noses and all other imaginable kinds of monstrosity" (1224). We might well see in these bestial revelers a parodic return of the novel's carefully controlled spaces of primitivism. The faun, a "delightful link" between man and animal, now reappears in grotesque form as creatures not quite human. With the image of the Carnival "orang-outangs," the notebook memory of the "bearded woman" with the orangutan father has materialized in the Italian streets. Like the narrator, we might read in the sight a displaced image of a mob of American "primitives": James's comment about Hawthorne's campaign biography of Pierce – that it was an attempt to quiet "the many-headed monster of universal suffrage" – suggests just such an identification, a link between these dog- and bear-headed creatures and the unrestrained clamor Hawthorne feared from abolitionists, slave mobs, anarchists, and urban masses. The once safely cordoned energies of primitivism here come alive as an "actual" welter of forces, foreshadowing American primitives in revolt. Interpreted in this way, Hawthorne's fear of "popular turmoil" in the United States is present in the novel after all: before Kenyon himself has left Italy, the novel stages a dumbshow of the atavistic return of the primitive in the streets of America.[51]

For Hilda the danger is not so much an atavistic assault as a transforming desire that comes from the wealth of feeling she finds in Italy. Hilda has an almost involuntary attraction to St. Peter's, where she discovers freeing consolations in Catholicism. The partitions that have confined these energies to the past seem to drop away, and the cathedral presents her "with all the effect of a *new* creation" (1143). She confesses to a priest; rather than merely observe, she participates in the rites that the novel's progressive, rational voices declare "gaudy superstitions" and "childish rites" (precisely the rites that Anglo-American ethnologists cited to link Catholicism with pagan and primitive tribes).[52] The superstitions assigned to history are rekindled into a new power to transform and express subjectivity. Like Kenyon, then, Hilda is swept up into participating in the primitive culture she disavowed, though in her case the experience does not evoke a fearful disgust but its twinned opposite, a seduction by Rome's spectacular spirituality that allows her piety to take the form of luxurious pleasure and emotional release.

It is the knowledge of these primitive excesses that Hilda and Kenyon bring back with them to America. Even as their return provides closure, the novel never buries what it has discovered in Italy. Instead, as in the discourse of ethnography, Hawthorne's novel performs the ambiguous act of rhetorical excavation: it keeps alive and visible what it declares dead. This may be the special brilliance of Hawthorne's fiction – not its celebrated ambiguity alone, but its ability to give such forceful illumination to what the narrative means fully to contain.[53] This narrative method, though, risks eliciting sympathies that may undercut its own structure of segregation. Indeed, the response of readers who are unwilling to leave Miriam and Donatello in the shadows suggests the risk may have been too great. On the other hand, Hawthorne's narrative excavation also shows that he means not to disavow but to retain and value the transgressive – but to value it *as a cultural relic*. Tellingly, Hawthorne closes the novel with an emblem that demonstrates the resources of cultural relics. The description of Miriam's bracelet symbolizes the elegiac value for what is consigned to the past. It gives, quite literally, a token value to the vitality of Miriam and her world through a commemorative act that seals her off in "an immemorial time."

> Before they quitted Rome, a bridal gift was laid on Hilda's table. It was a bracelet, evidently of great cost, being composed of seven ancient Etruscan gems, dug out of seven sepulchers, and each one of them the signet of some princely personage, who had lived an imme-

morial time ago. . . . It had been Miriam's; and once, with the exuberance of fancy that distinguished her, she had amused herself with telling a mythical and magic legend for each gem, comprising the imaginary adventures and catastrophe of its former wearer. (1238–9)

Like Tylor, who through his ethnographic analysis is able to master the "symbolic meaning" of such primitive objects as the "jewelry buried with the Etruscan dead," Hawthorne fixes Miriam and all she represents in the realm of primitive time and beautiful icons.[54] Hilda will bring back the "exuberance" of Italy in a form that can be safely imported to America: as fanciful "legend," reified even further as ornamental gems. Adventures and catastrophes are reassuringly imaginary. Exotic foreigners that had threatened violence and anarchic ridicule in the Carnival are replaced by the prehistoric and now "princely" Etruscan, the primitive preserved in a relic of culture.

So romantic an emblem should also remind us that the sphere of culture, for Hawthorne, is above all a sphere of the aesthetic. The word "culture," especially at this late moment in Hawthorne's career, had begun to call to mind elevated artistic achievements organized around new national and commercial institutions. The term would increasingly invoke the finest of the fine arts.[55] But at the same time, "culture" was beginning to assume the historical meaning bestowed by scholars of primitivism. These divergent meanings are perhaps nowhere yoked together so clearly as in Hawthorne's faun, the imaginative descendant of both a classical Greek statue and a creature of the "lower tribes." But as Hawthorne's fauns show, aesthetic value is never merely ornamental, and cultural relics are never simply historical. What we might call the aesthetic power to invent relics and to imagine the primitive had a particular urgency in this era. An aesthetics of the primitive provided resources for crucial relays: race may be defined as a matter of primitive culture, and culture may be measured by a scale of time. The particular social uses of these complex relays, from assimilation to discrimination, are inseparable from their imaginary quality, from the art and artfulness of a symbolics of primitivism.

In *The Marble Faun*, I have argued, primitivism performs mostly the work of confinement, bringing closure and control over volatile energies it values but also anxiously seeks to keep at a distance. It is important to remember, however, that virtually the same aesthetic

powers could support social transformation rather than confinement. High culture, for instance, was called upon to do what one
writer called "the special work of America at the present moment":
transform poor immigrants from Europe "as well as the emanci-
pated slaves of the South" into "thinking, knowing, skillful, tasteful
American citizens."[56] In making such a call, of course, the custo-
dians of culture shore up their own authority and confirm a structure of hierarchy, but they also commit themselves to the idea of
social change and a single citizenry. Such a mediation through art
was clearly Hawthorne's conscious aim in creating his faun. He
hopes to make the "mute mystery" of the Other into a romance
"without monstrosity." And he hoped, in part anyway, to dissolve
the perplexities about the Other into a beautiful tale of human
transformation.

In these particular aims Hawthorne seems to have failed. Instead of fashioning an ideal romance character, he complains in his
postscript of having created a creature that readers seemed to scrutinize like a specimen dissected by Cuvier: the modern faun is
"nothing better than a grotesque absurdity," he remarked, "if we
bring it into the actual light of day" (1239). The novel had apparently failed to purify romance of the "coarse" traces and perplexities of the lower orders. Moreover, the figure of the faun, however
potentially grotesque, would return to Hawthorne a year later in
his image of the slave-fauns of Virginia. But then we might also ask
if the modern faun was in fact a failure or whether it succeeded in
giving expression to an important historical conjunction of the categories of culture and race. We might even ask if the image is not a
successful expression today, if by success we mean the ability to give
form to powerful collective ideas and beliefs. For we can find yet a
further reincarnation of the black faun in Virginia, if a more insidious one, in the campaign rhetoric from the 1992 presidential elec-
tion, when candidate Patrick Buchanan announced that "I think
God made all people good, but if we had to take a million immigrants in, say, Zulus next year or Englishmen and put them in
Virginia, what group would be easier to assimilate and would cause
less problems for the people of Virginia?"[57]

A million Zulus in Virginia: exactly what is the incommensurability that Buchanan meant to signify with this image? Are we
speaking of an unassimilable culture or an incommensurate race? It
would not appear to be the difference of language, since many

Zulus speak English. It is unlikely to be color, or at least color alone, since the "people of Virginia" include millions of African descent (including acculturated descendants of Zulus). In his parable of the impossible Zulu American, Buchanan sought to conjure an image of supreme incongruity. What he imagined was a figure for the un-American, a trope with its own varied literary history, by turns a "mute mystery" and a "grotesque absurdity." Call it the continuing American fetish of race.

CHAPTER 3

The discipline of manners

The *manners*, the manners: where and what are they, and what
have they to tell?
                                  –Henry James, *The American Scene*

The figure of the savage has sponsored several kinds of fiction. By
the end of the nineteenth century, a number of subgenres of quasi-
ethnographic fiction were in place and flourishing, from the "imperial gothic" of exotic adventure novels to the highbrow primitivism
of writers like Joseph Conrad.[1] It might seem wrongheaded to place
the fiction of Henry James and Edith Wharton in this context. With
few exceptions, they write about the hypercivilized. Their characters, that is to say, are on the opposite end of E. B. Tylor's "scale of
civilization" from "savages" and their imputed traits. Tylor's savage was dominated by impulse and incapable of any sustained
reflection, while the typical Jamesian character is virtually defined
by the habit of reflection, a habit of sometimes bizarre proportions.
In one of the more familiar story lines from literary history, the
fiction of James and Wharton appears at the end of the tradition –
some would say the exhausted tradition – of the novel of manners. I
do not want to dispute their place in the genre but instead to
reconsider what it could mean to write about manners at the turn of
the century.

Unlike stories by Kipling and Conrad, James and Wharton's
plots rarely take us outside of a transatlantic world of cosmopolitan
capitals. But their novels are marked throughout with a metaphorical primitivism whose figures seem to signal a changed orientation
toward manners. Is it more than whimsy when, in *The Custom of the
Country*, Wharton called the old-money New York families "aborigines," "vanishing denizens of the American continent doomed to

rapid extinction with the advance of the invading race," or describes the climactic scene in *Age of Innocence* as a "tribal rally around a kinswoman about to be eliminated from the tribe"? What could it mean that the Ververs, in James's *Golden Bowl*, come to find the atmosphere at their English country estate "too tropical"? Why, for that matter, would one of James's contemporaries call his review of *The Wings of the Dove* "In Darkest James"?[2] It would be a mistake to see this exoticism as a spasm of stylistic excess coming at the end of an exhausted tradition of manners. The subject of manners, in fact, had been newly discovered in this era by social scientists. Anthropologists, social theorists, and psychologists increasingly located the source of all social praxis and regulation in cultural habits and customs. Read in a historical context of this professional analysis of manners, the fiction of James and Wharton, far from being anachronistic, returns to us as one of a number of emergent modern discourses on culture.

But although the novel of manners was not an exhausted genre, leisure-class manners were under suspicion of exhaustion in this era. As manners came under new scrutiny, observers charged that the moneyed classes suffered, in Veblen's words, an "arrested spiritual development" or, more drastically, a "reversion" to "archaic traits." The same professional interest in conduct and custom that revived the novel of manners also emptied those manners of their status as standards of civility. Among its early rhetorical effects, cultural relativism seems to have done less to suspend judgments about savage and civilized peoples than to invert the distribution of value on Tylor's scale of civilization. The lifeways of tribes are elevated to the dignity of cultures, while the practices and habits of the elite suffer a downward mobility, their religion no more than a variant of animism, their charities a species of aggression, the aspirations of their women a menacing atavism, their decorum a "pantomime of mastery."[3]

This critique of the rich, however, is both more and less than a demystification of the superiority of polite manners. On the one hand, there is certainly a moral condemnation in much of the analysis of class manners from this period. Energies of self-censure, anxiety, indignation, and, no doubt, envy motivate a portrait of a leadership class that is by turns ineffectual and crafty, weak and powerfully predatory. But on the other hand, to focus on the social

criticism alone is to miss the positive value that this vision of mid-
dle- and leisure-class culture might have held for writers and theorists, namely, its value as a source of knowledge about social power.
One of the most striking features of what we might call the ethnographic "savaging" of the leisure class is its concentration on a
sublimated violence among the elite, the "pantomime of mastery"
that Veblen discovered in the smallest details of social life. Veblen's
self-described ethnological analysis unveils the pretense and petty
cruelties of the rich, but, as his phrase suggests, it is also an anatomy of mastery, a close and sustained study of an apparatus of class
power that Wharton calls the "tribal discipline" of manners. Veblen's critique – especially the exotic terms of his critique – registers
a sense of a society in crisis. Yet like all critiques it aims to produce
knowledge, in this case a knowledge about the workings of social
power. Through an ethnographic lens, manners become the keys to
the secrets of social control and cohesion. When civilized manners
are subjected to the acid effects of relativism, what is lost in their
immanent worth is gained in insight into the workings of what
Malinowski called "the Mystery of the Social." This raises the
possibility that an anthropological relativism imported into class
analysis during this period was ultimately neither a neutral method
of study nor an instrument for correcting excesses of American
civilization, but rather a technique for pursuing a mastery of the
operations of everyday social life. From this perspective, the discovery of the relativism of elite manners, and the vision of WASP
decline that usually followed from it, might well have held a certain
value, if not an appeal, for those who wrote and warned about a
leisure class in crisis.

The fiction of James and Wharton shares with the era's ethnology a fascination with uncovering the power of manners. The perception of a cultural crisis finds one of its most complex expressions
when James and Wharton, at certain fictional extremes, make the
exchanges of drawing-room culture indistinguishable from acts of
coercive force. By giving rich narrative development to the oxymoron of violent manners, they could be said to introduce a fictional relativism to the novel of manners: the realism in their works is
produced out of a deliberate unmooring of codes of conduct from
assumptions about inherent civility, a disjunction that is the paradoxical foundation for a new representation of culture and new
institutions of cultural authority.

TRIBES, CITIES, DRAWING ROOMS

Henry James credited Matthew Arnold with having established "certain ideas and terms which now form part of the common stock of allusion," among them the "indispensable" notion of the Philistine, and the "now much abused name of culture." Of Arnold's "culture," James wrote, "I shall not go so far as to say of Mr. Arnold that he invented it; but he made it more definite than it had been before – he vivified it and lighted it up."[4] Arnold's success in making "culture" part of an educated vernacular owed something to the red-flag urgency he imparted by pairing the term with "anarchy" in the title of his 1869 volume. But like most powerful words, "culture" so readily became a new Victorian talisman not because Arnold gave it a fixed meaning but because the term was transferable: it circulated among diverse, even contradictory social idioms. Two years after *Culture and Anarchy* was published, E. B. Tylor's *Primitive Culture* made another claim on the word, and there is evidence that Tylor was responding to the special stamp Arnold had given to the concept of culture. In what may be an echo of Arnold's distinction between Hellenism and Hebraism, for instance, Tylor remarked that the "two great principles" of intelligence and virtue are often separated in human history. But in contrast with Arnold, Tylor argued that the rift was part of the very development of culture; such a separation "is continually seen to happen in the great movements of civilization." Where Arnold was at pains to distinguish culture from the Victorian notion of progressive civilization, Tylor makes the two nearly synonymous: culture becomes another name for the sweep of progressive historical forces that had brought "the educated world of Europe and America" to global preeminence, though those forces are now recognized as present – in due proportion – in the tribal societies Tylor saw as stages of "primitive culture." This usage returned the word to the very sense that Arnold had resisted: to Arnold culture was "at variance with the mechanical and material civilization in esteem with us."[5]

Despite these competing meanings, however, both Tylor and Arnold use the word "culture" to speak to a dimension of social life or experience that did not seem to be recognized in the eighteenth-century notion of society. Taken together, their divergent claims on the word are evidence of a new sphere that theorists were anxious to make intelligible. Both Tylor and Arnold, for instance, are concerned to include a dimension of "moral and social excellence" in their notion of culture, and both attempt to represent this immaterial sphere in their writing. For Tylor, however, the mentalistic expressions of social life – "belief, art, morals, law, custom" – are presumed to be governed by the same "general laws" of development as are technological advances. As his model of general laws suggests, the underlying referent of Tylor's analysis is natural science. Culture, like nature, is conceived as a scientific object – measurable, nameable, representable: "Just as the catalogue of all the species of plants and animals of a district represents its Flora and Fauna, so the list of all the items of the general life of a people represents that whole which we call its culture." Behind Tylor's title is the assumption that culture can be written, that lists and catalogues and books of anthropology can adequately represent and explain culture as a distinct object. Tylor's introductory chapter presents metonymic representation as the foundation of anthropology.

> The fact is that a stone arrow-head, a carved club, an idol, a grave-mound where slaves and property have been buried for the use of the dead, an account of a sorcerer's rites in making rain, a table of numerals, the conjugation of a verb, are things which each express the state of a people as to one particular point of culture, as truly as the tabulated numbers of death by poison, and of chests of tea imported, express in a different way other partial results of the general life of a whole community.[6]

The classic works of early anthropology – Tylor's books and Sir James Frazer's multivolume studies, for instance – are in essence vast compendiums of metonymic catalogues. They display in print form the collections of representative objects that ethnological museums arrange in glass cases. Arnold's "culture," on the other hand, as a name for general human perfection or an "inward condition of the mind and spirit," cannot be objectified – indeed, it seems to function as another name for the subject, an abstract "best self" set down amid the landscape of the Victorian city. But if Arnold's culture can never be represented by a list of the "items of the general life of a people," such catalogues do in fact figure prominently in Arnold's writing. For culture, as Arnold presents it, is also a powerful way of *looking* at social life, a manner of seeing and describing and classifying it that is remarkably like the anthropologist's. Arnold's culture is a standpoint from which to measure customs and habits of thought as elements of a distinct "way of life." Hence *Culture and Anarchy* contains its own species of the cultural catalogue: "Culture says: 'Consider these people then, their way of life, their habits, their manners, the very tones of their voice; look at them attentively; observe the literature they read, the things which give them pleasure, the words which come forth out of their mouths, the thoughts which make the furniture of their minds.'"[7]

Here Arnold represents a people through metonymic detail, sizing them up through concrete indices of their practices and tastes. It summarizes a style of seeing that Arnold shares with Tylor, and thus it is fitting that the label that Arnold gives to "these people" is tribal. Calling the British middle class "Philistines," after the biblical tribe that fought against Israel's "children of light," Arnold not only fashions a memorable emblem of the cruder traits he finds in the bourgeoisie, he also inscribes a way of seeing people that is based on otherness, a process that turns Englishmen and Englishwomen into foreigners and their everyday practices into strange, almost unaccountable customs. Emphasis in the passage is as much on a practice of observing ("look at them attentively") as it is on the way of life he represents. The two things are in fact mutually dependent; just as it is "culture's" perception which renders them Philistines, so the Philistines help to constitute culture by being its Other. Arnold's gaze imposes Michel de Certeau's "ethnological isolation," setting apart certain practices "as *a separate population,* forming a coherent *whole* but *foreign* to the place in which the theory is produced."[8]

Arnold's theory of culture performs upon British society what Tylor sets out as the fundamental act of anthropological analysis: "A first step in the study of civilization is to dissect it into details, and to classify these in their proper groups." The proper groups in Victorian civilization Arnold identifies as "Barbarians," "Philistines," and "Populace." By inventing this defamiliarizing taxonomy, of course, Arnold is following the established lines of socioeconomic classes – the aristocracy, middle class, and working class. But Arnold's playful act of naming ("this humble attempt at a scientific nomenclature") also changes our perception of these groups. Rather than classes, related through a common economic and political system – the "society" of eighteenth-century usage – they are fashioned as separate peoples living in geographic proximity like hostile neighboring tribes. To give vivid color to his sense of the lack of cohesion in British society, Arnold's rhetoric imitates the language of the scientist who studies and classifies the customs of distant natives.[9]

Common to both Arnold and Tylor, then, is a way of seeing that we can call "ethnological," though Arnold awards the name of culture to the "inward condition" that makes such vision possible, and Tylor gives the designation to the ethnological object. This state of things is paradoxical but not historically haphazard. Tylor and Arnold are repeating semantic skirmishes from the previous century: indirectly challenging the German nobles, the bourgeois German intelligentsia claimed *Kultur* as a special interior sensibility that contrasted with the merely formalistic civility of the aristocracy, whereas the more assimilated intellectuals of France and England conceived *civilisation* as an externalized code of manners that their class gradually reformed and appropriated. The semantic space of "culture" in the later nineteenth century, we have seen, included versions of both (Arnold's) internal cultivation and (Tylor's) external codes of behavior. But is also includes an important ethnological dimension, mostly absent from the earlier semantic field, that explains that rhetorical kinship between Tylor's primitives and Arnold's Philistines. Norbert Elias has shown how class and national rivalries embedded in eighteenth-century claims on "civilization" were transformed in the imperialism of the following century: in the nineteenth century, civilization was conceived as the common property of Europe and America in opposition to the savage world. Defined by this new binarism, the concept of *Kultur*, or civilization, came to carry a marked ethnological and racial meaning, and earlier class conflicts were flattened out as the term became a more monolithic one in the context of imperial expansion. But interestingly, the ethnological overtones associated with culture also could be doubled back on the domestic world. If class rivalries were effaced in the exporting of civilization to primitive outposts, they were reinscribed at home, where ethnographic description sprang up to mark class differences anew.[10] Arnold's mock classification of three British peoples or races, for instance, is a striking vision of the differences among economic classes. By fastening upon the small but significant details that give a class's social life its particular texture, he recognizes separate, lived realities that we are now apt to call "cultures" or "lifeways." The indices of taste and style represent a whole mentality, "the thoughts which make the furniture of their minds." But a description of class tribes, then, is also a recognition of competing social realities. What had been understood hitherto as the natural social difference among classes belonging to a single social world is reconceived as a stark heterogeneity of rival cultures.

These independent rivals, though, are not culturally relative rivals: Arnold's point in dressing up classes as races is to identify and criticize the characteristic moral failing of each – the lawlessness of the Populace, the boorishness of the Philistines, the social indifference of the Barbarians. In this Arnold's essay shares what Johannes Fabian has identified as the "intense concern" in much anthropology with representing "the unifying *ethos*, the common morality that accounts for regularities in the behavior of the members of a culture."[11] But in anthropology, of course, the concern to identify a "common morality" and ethos is intended precisely to replace moral judgment with a scientific knowledge of holistic, relative cultures. In fact the ability to represent a unified culture with "regularities" of moral belief is possible only with the advent of relativism.

Yet as Fabian also points out, anthropological relativism does not eliminate the kind of synoptic supervision of the moral that was Arnold's express purpose. The doctrine of cultural relativism, especially in the schools of anthropology that developed in the United States, made it possible to formulate "value studies," research projects devoted to discovering collective "personality" and "national character" writ large in culture. Relativism allows for the representation of an essential identity – or, as Fabian more contentiously argues, the methodological relativism of anthropology is "designed to get at the jugular of other cultures, that is, at their central values and vital characteristics." As would become clear in the twentieth century, the knowledge of culture produced through these projects is "easily put to work for such nonrelativist purposes as national defense, political propaganda, and outright manipulation and control of other societies." But the point here is not any insidious use of the knowledge of culture; it is rather that the culture concept operative in anthropology does not relinquish interest in value and moral ethos but rather converts a relativism of value into an instrument of knowledge. It is that conversion, made possible by the disinterested methods of science, Fabian argues, that makes works of anthropol-

ogy indistinguishable from "manuals" for "people who want to
get things done (diplomats, expatriate managers and supervisors,
salesmen and economic advisors)."[12]

Neither Arnold's nor Tylor's book was designed to be read as a
manual, though both were meant to prepare the way for social
action: *Cultural and Anarchy* was perhaps the most famous Victorian
jeremiad, and *Primitive Culture* ends with Tylor's claim that anthropology is to be a "reformer's science." But the view of culture
emergent in these works, while far from stable or monolithic, brings
with it new techniques for imagining and representing manners,
techniques that grant the writer an intellectual possession of culture that supersedes an English matron's merely personal possession of good manners or a Zuni priest's understanding of the meaning of his own prayers. The writer's discursive possession of
manners contains the power to define cultural identity: through
metonymic representation, Arnold's moral analysis confers on
classes the deep identity of a race, while Tylor's tribal analysis
confers on races the moral or spiritual identity that is culture.
Taken together, their books show the objectification of culture in a
master discourse, a discourse that also made culture an ineffable
subjectivity.

When social manners are recast as ethnographic data, then, a
notable transformation has taken place. Manners are able to en-
code an identity that has the ontology of a race and the holism of a
prehistoric tribe: hence the racial cast and taxonomic specificity in
a work like Henry Mayhew's study of the manners of the poor.
London Labour and the London Poor records the ritualistic details of
such spectacles as midnight rat killing and other antics of the many
"castes" of "street-folk," ordered through "a correct grouping of
objects into genera, and species, orders and varieties." The same
cultural analysis of manners allows Josiah Strong, in 1885, to present America's "present crisis" as an ethnological crisis, making the
American poor analogous to "cannibals of some far off coast" who
are not only foreign to the nation they live in but a "menace to our
civilization."[13] But it is not merely a desire for social control over
the "dangerous classes" that motivates an ethnographic analysis of
manners. There is as much to be gained from mapping the interior
spaces of the wealthy, their parlors and ballrooms and dining
rooms. Arnold, according to Henry James, had discovered and
charted the "middle region" of Philistinism, leaving signposts that

help the "earnest explorer to find his way." Veblen's innumerable catalogues of the culture of the rich, isolating "dwellings, furniture, bric-a-brac, wardrobe and meals," serve to transpose rooms and sporting fields into ethnographic spectacles. "Canons of taste," Veblen announces, "are race habits."[14]

The idea of a race habit, as we have already seen, is an elusive one. But when taste and habit have become "traits" comparable to the properties of race, class identity hardens into something far more rigid than mere social status. By the same token, the observer who analyzes race habits will acquire what could not be learned from observing manners in their naive sense, namely, an understanding of "general laws of culture." This gain offers a clue to writers' pronounced fondness for borrowing from the archives of anthropology in this era. What Veblen calls the "ethnological generalization" of manners was a method for acquiring a powerful rational mastery over even the most irrational of social phenomena. "Mr. Tylor's science" was a rich resource in an era when a "hunger for expert guidance" fostered, among other things, the rise of professionalism, the establishment of the social sciences, and the new organization of the modern university system.[15] Concepts and data from anthropology were adopted by the era's leading social theorists, including Durkheim, Marx, and Freud. In imagining the beginnings of the spheres they described – society, history, and the psyche – each relied on ethnological material and the narratives that gave it usable meaning.

But it is hard to overlook the fact that the writings of these three thinkers, for all their rational mastery, helped to make strange and almost unfathomable the territories of self and society that are usually the most familiar to us from everyday life. A certain irony obtains: ethnological analysis always makes partly alien what it masters. Moreover, as civilized manners were transformed into the stuff of ethnographic culture, the domain of culture seems never to have been free from a sense (to use Arnold's pairing) of encroaching anarchy. Mayhew's governing metaphor for the mixed population of London, lifted from a study of South Africa, was a figure that encoded class hostilities as it ethnologized class identity: "Each civilized or settled tribe has generally some wandering horde intermingled with, and in a measure preying upon, it." To explore and map the "unknown districts" of cities and "examine the customs, the amusements, and the social conditions" of the slum "aborigines" was, according to Thackeray, to apprehend a "vast mass of active, stirring life, in which the upper and middling classes form an insignificant speck." An ethnographic gloss lent a language of mastery, but it was also likely to install a matching ethnological anxiety. Interestingly, some of the same notes of worry that appear in anthropology proper were borrowed from descriptions of modern cities. Urban prostitution, for instance, was a model for the "horde marriage" that scholar John F. McLennan argued was practiced by earliest societies: "Savages are unrestrained by any sense of delicacy from a copartnery in sexual enjoyments; and indeed, in the civilized state, the sin of great cities shows that there are no natural restraints sufficient to hold men back from grosser copartneries." Nor in ethnographic accounts were the modern dangers located only in streetlife; Veblen's leisure-class "barbarians" have a "masterful aggression," the result of an "unrestrained violence [that] in great measure gave place to shrewd practice and chicanery." For Arnold, the British worship of the "fetish" of industry and of bodily strength inculcated a dangerous social and individual "confusion." An ethnographic representation did not eliminate the sense of threat from the phenomena it so powerfully explained but instead gave memorable, exotic expression to that threat.[16]

That details of "habits" and "amusements" might be the source of social disorder would seem as unlikely as the idea that such manners are the key to social knowledge. But as Pierre Bourdieu argues, it is everyday manners – and precisely the recognized "arbitrariness" of those manners – that could inaugurate a "crisis" for societies. "It is when the social world loses its character as a natural phenomena, that the question of the natural or conventional character (*phusei* or *nomo*) of social facts can be raised." At such moments, even the smallest conventions and habits, usually the unobserved "hum and buzz of implication" that surround everyday life, become newly visible. This moment of "objective crisis" brings "the undiscussed into discussion, the unformulated into formulation."

> If the emergence of a field of discussion is historically linked to the development of cities, this is because the concentration of different ethnic and/or professional groups in the same space . . . favours the confrontation of different cultural traditions, which tends to expose their arbitrariness practically, through first-hand experience, in the very heart of the routine of the everyday order.[17]

The "crisis" Bourdieu describes is in one sense the long process of disenchantment that is modernity, beginning with the ruptures with tradition that had their source in Renaissance cities. But historians have argued for an especially pronounced sense of disquiet in this era. Thus Jackson Lears describes a new "crisis in cultural authority" felt by America's educated classes at the turn of the century. It is true that precisely those elements of modernity that Bourdieu names – urbanization and the close contact of different ethnic and professional subcultures – were greatly accelerated in America and England during this time. Certainly, Lears describes a pervasive social anxiety. Official creeds of optimism and progress were eroded by fears of class and ethnic violence and challenged by a changing urban landscape. The sense of a crisis was internal as well, prompting many to write of feelings of "weightlessness" and mental breakdown. "Reality itself began to seem problematic, something to be sought rather than merely lived."[18]

Yet this prospect – a leadership class dispossessed of its claims to the real – is a surprising one when we contemplate that it is precisely the prerogative of that class to put in place and enforce a hegemony that perpetually transforms ideology into reality. The feelings of loss and disorientation, amply documented by Lears and others, represent a profound historical experience. But the laments and complaints, however deeply felt, can mask what Bourdieu calls the "objective" nature of the loss, the necessary place of crisis in a structure of social legitimation. The kind of objective crisis of manners that Bourdieu describes is not a dispossession but rather a crucial part of a production of authority. The unnerving arbitrariness of manners is one of the necessary ingredients for the formation of social knowledge and the experts who possess it. Urban dislocation, with its corrosive effect on manners, in fact "permits and requires the development of a body of specialists charged with raising to the level of discourse, so as to rationalize and systematize them, the presuppositions of the traditional world-view, hitherto mastered in their practical state."[19]

A crisis of authority, then, is also likely to be the origin of an authority. With the existence of a body of experts, manners "in their practical state" lose their immanent meaning. At the same time, ethnology and its special expertise on the subject of manners brings about a colonizing of ordinary social life, an infiltration of the quotidian surface of a world that can no longer be understood in its own terms. "To expect to look modern life in the face and comprehend it by mere inspection," Tylor writes, "is a philosophy whose weakness can easily be tested." The arcane relics of anthropology contain what turns out to be the most direct and practical knowledge: scholars look to primitive culture "not merely as a matter of curious research, but as an important practical guide to the understanding of the present."[20] With the ethnographic turn in social analysis, the social life in city streets, public buildings, even drawing rooms makes possible both new kinds of social anxiety and new forms of intellectual mastery.

It is fitting, then, that Tylor himself introduces his masterwork on primitive culture by inviting readers to dissect the eclectic ornamentation of a Victorian drawing room.

> It needs but a glance into the trivial details of our own daily life to set us thinking how far we are really its originators, and how far but the transmitters and modifiers of the results of long past ages. Looking round the rooms we live in, we may try here how far he who only knows his own time can be capable of rightly comprehending even that. Here is the "honeysuckle" of Assyria, there the fleur-de-lis of Anjou, a cornice with Greek border runs round the ceiling, the style of Louis XIV and its parent the Renaissance share the looking-glass between them. Transformed, shifted, or mutilated, such elements of art still carry their history plainly stamped upon them; and if the history yet farther behind is less easy to read, we are not to say that because we cannot clearly discern it there is therefore no history there.[21]

Tylor presents Victorian decorative styles primarily as a heuristic for thinking about primitive society. The drawing room is an object lesson for reading the ethnological materials that will disclose the origins of civilization. Tylor gives us a parable of primitive culture quite literally domesticated: the primitive is present in the rooms of civilization, though present in "transformed, shifted, or mutilated" traces of other social worlds. But Tylor's drawing-room example also points to the fact that Victorian interiors were a domestic counterpart to the cultural heterogeneity that Victorians faced in foreign lands and immigrant-filled cities. As Tylor's allusions to Greek and Assyrian motifs indicate, the art and decoration in this period had appropriated their own symbols of primitivism. An Egyptian sphinx head or a Dionysian staff might appear on anything from a teapot to a curtain rod. A wave of revivals – the vogue for Tuscan and Gothic as well as Asiatic and ancient styles – corresponded with the period of nineteenth-century empire building, the global reordering that was registered in the visual environment of imperial capitals. Architectural façades, furniture, even clothing bore witness to the absorption of non-Western artifacts and histories made possible by imperial travel. When both Wharton and James refer to the impressions and observations garnered for fiction as "loot," their figure echoes a global process of cultural transfer that changed the look of European cities and imperial outposts alike. By the end of the century, these successive revivals made for a sometimes wild eclecticism in the decorative arts, a mingling of cultural images that is a visual parallel to similar syncretic representations in texts.[22]

As expressions of taste and beauty, the mingling of styles was largely a matter of pleasure. But the heterogeneity that reigned in design and decorative arts was a symptom of a larger social reordering that produced confusion as well as excitement. The exotic mixing of styles in decoration and design seemed to many to concretely realize the disorder they felt in society. Tracing the lines of world history in his work *The Law of Civilization and Decay*, Brooks Adams saw the eclecticism as a sign of the unraveling of social order: "the ecstatic dream, which some twelfth century monk cut into the stones of the sanctuary hallowed by the presence of his God, is reproduced to bedizen a warehouse, or the plan of an abbey, which Saint Hugh may have consecrated, is adapted to a railway station." Architectural historian Siegfried Giedion describes the nineteenth century's attraction to Gothic and primitive images as part of a "devaluation of symbols" that had its roots in the Napoleonic Empire style. Isolating once-sacred symbols from traditional cultures, designers recontextualized them in a modern aesthetic that favored exotic appeal over compositional space and function.[23]

In Wharton's novels, the appetite for mixing styles that created "polyphonic drawing-rooms" and amalgamated architecture often represents an invasion of the elite social strata by more vulgar castes from below. Ralph Marvell, in *The Custom of the Country*, finds "social disintegration expressed by widely-different architectural physiognomies" of the newly fashionable district of Fifth Avenue. Like Arnold discovering the Philistine "way of life" in the evidence of their tastes and the "furniture of their minds," Ralph finds an "inner consciousness" of his family and their social universe in the "very lines of the furniture in the old Dagonet house." The mixing of styles in architecture and interior furnishings, therefore, represents a "monstrous" symbolic miscegenation between different social castes:

> What Popple called society was really just like the houses it lived in: a muddle of misapplied ornament over a thin steel shell of utility. The steel shell was built up on Wall Street, the social trimmings were hastily added in Fifth Avenue; and the union between them was as monstrous and factitious, as unlike the gradual homogeneous growth which flowers into what other countries know as society, as that between the Blois gargoyles on Peter Van Degen's roof and the skeleton walls supporting them.[24]

To observers like Brooks and Wharton's Ralph Marvell, the amalgamation of different styles and symbols could be read only as cultural decay. But the same syncretism of internal difference, in rooms as well as cityscapes and texts, was also the basis for the construction of new theoretical knowledge. The introduction of exotic and disparate styles in decoration converted buildings and interiors into objects of professional analysis. Before the influence of the Empire style, the design books of furniture builders were directed toward problems of technique and efficiency. But Napoleon's designers, whom Giedion charges with setting off the nineteenth-century vogue for eclecticism and archaic motifs, made decoration itself their central object, and their volume *Interior Decorations* no longer presents design as the artisan's praxis but as an autonomous cultural field. Decorated rooms and furniture, then, gained an autonomy in part through a mixing of cultural symbols.[25] If symbols were thereby devalued, they were also newly visible, placed into relief as discontinuous cultural references composed in a new totality. At this moment rooms become something that can be theoretically described and composed – analyzed as a discreet object, corrected or praised, described and explained. Edith Wharton's career as an author begins with her *Decoration of Houses,* a book that analyzes a social hierarchy of values in home decoration. Although Wharton disapproved of the extremes of Victorian eclecticism, it was the enabling condition for her writing: she wrote against it, producing a text that reformed the disorder of contemporary drawing rooms in order to produce the cultural space she called "interior architecture." The new genre of interior design is a cognate to the

ethnologies of leisure-class manners undertaken by writers like
Veblen and Georg Simmel. In both kinds of writing, the habitats
and practices of the wealthy are constituted as a theoretical object,
a distinct and self-contained world to be discussed and critiqued.
This is the "recipe" that Certeau ascribes to the long history of
ethnological writing, "the double move delimiting an alien body of
practices and inverting its obscure content into a luminous writing."[26] A decay of symbols is in this sense the ground for constructing a new discourse of culture, though it is a discourse that requires
writers to convert its "obscure content" into cultural illumination.

That a decorated interior was also an ethnological space for
Wharton is clear from the travel writing she produced throughout
her career. From the lavish rooms of French villas to the "arcaded
courts" of Moroccan houses, Wharton analyzes interiors as maps to
the local cosmology of a people. In Wharton's fiction as well as her
travel books, rooms and furniture are codes that call for a translation into writing. Edmund Wilson recognized this when he penned
his well-known description of Wharton as "the poet of interior
decoration." But critics have generally perceived Wharton's interest in interior design too narrowly. The close attention her fiction
pays to the manners of the social elite – their clothing, homes,
amusements – has often been cited as evidence of Wharton's social
myopia. Far from indicating a limited class vision, however, Wharton's concern with the details of manners is evidence of her intellectual sympathy with the social science that people of "advanced"
tastes (as Newland Archer phrases it) read and wrote. For both
Wharton and James, rooms are the equivalent of the anthropologist's "field," a territory in which objects and actions take their
meaning not from any single economic, rational, or functional measurement but from an invisible cultural whole. That their descriptions of drawing rooms can be read as anthropological signs has not
escaped anthropologists: Mary Douglas and Baron Isherwood begin their effort at an anthropology of consumer goods with a close
analysis of interiors in James's *Ambassadors* and his *Bostonians*. Unlike the perspective that economists bring to goods, Douglas and
Isherwood argue, James recognizes that possessions are "part of a
live information system" that has the "function of creating meanings."[27]

Reconceived as an "information system," the manners in James's
novels are the site of the production and control of a certain kind of

knowledge. Yet the information coded in those pages is often a strange, almost unreadable knowledge that seems designed to surprise and shock and perhaps even to confound. The effect is something far different from what the bloodless image of an "information system" implies. What is more, Douglas and Isherwood, with their cool semiotic analysis, fail to hear an anthropological note that was obvious to James's contemporaries. They miss, that is, the particular tone of a suppressed violence that is sounded in much of James's work, a tone common in early anthropology though often elided in later work bent on eliminating crass sensationalism. Likewise, the rituals enacted in the rooms of Wharton's novels are not as tranquil as the daily rites presumed in *The Decoration of Houses.* If we read their novels for anthropological signs as they were historically inscribed, we must confront the special information that was thought to be lodged (to borrow a Malinowski title) in "savage crime and custom." Both James and Wharton are able to imagine drawing rooms as sites of modern sacrifice. They feature, that is, acts of subtle coercion that make a sacrificial figure expendable in the name of a more powerful community united in desire or social law.

These are by no means the only rites carried out by the novelists' tribes of the rich. But the disguised punishments and expulsions are at the core of some of the most puzzling yet insistent themes in the fiction. Certainly these acts are among the most strongly accented. James marks his plots with images of blood sacrifice, as when he speaks of Nanda Brookenham, in *The Awkward Age,* as a lamb prepared for slaughter that "struggled with instincts and forebodings, with the suspicion of its doom and the far-borne scent, in the flowery fields, of blood." Milly Theale, Verena Tarrent, and Hyacinth Robinson are all figures in an economy of substitute violence akin to the primitive logic of sacrifice that fascinated contemporary anthropologists. Wharton chronicles the sacrificial rites of the wealthy often with an explicit anthropological gloss, recording varieties of the "New York way of taking life 'without the effusion of blood.'" Like Veblen's dissection of the "masterful aggression" of everyday leisure-class habits, the extraordinary imagery and plotting in these novels posit a crisis of manners, an internal, invisible rift that has opened up between class decorum and a hidden store of coercive machinations. With or without direct references to primitive practices, the novels of James and Wharton frequently present a world that to many readers seemed distinctly uncivilized; in the words of one contemporary reviewer, James seems to paint "society as organized cannibalism."[28]

How are we to read these acts of sacrifice? Many of James's later critics would discuss the theme of sacrifice in a quasi-transcendent vocabulary of self-abnegation and renunciation, the self-sacrifice of society's lambs. But his contemporaries were more likely to fix upon the theme as a mark of acts of control and aggression they found in his fiction, especially the late novels, which at times "inspire horror without pity." The perceived "horror" was described by more than one reader in the idiom of primitivism. To find a way through the "jungle of mixed motives" of James's dramatis personae, wrote a contemporary reviewer, one must have "the persistence of an African explorer seeking to penetrate the gloom of the Aruwhimi forest." Readers recognized that this tendency to portray a darker, coercive side to society was not a departure from James's role as a novelist of manners but a peculiar extension of it. "No word or look or act in their lives had escaped the author's attention," a critic writes of the characters in *The Awkward Age:* "His observation and knowledge seem to grow keener with each new novel. But where will they end, that observation and knowledge? Will they swamp themselves finally in pessimism and unpleasantness and horrors?"[29] Interestingly, contemporary readers showed less resistance to very similar acts of sacrifice in Wharton's fiction. Yet Wharton herself, influenced in particular by Frazer's *Golden Bough* and its global survey of sacrificial rites, explicitly presents these collective acts in tribal terms of "rites and sanctions," with victims "offered up unflinchingly" according to fashionable society's codes of taboo and obligation.

There can be little doubt that James and Wharton mean to expose and condemn a subtle species of social cruelty when they use this language. But the complex discourse of sacrifice in their fiction, in its sheer excess and its ability to elicit similar language from readers, is really an index to something broader: a perceived crisis of cultural authority. When analysis of manners can with some consistency convert to analysis of "horrors," it registers a shared alarm at a decline in the moral and social leadership of the educated classes. Yet, as the reviewer of James's *Awkward Age* suggests, the perception of "unpleasantness and horrors" in the novel seems to be the product of James's keen "observation and knowl-

edge." In James's fiction, as in contemporary social theory, the
sense of crisis coexists with the emergence of a special understanding and penetration of the operations of social life, a knowledge that
surpasses the ordinary perceptions of social actors, whose own understanding – or at least their own explicit account – must now be
regarded as naive. What we have called the "sacrificial" dimension
of James and Wharton's fiction, then, connects the novels not only
with a perceived crisis but with an implied body of expert knowledge. When contemporary readers found an "organized cannibalism" in these novels, they brought to the fiction the same categories
through which leading theorists thought about social power in their
own society. In the nineteenth century, a fascination with the dramatic rites and punishments of tribal societies had inspired a "positive epidemic of research into primitive law," according to Malinowski, in the search for the "forces which make for order,
uniformity and cohesion" in social groups. When it came to analyzing modern social force and obedience, theorists were drawn to the
example of tribal life not so much for any literal violence of sacrifice
or cannibalism (although the more sensational rites had a symbolic
resonance) but for the almost perfect social control that seemed to
be exercised through tribal custom. "The unwritten laws of customary usage," wrote Robert Lowie, "are obeyed far more . . . than our
written codes."[30] Like many contemporary anthropologists and sociologists, James and Wharton view manners not just as a heritage
or legacy continuing from the past but as a structure for securing
compliance in the present. Manners are not traditional but political.

Any matters of taste and conduct, therefore, can be what James
calls a "battlefield." Wharton's Ralph Marvell, we have seen, finds
"social disintegration" in the nouveau riche taste for the mixed
architecture of Fifth Avenue. Deployed at public sites such as architecture, tactics of power can also obtain in the smallest details of
personal life and of the body itself. When James tells of the duchess's efforts, in *The Awkward Age,* to keep up the "cultivation" of her
figure and looks, he acknowledges that her battle is a class warfare
against an absent but "lurking" foe, waged in the subtlest details of
her features and in her ineffable "air."

> There were definite ways of escape, none of which she neglected and
> from the total of which, as she flattered herself, the air of distinction
> almost mathematically resulted. This air corresponded superficially

with her acquired Calabrian sonorities, from her voluminous title down, but the colourless hair, the passionless forehead, the mild cheek and long lip of the British matron, the type that had set its trap for her earlier than any other, were elements difficult to deal with and were all, at moments, that a sharp observer saw. The battleground then was the haunting danger of the bourgeois.[31]

Direct glimpses of class competition such as this, however, are not common, especially in James's work. More often James and Wharton show the subtle internal forces that members of a social caste exert upon each other in their efforts to keep up standards of taste or brilliance, which in turn are the regulating boundaries that determine class power. The most refined shades of decorum are able to be converted into what Wharton calls "tribal discipline," a phrase linking manners to the ethnographic record in which theorists believed they had found an archetypal system of social regulation.

COMPOSING POWER

The early classics of anthropology provided a scientific discourse for explaining the relation of civilization to sin, violence, and crime. From Montaigne onward, talk about the primitive has also been talk about what is brutal and improper in Western civilization. Whether civilization is by definition deemed superior to primitivism, or whether in the vein of Rousseau it is held up as inevitably worse than any savagery, describing tribal societies – real or imaginary – has been a vehicle for working out the riddle of civilized crime. For Western religion, of course, it is no riddle at all: human beings are wont to sin, no matter what their social condition. But in the enlightenment tradition, the persistence of degraded behavior among educated peoples posed an acute problem. It has been suggested that with the decline of Calvinism, Gothic fiction filled the vacuum left in its wake with a new descriptive vocabulary for the depravities that had formerly been called sin.[32] We might view early anthropology in the same light, as a kind of scientific, rationalized companion to the Gothic, a discourse that records human behavior – especially what appeared to be the extremes of sexuality, aggression, and supernaturalism – through a framework that lacks the theological condemnation of Judeo-Christian law but retains the psychic investment in its taboos. But unlike Gothic fiction, anthropology explores human aggressions and crimes as a histori-

cal resource, a violence that seems to offer knowledge about fundamental operations of social power. Eric Hobsbawm argues that after
the 1870s, "almost certainly in connection with the emergence of
mass politics," the "intellectual study of politics and society was
transformed by the recognition that whatever held human collec-
tivities together it was not the rational calculation of their individual members." Anthropology and folklore offered a rich, multifarious record of the "social bonds and ties of authority taken for
granted in earlier societies" but that now appeared severely eroded
by the very successes of liberal ideologies.[33]

With a characteristic logic of inversion, anthropology looked for
the origins of tribal bonds in acts of tribal violence. Beneath the
documentary surface of ethnographic works from this period, there
often lies a substratum of the lurid. In its early stages, the anthropological imagination envisioned the origins of civilization in spectacular crimes. J. F. McLennan traced the rise of modern marriage
back to a custom of violent "wife capture." For McLennan, this
practice was the matrimonial equivalent of discovering fire, a great
leap upward from the indiscriminate promiscuity of the earliest
human tribes. In Frazer's magisterial work *The Golden Bough*, the
primal act of regicide is at the heart of customs and beliefs in
virtually every world civilization, from the *Panes* bird-fest of the
California Acagchemem to the Whitsuntide ceremonies of lower
Bavaria and the snake rites of the West African Issapoo. Bronislaw
Malinowski, in his *Crime and Custom in Savage Society*, claimed to want
to rid the discipline of its penchant for the sensational: "Savagery is
still synonymous with absurd, cruel, and eccentric customs, with
quaint superstitions and revolting practices. Sexual license, infan-
ticide, head-hunting, couvade, cannibalism and what not, have
made anthropology attractive reading to many, a subject of curiosity rather than of serious scholarship to others." The book that
established Malinowski's fame among a broad audience, however,
carried a title that was less than staid: *The Sexual Lives of Savages*.[34]

Could it be that the sensationalism is fundamental rather than
incidental? It is precisely at crucial moments in anthropological
analysis that we often find scenes of Gothic intensity. Frazer establishes the center of gravity for his enormous compendium of rites by
describing Turner's dreamy landscape painting of the Golden
Bough, only to strip away the pastoral and uncover the "strange
and recurring tragedy" enacted there in a "barbarous age": "In this

sacred grove there grew a certain tree round which at any time of the day, and probably far into the night, a grim figure might be seen to prowl. . . . He was a priest and a murderer; and the man for whom he looked was sooner or later to murder him and hold the priesthood in his stead."[35] An ethnographic account of the "Australian Blacks" that McLennan includes as proof of wife capture reads like a tabloid crime story: "Slowly and silently, they [two "wife-stealers"] creep close enough to distinguish the figure of one of those leubras [women]; then one of the intruders stretches out his spear, and inserts its barbed point amongst her thick flowing locks; turning the spear slowly round, some of her hair speedily becomes entangled with it; then, with a sudden jerk, she is aroused from her slumber, and as her eyes open, she feels the sharp point of another weapon pressed against her throat."[36] Vividly staged, such moments reanimate a violence said to be from the primitive past and present it in the same style of breathless scandal that colors crime stories. The similarity is not random. Ethnological authors frequently drew parallels between the ritual practices of tribes and the more sensational goings-on of the urban world. McLennan saw the promiscuity of the primal horde repeated in the "sin of great cities." Tylor imagined a North American Indian watching a London seance with perfect comprehension. Frazer's note of alarm is characteristic: there is "a solid layer of savagery beneath the surface" of "polite society," he writes, and "we seem to move on a thin crust which may at any moment be rent by the subterranean forces slumbering below."[37]

Remarks like these show that, paradoxically, anthropologists exploring what they supposed was the distant cultural past also felt an alarming nearness of primitivism. Alongside the modern savagery they believed might erupt from below, anthropologists also discovered echoes of violent origins in the simple, often pleasing customs that survived in the very fabric of civilized life. The happy tradition of the bridegroom carrying his bride over the threshold, McLennan suggests, replays the original act of marriage by capture. The sentimental image conceals the germ of an earlier brutality. In such "survivals," savagery has moved indoors. Reading *The Golden Bough*, we see a host of benign gestures – gathering mistletoe, chanting a nursery rhyme, lighting a bonfire or Yule log – changed into ominous reverberations of acts of human sacrifice. A menacing otherness, absent but determinate, lives on in the manners of the civilized.

In this way the ethnographic record made visible what the anthropologists felt were unacknowledged forces in modern social life.

Yet in locating such forces at the foundations of culture, anthropologists submitted the record of human violence and sexuality to
certain restraints. Evolutionist theories served to quiet or compose
violence in a historical narrative, locating its rightful place in a
space of origins. The temporal plot governing these works offered a
unique solution to the problem of evil: human aggression is admit-
ted in civilization as both inherent (in the past) *and* pathological or
criminal (in the civilized present). Ethnography thus gives violence
a structure of irony. The "atrocious life which the real savage may
lead with impunity and even respect," Tylor writes, would make
the modern Londoner a criminal, only able to lead the life of "his
savage models during his short intervals out of gaol."[38] Field-
workers like Malinowski brought their own kind of narrative composure to topics of savage crime and sexuality by constructing sociological models of tribal functionalism. The anthropologist takes
a worldly tone toward these primitive crimes, presenting them not
as scandal but as data. Like the new science of urban statistics,
anthropology translated its often sensationalist material into regular laws and classified phenomena.[39]

In anthropology, then, an essential human aggression is both
lurid and rationalized, regular if not regulated. Though civilization
has its origins in acts of hostility and conflict, what Tylor called the
"doctrine of development" ensures that such acts are now pathological or criminal, or both, and therefore subject to penal and well as
cultural laws. To this end, anthropology did indeed regulate what it
deemed primitive: the subdiscipline of criminal anthropolgy, for
instance, makes clear the potential administrative uses of primitivism, drawing on ethnological categories as a basis for policing the
territories of the dangerous classes. More typical, though, is Tylor's
claim that anthropology will foster social reform, that the "painful"
but necessary "office of ethnography" is "to expose the remains of
crude old culture which have passed into harmful superstition, and
to mark these out for destruction." Moreover, as Hobsbawm argues,
once "rulers and middle-class observers rediscovered the importance of 'irrational' elements in the maintenance of the social fabric
and social order," it appeared that it might not be possible or even
desirable to eliminate the surviving energies of "old culture."[40]

Unlike a Gothic literature designed to give free reign to occult energies, then, ethnographic writing conjures those powers only to derive from them a controlling knowledge of the prehistoric past and its precise legacy in the present. It therefore could be said to partake of the "rediscovery" of a reservoir of violent passions behind civility, what Lears calls a "fin-de-siècle fascination with primal, aggressive impulse." Yet importantly, ethnographic writing never presents an aggression hidden in the deep recesses of the psyche or in blind biological drives but rather in the delineated details of social rites and customs. In culture such power can be observed, described, recorded, marked. It can, in Tylor's language, be *marked out*, either for "destruction" or for some other end – modification, manipulation, even emulation.[41]

Marking the primitive was therefore an enormously resourceful social practice, a practice linked in important ways to what Hobsbawm has called the "invention of tradition." In this sense, the scientific composing of aggressive power is also a principle of composition, making possible a rewriting of modern social life that connects it with an imagery of elemental customs and rituals.[42] Hence Durkheim's claim that the forces of religion and its once violent rites still carry out the "essential task" of maintaining "the normal course of life." Hence the details of conduct, dress, and taste in Veblen's leisure-class world could be reconceived as a display of "prowess" and "masterful aggression" motivated by "predatory traits." Even Freud turns to a litany of rites and tribal acts to substantiate his claim that "the past lives on in mental life." In *Totem and Taboo*, the slaughter of a camel by Sinai Bedouins and the killing of a holy turtle by Zunis lie encoded within the actions of "little John" and his fear of dogs.[43] The exoticism of these narratives of occult power and aggression, their reliance on strange codes and symbols to describe everyday life, registers anxiety even as it announces the importance of a special analytic expertise.

A literally outlandish imagery of ritual power governs much of Henry James's late fiction, imagery that bears the same double structure of crisis and knowledge.[44] In part because of the spectacular excesses of such imagery, James's novels have been aptly characterized as a species of melodrama. But in a fiction of manners, this very spectacularity makes for an opacity quite at odds with the immediacy of theatrical melodrama. What is most striking about James's narrative economy is that the melodrama of manners, however extravagant and outsized the imagery, never departs from a close and sustained examination of the nuances of social sensibility and manners. The refinements of the drawing room serve as the precise site at which conflicts are generated, staged, and executed.[45] *The Golden Bowl* contains some of James's most pronounced moments of well-mannered violence, moments that therefore resemble the lurid composure that characterizes ethnographies. In one of the most critically analyzed images, Maggie Verver's suppressed urge to blurt out her knowledge of her husband's affair ("she might sound out their doom in a single sentence, a sentence easy to choose among several of the lurid") is transformed into an image of her doom as a sacrificial scapegoat: "They thus put it upon her to be disposed of, the whole complexity of their peril . . . as the scapegoat of old, of whom she had once seen a terrible picture, had been charged with the sins of the people and had gone forth into the desert to sink under his burden and die."[46] The image enacts a doubling of Maggie's self-sacrifice with her fate as a sacrificed victim, a narrative fold that will double on itself yet again when Maggie seizes her own powers of "terror" to sacrifice her husband's mistress, Charlotte Stant. Such dizzying placements and displacements of power, switching sides to the very end, induce in readers a vertigo that is the antithesis of the novel of manners' usual office of moral grounding. This last major novel of James's would show as never before the ability of his fiction to seem maddeningly amoral as it limned the genre's most profound moral questions of adultery, familial loyalty, and social continuity.

In what is the most penetrating reading of the novel's operations of uncanny force, Mark Seltzer argues that *The Golden Bowl* ultimately disavows the power it so cannily anatomizes. In the novel, according to Seltzer, the "shame of power" disappears into an immanent policing that acts through "irreproachable" acts of social decorum and intimate exchange, acts that have the unspoken power to claim and impose what is right and normal. At the level of James's own art, any potentially shameful authorial power is effaced through the capacity of James's organicism to define aesthetic norms.[47] The story does indeed show the remarkable force that can be wielded by the minute forms of social observances. What allows Maggie to triumph over Charlotte is not will or charismatic power but her position in the network of social forms, the "silver tissue of decorum" that works to repress acknowledgment of the sexual betrayal. Manners are thus the very medium in which the novel's characters try to exert force on one another. One sign of the rise of Maggie's "feverish success," for instance, is the enhanced sensitivity with which Charlotte begins to ritually observe the grades of disparity between their respective social positions: "Charlotte's attitude had, in short, its moments of flowering into pretty excesses of civility, self-effacements in the presence of others, sudden little formalisms of suggestion and recognition, that might have represented her sense of the duty of not 'losing sight' of a social distinction." As Maggie intensifies Charlotte's "torment," the only traces of either Maggie's efforts or Charlotte's resistance are these forms of hypercivility. At the same time, however, Maggie begins to sense that Charlotte's new deference is also a counterattack, that "Charlotte's alacrity in meeting her had, in one sense, operated slightly overmuch as an intervention" and was part of a strategy to effect a "readjustment of relations to which she was, once more, practically a little sacrificed."[48]

Seltzer aptly describes a power in James's novel that is "finally indistinguishable from manners."[49] Yet by the same token, the images that trace a spectacular story of power – figures in high relief, like the famous scapegoat image – so utterly change the novel's fabric of manners that social observances no longer provide any grounds on which to normalize power in the forms of intimacy and sociability. Thus, while manners are "indistinguishable" from power, the effect of James's images, and the cumulative effect of reading the whole novel, is precisely to *distinguish* manners, to end forever any naive sense of manners and give them an almost unbelievable interpretive weight. As in the archives of anthropology, the lurid and extravagant images are signposts designed to mark essential operations of power, operations requiring special knowledge to decipher. What I am suggesting is that James means less to disavow power than to master it as an expert, a position that is less disingenuously detached from the "excesses of civility" that channel power in his extraordinary novel of manners.

Edith Wharton's novels also fuse a surface of manners with an exotic "nether side" where unacknowledged forms of social punishment and aggression can be represented in the text. When Lily Bart in *The House of Mirth* reads a letter Bertha Dorset had sent to her one-time lover Lawrence Selden, the novel opens up the first glimpse of the powerful forces of collective taboo and revenge that will eventually make Lily their victim.

> Now the other side presented itself to Lily, the volcanic nether side of
> the surface over which conjecture and innuendo glide so lightly till
> the first fissure turns their whisper to a shriek. Lily knew that there
> is nothing society resents so much as having given its protection to
> those who have not known how to profit by it: it is for having be-
> trayed its connivance that the body social punishes the offender who
> is found out.[50]

Wharton's "nether side" is the space of an operative discrepancy
within manners, an internal difference through which wounds can
be inflicted by the very acts of decorum one performs in the name of
graciousness and good form. Thus Lily will be marked as a
"doomed" and abandoned "castaway" by nothing more than the
"loudly affirmed pleasure" expressed in a matron's greeting, or
rather in what is omitted from that greeting, the "nebulous generalization, which included neither enquiries as to her future nor the
expression of a definite wish to see her again." And in the novel's
climactic scene, the ordinary rites of "leave-taking" from a restaurant dinner become the forms for Lily's abrupt sacrificial expulsion
from society. "Miss Bart is not going back to the yacht," Bertha
Dorset proclaims. The sentence forces Lily to act as the executioner
at her own social death taking place before a shocked audience: "I
am joining the Duchess tomorrow," Lily explains, "and it seemed
easier for me to remain on the shore for the night."[51]

Though the script of this exchange is indistinguishable from
polite after-dinner chat, the rite as performed is a sacrificial act, and
every onlooker knows it. Indeed, the spectators must recognize and
be a witness to it for the expulsion to have its power. In this sense
the fatal exchange is remarkably like the "chasing away" ceremony
Malinowski represents as the culminating act of a village crisis, an
expulsion achieved through the magical power of words alone: "You
are a stranger here. Go away! We chase you away! We chase you out
of Omarakana." Once an offense is publicly charged and retribution demanded, a new reality is collectively defined and accepted,
and the ceremony has a "binding force" on both the members and
the now official "stranger." Similarly, a new truth is put into place
by Bertha Dorset's words in *The House of Mirth:* "the truth about
any girl," Lily tells Gerty Farish, is what is spoken publicly about
her by the rich. Bertha's sentence acts with a kind of verbal magic,
a force that requires "no bodily force," as Malinowski writes of
Trobriand spells, but that puts into place a new order.[52]

The force that is figured in Wharton's "nether side" thus marks an otherness within the everyday acts of decorum, an invisible "fissure" in the conventions of polite behavior out of which comes the power to impose and enforce a social reality. The drama of social life, in this view, is shaped by something absent or off the scene, by occluded energies of coercion or transgressive desire that still can be perfectly executed in civilized manners. The silent "shriek" articulated in this moment of leave-taking, like the "primitive wail" James's narrator attributes to a mute Charlotte Stant, marks what is certainly a melodrama of manners. Less certain, though, is the exact valence inscribed through this extravagant portrait of power. Is language of this sort designed to stage the open struggle between good and evil that is the aim of theatrical melodrama? Alternatively, does the representation of polite sacrifice partake of what Lears calls the turn-of-the-century "worship of force"?[53] These quite different motives, moreover, might well coexist: the irony, not to mention the efficiency, with which James and Wharton's narratives dispatch social victims cannot help but suggest that they harbor a fascination for the well-mannered coercion they also indict.

But both the glamor and the condemnation James and Wharton attach to "tribal discipline" are finally less important than the social position from which they write. For both admiration and condemnation come together in a narrative analysis of power that was part of an institutionalized, a *disciplined,* crisis of cultural authority. The "discovery" of occult power in manners, that is, was most overtly the work of new disciplines of culture, discourses that made visible the threats of decline or of a loss of moral grounding even as they organized new forms of expert authority to meet those threats. The very extravagance with which James and Wharton rewrite the novel of manners is a sign of the place of their fiction within new institutions of cultural knowledge. Their novels, even today variously called anachronistic, eccentric, predatory, vertiginous, and anomalous, by admirers as well as detractors, are nevertheless rich examples of a far-reaching social enterprise: the effort to define and master an uncanny power in everyday life. The language of drawing-room sacrifice signals one obvious way that their fiction takes its place within a body of "extraordinary discourse" that, as Bourdieu tells us, was invented to capitalize on a disruption of ordinary experience:

The relationship between language and experience never appears more clearly than in crisis situations in which the everyday order (*Alltäglichkeit*) is challenged, and with it the language of order, situations which call for an extraordinary discourse (the *Ausseralltäglichkeit* which Weber presents as the decisive characteristic of charisma) capable of giving systematic expression to the gamut of extra-ordinary experiences that this, so to speak, objective epoche has provoked or made possible.[54]

In his *Remarks on Frazer's Golden Bough*, Ludwig Wittgenstein suggests that the melodrama of early anthropology is not the discipline's embarrassment but its most important feature, for Frazer's extravagant "tone" is the key to understanding the way an extraordinary discourse (in Bourdieu's sense) produces knowledge. Critical of Frazer's historical explanation of tribal beliefs and rites as primitive "errors," Wittgenstein instead points to a significance that both Frazer and his "savage" find in sacrificial rites.

> When Frazer begins by telling the story of the King of the Wood at Nemi, he does this in a tone which shows that something strange and terrible is happening here. And that is the answer to the question "why is this happening?": Because it is terrible. In other words, what strikes us in this course of events as terrible, impressive, horrible, tragic, &c., anything but trivial and insignificant, that is what gave birth to them.[55]

Frazer's ominous "tone," Wittgenstein argues, does not come from an effort to present the savage's point of view. Rather, Frazer is himself "already impressed by the material." Wittgenstein does not mean the impression is inherited, genetically or archetypically, but that it is present in Frazer's own experience: what seems significant is "what connects this picture with our own feelings and thought." "There is something in us too that speaks in support of those observances by the savages." What impresses us about such customs – what impressed Frazer enough to write thirteen volumes, Wittgenstein implies – is not a historical hypothesis about its origin but something "deep" that "*we* impute . . . from an experience in ourselves":

> For when I say: what is deep in this practice lies in its origin, if it *did* come about like that, then either the depth lies in the idea (the thought) of [its descent from] such an origin, or else the depth is itself hypothetical and we can only say: *if* that is how it went, then it was a deep and sinister business. What I want to say is: What is sinister, deep, does not live in the fact that that is how the history of

this practice went, for perhaps it did not go that way; nor in the fact that perhaps or probably it was that, but in what it is that gives me reason to assume it.[56]

Faced with a record of primitive rites, Wittgenstein gives the weight of causality to "something" in contemporary experience, a priority that reverses the positions of ethnographic origins and present-day survivals. From this perspective, our own "reason to assume" a violent origin to culture is the real basis of anthropological reasoning. Our own experience and manners thus precede the primitive: "modern" life is the ground for the historical knowledge of anthropology. For Wittgenstein, then, the significance of exotic anthropological writing was its ability to give what he calls "depth" – not historical but cognitive depth – to ordinary acts and exchanges in modern experience. In this way, Wittgenstein can conceive an everyday encounter, one man "speaking sternly" to another, as another kind of ethnological survival:

> If I see such a practice [as the ceremonial eating of the Beltane cake], or hear of it, it is like seeing a man speaking sternly to another because of something quite trivial, and noticing in the tone of his voice and in his face that on occasion this man can be frightening. The impression I get from this may be a very deep and extremely serious one.[57]

This passage could pass for a synopsis of a scene from a James novel, describing as it does a thoroughly banal occurrence that is made to bear the weight of analogy with a violent and dramatic primitive practice. This substitution of survivals for origins, of impressions from modernity for ethnographic data, makes for a radical change in perspective. What if anthropology is really a way to write "our own" social life? What if the literature of tribal discipline is the record of a disavowed terror in modern manners? The discourse of anthropology – its terms, its voluminous material, and its imaginative structures – is then an extraordinary record of modern life, and the representation of primitive "terror" is actually prefigured by acts of power enacted in ordinary words and actions.[58] The "strange and terrible" moment of the savage in Frazer's Nemi Wood is thus a prehistoric event descended from Frazer's own experience in modernity – or equally, we might say, descended from James's experience. Such a view makes the nighttime vigil of the Nemi savage a survival of Charlotte Stant's afternoon ordeal at the Verver estate, an afternoon during which all her ordinary actions –

absenting herself from a family luncheon, walking in the garden –
are signs that betray her sense of being stalked: "there were always
too many [suspicions], and all of them things of evil when one's
nerves had at last done for one all that nerves could do; had left one
in a darkness of prowling dangers that was like the predicament of
the night-watcher in a beast-haunted land who has no more means
for a fire."[59] Wittgenstein's attention to the production of anthropology through its "tone" invites us to see the history of culture as a
history of the discourse of culture. Viewed in this way, we could say
that anthropological culture is a variant of fictional realism and
that the archives of tribal discipline are not a preserved history but
a literature produced by a new imagining of manners.

REALISM, RELATIVISM, AND THE DISCIPLINE OF MANNERS

Culture, as Tylor described it, holds the key to "the remarkable
tacit consensus that induces populations to unite in the use of the
same language, same religion, and settle to the same general level
of art and knowledge." Malinowski dubbed this cohesion the "Mystery of the Social."[60] In *Folkways*, William Graham Sumner insisted
that only an impartial scrutiny of the widest range of human customs could yield knowledge about the social.

> When, therefore, the ethnographers apply condemnatory or depreci-
> atory adjectives to the people whom they study, they beg the most
> important question which we want to investigate; that is, what are
> standards, codes, and ideas of chastity, decency, propriety, modesty,
> etc. and whence do they arise? The ethnographical facts contain the
> answer to this question, but in order to reach it we want a colourless
> report of the facts.[61]

Here the question of manners and conduct is no longer a matter of
their propriety, or even of their "stage" of civilization. It is rather a
question of social "codes" themselves, what they are and how they
work. Through unbiased global comparison, manners become an
objective "report of the facts." Even as the great encyclopedic works
like *The Golden Bough* reached their largest audience (around 1910),
ethnographers began to turn from evolutionary comparisons to
more concrete analyses of particular tribal societies. Increasingly,
the object of ethnographic works in this period was not the reconstruction of a grand "scale of civilization" but analysis of closely

observed and fully realized rites and manners. This shift brought a heightened realism – the reporting of actual field observations, attention to detail and everyday behavior – and at the same time an increased relativism – a representation of multiple realities born of a universe of multiple cultures. For the ethnographic observer, Malinowski insists, "the culture of his tribe" must be grasped and presented "as a self-contained reality."[62] The mystery of the social is to be discovered in writing the special realism of culture.

What did it mean at the turn of the century to recognize the "reality" of cultural manners, to scrutinize and record them in books? Norbert Elias notes that the social manners of Western cultures have long been observed and recorded, from the Renaissance books of courtesy to etiquette manuals that guided the rise of the middle classes. A "direct line of tradition" connects such texts to the courtly portraits of Saint-Simon and the English character writers, and later to the realist novels of the nineteenth century: all are genres created out of a keen "lucidity of human observation" and a "capacity to see people in their entire social context and understand them through it."[63] Elias shows that the lucidity of observation that fosters realism was itself a tactic for bourgeois advancement, a practical skill for perceiving and judging nuances of social relations and distinctions crucial for success in increasingly interdependent societies. The realist novel, then, is an artifact of what could be called "realist observation," a practice central to the ascendance of the middle class and necessary for any individual who wanted to rise. But with the advent of professional anthropology, manners had become the special concern of more than just of the socially ambitious and the novelists who chronicled them. Manners were also the business of scientists. Customs and rules of behavior were not merely a canon transmitted to the young but an object of reflection from which to extract rational knowledge about culture. Indeed, for anthropologists and sociologists, the customs and conventionalized wisdom Sumner called "folkways" held the ultimate keys to social power: "The folkways are the widest, most fundamental, and most important operation by which the interests of men in groups are served."[64]

As anthropology was organized into a professional discipline, the realist observation embedded in a field of private social praxis moved into public institutions of knowledge and social administration. A view of culturally constructed self, a *homo habitus*, became an academic truth. John Dewey's axiom that "Man is a creature of habit, not of reason nor yet of instinct" is echoed decades later when Lévi-Strauss remarks that "between the instincts inherited from our genotype and the rules inspired by reason, the mass of unconscious rules remains more important and more effective."[65] At the same time, cultural customs interested makers of public policy. Folkways are "the dominating force in history," Sumner writes, and "a condition as to what can be done, and as to the methods which can be employed." A study of folkways was the necessary groundwork for any systematic regulation of society. The 1878 silver agitation or the "mob gathered in the slums of a great city" could only be understood in a global context that included the rise of Moslem prophets and the power of the Mahdis in Africa. "What is the limit to the possibilities of fanaticism and frenzy which might be produced in any society by agitation skillfully addressed to the fallacies and passions of the masses? The answer lies in the mores."[66] Mediating between mobs and etiquette manuals, the folkways are the basis for establishing a professional "lucidity" of cultural observation.

The realism of James and Wharton, I have argued, is similarly situated at the intersection where private social life becomes the province of institutions of cultural knowledge. For that reason, it is possible to find a resemblance, for instance, between their fiction of manners and William James's well-known analysis of the power of cultural habit. Habit, according to William James, is the "fly-wheel of society":

> It alone is what keeps us all within the bounds of ordinance, and saves the children of fortune from the envious uprisings of the poor. It alone prevents the hardest and most repulsive walks of life from being deserted by those brought up to tread therein. . . . It keeps different social strata from mixing.

Through habit, these most far-reaching questions of social order and anarchy are rooted in manners, including the cultural conditioning of the body itself – "vocalization and pronunciation, gesture, motion, and address."

> Already at the age of twenty-five you see the professional mannerism settling down on the young commercial traveller, on the young doctor, on the young minister, on the young counsellor-at-law. You see the little lines of cleavage running through the character, the tricks of thought, the prejudices, the ways of the "shop."

It is these minute aspects of manner, rooted in details of speech, clothing, carriage, and taste, that constitute an invisible force keeping "different social strata from mixing."

> Hardly ever can a youth transferred to the society of his betters unlearn the nasality and other vices of speech bred in him by the association of his growing years. Hardly ever, indeed, no matter how much money there be in his pocket, can he even learn to *dress* like a gentleman-born. The merchants offer their wares as eagerly to him as to the veriest "swell," but he simply cannot buy the right things. An invisible law, as strong as gravitation, keeps him within his orbit, arrayed this year as he was the last; and how his better-bred acquaintances contrive to get the things they wear will be for him a mystery till his dying day.[67]

The rich parvenu who attempts to enter "society," the subject of so many stories by Henry James and Edith Wharton, is here transposed to a social science textbook. As manners enter the discourses of social science, they are analyzed explicitly as signs of a silent network of social power rather than inherent propriety. The "mystery" of clothing and taste, the mute manners of the body, all heed an "invisible law" that governs society and its interlocking orbits. In the hands of James and Wharton, the novel of manners is also able to trace powerful, exquisitely subtle mechanisms of social force. James's *Sacred Fount* shows most clearly the degree to which the novel could recast manners as the stuff of quasi-scientific "law" and deep forces of social discipline. *The Golden Bowl* takes to its logical limit the idea that polite observances might be indistinguishable from tactics of power. Yet what Henry James called the "mystery of manners" is also importantly different from the mystery his brother describes as a set of opaque forces that, like gravity, keep diverse social strata "from mixing." When the drama of manners comes alive in James's fiction, the social life he depicts is never predictably governed by laws, even though something very like "invisible laws" seems everywhere to call out to be identified and interpreted. William may have observed a world without social "mixing," but Henry's narratives tell precisely of a subtle but disturbing social disorder – not only the mixing of class strata, with all the anxieties that attend it, but the "mixed motives" James's reviewer compared to a tropical jungle, and the recognition of social forces that Maggie Verver calls "an awful mixture in things." [68] Henry's penetrating observation of the social always produces a sense of a disturbance in the sphere of manners as it simultaneously evokes a special kind of cultural knowledge. The result is a realism constructed through a mutual instantiation of crisis and culture.

Edith Wharton's realism is even more clearly articulated through what Ruth Benedict called "culture consciousness" and the institutions that fostered and codified it. As in ethnography, representing a reality of manners for Wharton rests on a principle of relativism, a principle that brings about her own version of a crisis of manners. But the "culture consciousness" in Wharton's fiction, I want to argue, allows her fiction both to critique and to preserve the authority of the turn-of-the-century leadership class, a double strategy that finally serves to accommodate the very changes that the class appeared to oppose. Like Benedict in her essay "The Science of Custom," Wharton presents culture as a "flexible instrument" for "divesting" a society of rigid absolutes while "reinstating and reshaping" the local values that sustain a particular social existence.[69]

To Wharton, scientific knowledge is indispensable for discovering our "inward relation to reality." She immersed herself in what her contemporary Marcel Mauss called "the science of manners." Favorite works included the volumes of Spencer, Frazer's *Golden Bough*, E. A. Westermarck's *History of Primitive Marriage*, and the "remarkable books on tribal life in Melanesia" by Malinowski (whom she came to know socially). Like these authors, however, Wharton had discovered that the reality of manners contains a crucial relativism: the real includes not only material forces and human instincts but the irreducible reality of social forms, a reality that is always both essential and equivocal. For although there is no human life outside of a web of mutual relations ("man is human only because he is socialized," Durkheim writes), still no particular social feature – this form of marriage, that division of labor or gender roles – is in itself either necessary, unalterable, or permanent. Wharton's *Age of Innocence* explores precisely this tension between the real and the conventional – or, in terms that Wharton grafts onto her novel, between nature and culture, the submerged faultline that was also at the heart of anthropological studies.[70]

Interestingly, anthropologists helped to construct the idea of culture in the "wide" sense by calling upon drawing-room manners. In their effort to present tribes as complex, full-bodied societies, anthropologists turned to the domain of Western taste, etiquette, and civility, creating an ironic register of cross-cultural manners. Franz Boas made class etiquette a touchstone for his attempt to frame ethnological questions in terms of cultural history rather than racial capacity. What is "purely traditional," like our rules of modesty or table manners, Boas writes, nevertheless constitutes our whole social and moral equilibrium: "to eat with people having table manners different from our own seems to us decidedly objectionable and causes feelings of displeasure which may rise to such intensity as to cause qualmishness." Our taboo on eating dogs, Boas argues, is no different from the southwestern tribes' taboo on eating fish: "the customary action is the ethical action, a breach of custom is everywhere considered as essentially unethical."[71] Manners here locate the modern sense of relative culture: no longer a monolithic scale with a succession of stages stretching from savagery to civilization, culture is the whole body of local explanations and rules, historically rooted sentiment and feeling, customs, and habits of thought.

"The savage rules of etiquette are not only strict, but formidable," Robert Lowie writes, "nevertheless, to us their table manners are shocking." In ethnography, all manners and rules of custom carry a doubleness; they are simultaneously proper and strange. Lèvi-Strauss, in *Tristes Tropiques,* describes this structure of feeling when he writes that "for the first time in my life, I was on the other side of the equator in the tropics, and I felt I was in a drawing room."[72] In his *Argonauts of the Western Pacific,* Malinowski mocks the colonial magistrate who, when "asked about the manners and customs of the natives answered, 'Customs none, manners beastly.'" The joke depends on the magistrate's priggish confusion of the category of culture with bourgeois cultivation. But Malinowski's aim is to take this confusion seriously, to show Western readers that the natives possess "excellent manners in the full meaning of this word" – to show, that is, that within the foreign customs of a savage tribe are all the internally differentiating codes that articulate the complex fabric of Trobriand reality: the tacit rules that define propriety for men and women, the value attached to possessions and gifts, the boundaries that separate the ceremonious from everyday life, the internal codes of decorum, prestige, and "glamour."[73]

It is in fact the glamor of the elaborate *kula* gift-exchange system that Malinowski is most concerned to convey and analyze, even as he concedes that *kula* objects are, to European eyes, little more than "greasy trinkets." By drawing upon the disparity within the meaning of manners, Malinowski opens up a new way of representing the real: neither glamorous nor greasy, the *kula* treasures belong to a new "ethnographic reality" that is founded on precisely the difference between the two views. Like fiction writers, Malinowski writes in a space that mediates between the real and the imaginary:

> The objective items of culture, into which belief has crystallized in the form of tradition, myth, spell and rite are the most important source of knowledge. In them, we can face the same realities of belief as the native faces in his intimate intercourse with the magical, the same realities which he not only professes with his tongue, but lives through partly in imagination and partly in actual experience.[74]

Claiming to have discovered the "full meaning" of manners, Malinowski establishes a kind of writing that combines a dimension of cultural strangeness and arbitrariness we perceive in customs not our own with a structure of realism in which those same customs appear inevitable, natural, and necessary, as they do to native inhabitants. "Ideas, feelings, and impulses," Malinowski writes, are "an ethnic peculiarity of the given society."[75] Through relativism, ethnographic realism transforms the most immediate texture of subjectivity into an "ethnic" signature.

By holding itself out as a special realist register of subjectivity, ethnography was poaching on the territory of the novel. Lionel Trilling, in his essay "Manners, Morals and the Novel," described the novel as the leading agent of "moral realism" in the two-hundred-year history of the bourgeois transformation of literature: from Cervantes onward, the novel pursues its "quest for reality" beneath the illusions generated by "snobbery" and money, with "manners as the indication of the direction of man's soul."[76] Within ethnographic realism, however, a gap opens up between manners and morals: there is no way to read the canons of behavior as moral imperatives, no way to place taste and grace within a universal aesthetics, no measurement of sensibility against an irreducible common sense. Similarly, in Wharton's fiction the novel has become a vehicle of what might be described as a "realism of custom," writing that represents through a fine-grained verisimilitude of social detail a world that is nevertheless relative and ungrounded, while still claiming to uncover and display the essential workings of culture. In their novels both Wharton and James often seem to expose, even to flaunt, a loss of what Trilling calls the

genre's accumulated "moral realism"; to many contemporary observers this fact was further proof of an erosion of civilized values.
But the loss of a universal moral ground in their fiction, I have
argued, is answered and composed in the novels in a way that
corresponds closely to the *composure of culture* in social theory: the
construction of a culture concept based precisely on a recognition of
both the reality and the relativism of different social worlds. To
trace this in greater detail, I want to analyze Wharton's *Age of
Innocence* for the way it constructs a new realism of culture out of the
discovery of ungrounded and competing social realities. Invoked by
a crisis of relativism, the novel's culture concept is founded upon
"tribal discipline," a class power that is at once tragic (for its own
members) and effective (against class outsiders) and finally adap-
tive (to the new conditions that the discipline of manners is designed to oppose).

Until the arrival of Ellen Olenska, Newland Archer accepts even
the most baroque observance and distinction of his circle as a
natural, almost "congenital" inheritance.[77] But when he falls in
love with Ellen, the New York "tribal" life and its worship of
" 'Taste', that far-off divinity," (1026) begin to appear as an archaic
formalism, a "parody of life." A gulf opens between the world of
social convention and a private, alternative world he calls "reality":

> he had built up within himself a kind of sanctuary in which she
> throned among his secret thoughts and longings. Little by little it
> became the scene of his real life, of his only rational activities. . . .
> Outside it, in the scene of his actual life, he moved with a growing
> sense of unreality and insufficiency, blundering against familiar prej-
> udices and traditional points of view as an absent-minded man goes
> on bumping into the furniture of his own room. (1224)

Newland's crisis is a personal and emotional one, of course, but its
repercussions have the broadest possible social range. His illicit
desire triggers an estrangement at the level of the smallest details of
social life and spreads into the very "structure of his universe"
(1097).

As the larger contours of the novel make clear, Newland's sense
of "unreality" dramatizes the forces of dislocation pressuring a
whole social group. The Archer family, for instance, feels keenly the
changes in New York society, vigilantly tracing "each new crack in
its surface" (1210). The novel provides hints about the sources of
the ruptures – new technologies, a changing cityscape, novel ideas

about woman and marriage, the perception of "a country in possession of the bosses and the emigrant" (1115). The characters themselves, however, say almost nothing about these large-scale
changes. Instead, they focus on small, discrete adjustments in their
own social habits, a slight increase in "extravagance" of dress or a
shift in the customary round of leisure entertainments.

For the reigning clans of Old New York, though, change and
heterogeneity do not prompt a perceived erosion of reality as they
do for Newland. Instead, change is understood as a threatening
challenge to universal standards of propriety and taste. What is
more, the elders absorb the very marks of change into their patterns
of social ritual: without fail, Mrs. Archer will ceremoniously "enu-
merate the minute signs of disintegration" during the mid–October
"household ritual" (1219) of assembling the proper carpets and
curtains. Like the rector's jeremiad, delivered every year in his
Thanksgiving sermon, Mrs. Archer's laments about social decline
become part of the linked institutions that actually foster continuity
and strength for her social circle. On one side, therefore, even the
effects of a crisis in manners becomes a process by which New York
"managed its transitions" (1222). Social energies marshaled under
the banner of "disintegration" help to convert the very arbitrariness
of manners into a continuing source of meaning and cohesion.

On another side, however, exposing the contingency of culture
produces a different kind of energy, a restlessness represented by
Newland's agitated sense of "unreality." For Newland, we have
seen, manners are no longer a matter of natural decorum. Performing the round of social calls expected of a fiancé, he feels "trapped"
as they "rolled from one tribal doorstep to another" and wonders if
"his readings in anthropology caused him to take such a coarse
view of what was after all a simple and natural demonstration of
family feeling" (1069–70). Here anthropological allusions make
vivid Newland's sense of estrangement: what was natural is now
hollow, even coercive. Newland seems to be directly at odds with
his family on the question of social "form" and manners. Through
ritual repetition, the Archers and their circle confirm their customs
as a "natural demonstration" of feeling, while for Newland repetition serves to empty those customs of any inherent meaning. The
novel stages a clash between two versions of culture, between
drawing-room culture ("decent people had to fall back on sport or
culture" [1115], in one of the Old New York axioms) and anthropo-

logical culture (Tylor's "culture in the wide ethnographic sense"). The conflict is between manners as inherent values of propriety and manners as local forms of human society. But although these paradigms are at odds, the conflict actually belongs to the novel's larger solution to the problem of social change. By displaying the tension, Wharton makes visible the particular "crisis of cultural authority" among the educated classes. Yet the tension itself, as we will see, is put into the service of cultural continuity. By illuminating the difference between absolute and relative manners, the novel provides for a heightened "culture consciousness" that finally serves to revitalize the world of the Archers and the social power of their kin and kind.

What is real in the novel becomes intelligible precisely through a dialectic of the traditional and the personal, the arbitrary and the actual. And the medium for this dialectic is custom, the locally rooted but contingent forms that can be disowned or disobeyed but never transcended. When Newland Archer calls his very real passion for Ellen the "only reality," Ellen confronts him with the reality of bourgeois kinship: "Is it your idea, then, that I should live with you as your mistress – since I can't be your wife?" Newland's answer resists these social classifications: "I want somehow to get away with you into a world where words like that – categories like that – won't exist" (1245). But Ellen's reply, "Where is that country? Have you ever been there?" returns the novel to its foundation in the cultural – the variable but irreducible categories of countries, classes, regions, and urban castes. Ellen's response acknowledges both their mutual desire and their mutual relation to New York kinship (we are "Newland Archer, the husband of Ellen Olenska's cousin," she recounts for him, "and Ellen Olenska, the cousin of Newland Archer's wife"), and the novel's poignancy comes from the inevitable tension between the unassimilable realities of kinship and illicit passion. Wharton thus uses a love story to install a certain space of culture, the same space Malinowski represents in the Trobriands, where an ethnographic reality emerges out of "the power of tribal law, and of the passions which work against and in spite of these."[78]

Wharton underscores this double structure of culture, at once conventional and actual, in the scene that places Newland and Ellen within the "queer wilderness of cast-iron and encaustic tiles known as the Metropolitan Museum," in front of the glass cases housing the "Cesnola antiquities" (1261). As the lovers struggle with a painful recognition of the real force of New York kinship taboos, Wharton balances the scene's emotion with a cooler, detached view of culture itself, represented by the fragments of a now-vanished ancient community. "Its glass shelves were crowded with small broken objects – hardly recognizable domestic utensils, ornaments and personal trifles – made of glass, of clay, of discoloured bronze and other time-blurred substances" (1262). Gazing on the display, Ellen points to the tension that Wharton has built into the novel as a whole, noting that these reified, frozen pieces of an exotic world carry a life and meaning now inaccessible but once as real as her own: "these little things, that used to be necessary and important to forgotten people, and now have to be guessed at under a magnifying glass and labelled: 'Use unknown.'" While Ellen dwells on the historical contingency of experience, Archer returns the dialectic to its opposite pole of immediacy – "Meanwhile everything matters" – though this declaration is ultimately framed by a "vista of mummies and sarcophagi" (1263), another reminder of the mutability of cultures and their customs. Shifting rapidly between the two perspectives, Wharton creates a wider consciousness of culture out of the reader's heightened sense of the difference. By juxtaposing the exotic and the immediate, Wharton turns the "unreality" of the New York scene into the permanence of culture, converting the drawing-room crisis into the authority of the museum. The "queer wilderness" of the Metropolitan Museum becomes the field for securing the real. It is precisely the decentered nature of museum culture, its relativism of customs and manners, that recovers reality and authenticity.

Examining the "strange organized disorder" of museums, Paul Valéry would critique that authority in an essay, published one year after *The Age of Innocence*, entitled "The Problem of the Museum." But Valéry's very challenge illuminates both the logic and the strength of the culture concept that had begun its ascendancy during the years of Wharton's story (proleptically, Wharton has Newland inscribe the dominant authority of museums like the Metropolitan: "Some day, I suppose, it will be a great Museum"). Valéry complained of the "abuse of space known as the collection," a disorder created in museums by the radically decontextualized objects reassembled and competing for attention in the same rooms. But the process of collection and display that Valéry calls "abuse" had been established as the most powerful means to sanction cultural value and authenticity, and his attack is in part a reflection of the now-dominant authority of the museum model, which had been extended from art and antiquities to ethnographic collections. The logic of the museum collection is based precisely on an "organized disorder," on a coordination of disjunctions and juxtapositions – objects from vastly different worlds – that by their very disparateness are made witnesses to a larger continuity: the wholeness of art, and the authenticity of culture, broadly conceived.[79] A similar logic governs Wharton's fiction, ordering the textual juxtaposition of "Old New York" with prehistoric antiquities and tribal metaphors. Taken together, the very gaps and discrepancies between utterly different social worlds produce a coherent discursive space unified under the concept of "culture."

Writing of the social function of museums in this era, Philip Fisher analyzes the new role of the museum in creating authenticity for societies now fully committed to industrial mass production. In the age of factories, "the British Museum in London and the Metropolitan Museum in New York represent a new kind of institution. No longer do they provide a visible history of the culture itself: that is, a display of objects rich with symbolic, local significance. Instead they are storage areas for authenticity and uniqueness per se, for objects from any culture or period whatever that were said to be irreplaceable."[80] It is not just the choice of the Metropolitan as a setting in *The Age of Innocence*, then, that links Wharton's fiction to the new institution of the museum. Wharton shares the assumptions that made modern museums possible, assumptions that the authentic and the real are in some sense precarious, in need of preservation, and that they reveal their purest meaning in the form of collections and the apparatus of archival representation. "The compact world of my youth has receded into a past from which it can only be dug up in bits by the assiduous relic-hunter," Wharton writes in *A Backward Glance*, "and its smallest fragments begin to be worth collecting and putting together before the last of those who knew the live structure are swept away with it." [81] Here culture is that which is "worth collecting." Conceived as "relics" and "fragments," the past is reassembled according to new dual principles of "worth": cultural wholeness, and cultural extinction – on the one hand a comprehensive "live structure" analogous to Tylor's definition of culture as a "complex whole" and, on the other, the imminent loss of that living whole.

Collected and displayed as "relics," the manners of the New

York circle in *The Age of Innocence* are vested with a rich realism even as they signify what Malinowski calls an "ethnic peculiarity." But the novel also asserts that the "real" is held in place by subtle yet highly effective techniques of social force. The plot of *The Age of Innocence* shows that the very boundaries that determine cultural identity and meaning are silently – and in times of crisis, actively – policed. Had the plot line allowed Archer and Ellen to escape the claims of kinship, the narrative would have swerved from its terms of realism into romance, the utopia of a "country" without cultural categories – the husband, the wife, the mistress. Keeping the realist plot in place, however, requires every resource of the families' "tribal discipline," not only the ritual sacrifice of Ellen but the imprisonment and surveillance of Archer.

May's elaborate dinner party, the narrator says, is a "tribal rally around a kinswoman about to be eliminated from the tribe" (1281). As Ellen is ceremoniously expelled, Archer realizes that he is also being subjected to the same forces that Pierre Bourdieu has called the "symbolic or euphemized violence" of custom.[82] Dinner conversation dwells on the recently exiled Beauforts, cast out for a financial scandal, and by the "inexorableness" of its tone Archer knows the discussion is a collective threat issued to him: "'It's to show me,' he thought, 'what would happen to me – '" (1282). The family has issued what anthropologists in their fondness for classifying species of magic termed a "conditional curse," a protective spell that calls down in advance the punishment that will befall anyone who transgresses it. Like Wharton, Malinowski presents conditional curses as part of an implicit legal structure that serves to enforce the tribal code. Where Western law requires separate institutions of courts and prisons, Malinowski sees tribal law is part of an entire "social machinery of binding force."[83] Archer realizes that the unspoken ceremony enacted at the dinner is merely the culmination of forces of daily, ongoing tribal regulation: "He guessed himself to have been, for months, the centre of countless silently observing eyes and patiently listening ears, he understood that, by means as yet unknown to him, the separation between himself and the partner of his guilt had been achieved, and that now the whole tribe had rallied about his wife on the tacit assumption that nobody knew anything" (1282). As Bourdieu notes of euphemized violence, its power lies in the collective denial that any coercion is taking place, making direct resistance inappropriate or even absurd. Archer knows that the conspiracy to ignore the crime, a "tissue of elaborate mutual dissimulation" (1285), is the family's most effective way of subduing him. He eats Florida asparagus and smokes with the men in the drawing room, but by these very acts knows he is a "prisoner in the centre of an armed camp" (1282).

By presenting the silent punishment enacted through the conventions of a dinner party, Wharton addresses what Malinowski singled out as one of the "riddles of Culture" that most intrigued anthropologists: the power of tribal discipline. Once the myth of the wild savage was dismissed and "it became plain that hypertrophy of rules rather than lawlessness is characteristic of primitive life," the savage came to represent "a model of the law-abiding citizen." As Malinowski wryly notes, this did not prevent ethnologists from being drawn to sensational cases of "blood-curdling crime, followed by tribal vendetta, in accounts of criminal sorcery with retaliation, of incest, adultery, breach of taboo or murder." But such acts of violent retribution were now seen as contributing to a "transcending solidarity of the kindred group." (Malinowski himself was at pains to disprove the notion of a "mysterious 'group-sentiment'" that he imputed to Rivers, Durkheim, and others, but he too saw in tribal life remarkable "forces of cohesion.")[84] Wharton borrows from this literature of savage crime and ceremonial discipline to represent acts of power inherent in the genteel decorum of New York society. The anthropological perspective not only accepts the fundamental reality of custom, it also perceives custom as an active, always-present web of force. This represents a considerable transformation of the traditional novel of manners. Although the genre had always recognized the pressures of social and sexual politics, it rarely if ever pictured those pressures as a machinery of punishment and coercion. Retaining the drawing-room settings and the portraits of sensibility of a Jane Austen novel, Wharton adds a subtext of crime, surveillance, and punishment more likely in a Dostoyevsky novel, or, more to the point, in a work like Malinowski's *Crime and Custom in Savage Society*.

Although duplicitous, May's dinner is a ceremony of "rehabilitation and obliteration," carried out in much the same way as the Trobrianders' "magic of oblivion," ritual spells that restore marital happiness after the wounds of adultery. For Malinowski, what is real in a "fetching back" rite is its effectiveness: "This formula is said to be very powerful, and to have restored married happiness to

scores of broken households."[85] The same is true of the New Yorkers' willful denial of the love affair: what matters is not the denial's
falsity but its power. By resolving the novel as she does, Wharton
completes the work of "obliteration." After the climactic sacrifice,
Ellen Olenska is never again seen or heard from in the narrative.
Even after thirty years of social change and moderation, the ritual
act holds: when Newland gazes at Ellen's Paris house in the book's
final scene, unexplained forces keep him from crossing the threshold. The magic of the Wellend's "fetching back" rite is as strong as
ever.

Once manners are recast as performative ritual rather than a
measurable propriety, the novel has transformed an analysis of
moral meaning into an anatomy of social power. Questions of social
discipline, of course, have always been implicit in the novel of
manners. But by detaching manners from any definitive set of moral imperatives and binding them to a complex machinery of decorous force, Wharton's realism comes to match the vision of contemporary social theorists, who saw manners not as immanent values
but as a permeating "system," like trade or law or government. The
result, for James as well as Wharton, is the creation of an "extraordinary discourse" to register perceived ruptures in the substance of
ordinary social life. But if descriptions of drawing-room sacrifice
and other civilized blood sports bespeak cultural disruption, we
should see in the same language a discourse of mastery – not only
the intellectual mastery of "laws of culture," but a language of
social mastery "discovered" in tribal life itself. The novelists are
members of the "body of specialists" Bourdieu describes as necessary in times of cognitive crisis, experts charged with formulating in
new kinds of discourse all of the practices and beliefs that were once
accepted as natural and unremarkable phenomena, and thereby
transforming them into objects of a new cognitive mastery.

Thus if rewriting the novel of manners is an act of preservation
directed against the threat of an exhausted tradition and a menacing modernity, it is an act that renews the genre for the world it
appears to resist, sharing and circulating through the institution of
fiction the authority of modern institutions – museums, social sciences, popular discourses of primitivism.[86] *The Age of Innocence* displays the paradoxical modernity that could issue from the "relics"
of culture. Archer's ultimate surrender to the tribal ways brings a
restored sense of reality, yet at the same time it provides the basis

for a transition to a modern society of technology and a liberal hegemony. Ellen's expulsion, at once a stunning tribal sacrifice and a tribal "victory," is the emotional center of the novel; Wharton's aesthetic energies have their most brilliant play in this scene, perfectly harmonizing drawing-room and ethnographic manners. But it is the novel's final chapter, set twenty-six years later in Paris, that reveals the full implications of Wharton's realism. In modern Paris, Newland himself is now a relic ("Don't be prehistoric!" his son tells him). But it is precisely as an antiquarian object that Newland achieves a poignant sense of reality, though a reality now recognized as customary, fragile, and in need of preservation. Newland finds himself unable to cross the threshold to Ellen's apartment: "'It's more real to me here than if I went up,' he suddenly heard himself say; and the fear lest that last shadow of reality should lose its edge kept him rooted to his seat as the minutes succeeded each other" (1302).

The moment is preserved in museumlike stillness. But with a precious reality "rooted" with Archer in this scene, the chapter also embraces the opposing forces of modernity that had produced the extinction of Old New York. Telephones and electric lighting, Roosevelt's politics, and rapid overseas travel have been integrated into the life of the next generation of leading New Yorkers. Even more importantly, the taboos against exogamous marriage to the sons and daughters of business and politics have been lifted. Now society is a "huge kaleidoscope where all the social atoms spun around on the same plane" (1296), but the disorder is an energy harnessed by Archer's children. Wharton's portrait of a class that in fact retained and strengthened its claim to power and wealth through the tumultuous social changes of fin-de-siècle America is demographically correct. In spite of a pervasive sense of WASP decline – indeed, in part through that very sense – the northeastern elite expanded its social influence and helped to acculturate the American polity to a new society of consumption and corporate capitalism. Newland Archer's story is a story of culture consciousness and the new social life it produced in the name of cultural preservation.

CHAPTER 4

Henry James and magical property

The classification of things reproduces the classification of
men.

Emile Durkheim and Marcel Mauss, *Primitive Classification*

As in the kula, so in such tournaments of value generally,
strategic skill is culturally measured by the success with which
actors attempt diversions or subversions of culturally conventionalized paths for the flow of things.

Arjun Appadurai, *The Social Life of Things*

Edith Wharton, discussing favorite kisses in literature with a dinner
companion, gave as her "crowning" example the kiss on the stairs
in James's *Spoils of Poynton*. She called it "one of the most moving
love-scenes in fiction."[1] But in spite of this impressive kiss, the love
story in *Poynton* is a curious one. For the story of the love between
Fleda Vetch and Owen Gereth is often eclipsed by a property story,
the tale of the even more intimate attachment between Mrs. Gereth
and her furniture. Or perhaps it would be more accurate to say that
the love story is utterly entangled with the property story: Fleda,
with her complex passion for both the Poynton property and its
legal owner, Owen, fuses the novel's two inseparable plots. That
James so tightly wove together ambiguities of marriage, sexuality,
and property has earned the novel a reputation as one of his most
problematic fictions. Yet for all its complexities, the novel's explicit
focus on relations between people and their property throws into
relief a theme that preoccupied James throughout his career. *The
Spoils of Poynton* makes an open analysis of the relations linking art,
property, and women through the exchange medium of marriage.
From his early novel *The American*, in which James first examines
the parallel acquisition of art and women, to *The Golden Bowl*, where

114

the links between kin, marriage, art, and wealth multiply exponentially, James creates a narrative form in which "relations stop nowhere" in order to trace a social circuit crossing even the boundary between people and things.

Many modern critics have found these themes unnerving, a sign of something pathological in James's fiction – in the words of one scholar, "his novels and tales move relentlessly toward the *perversity* of family and marital relations." In this view, the feelings Mrs. Gereth bears for the Poynton furnishings show her "warped" nature, and Fleda's similar sentiments betray a "sexual fetishism."[2] James's contemporary readers were startled as well: "Few, indeed, would have considered favourably, as the theme of a story, the fondness of a middle-aged lady for the furniture she and her late husband have collected."[3] But if late nineteenth-century readers found a "fondness" for things an unlikely subject for a marriage novel, the topic was nevertheless of sharp and widespread interest in that era. Marx was only one observer among many to describe a growing "mania for possessions." Radicals and apologists alike warned of the confused and morbid strains of feeling they saw springing up in an age of luxury, while still others testified to the "restorative powers" of objets d'art and beautiful home decoration.[4] In a variety of ways, writers expressed a shared sense that new relations linking people and things were a pronounced social fact, an uncanny but powerful reality.

Today scholars have a ready label for that emergent world: the culture of consumption. Increasingly, the strata of society were wedded to the world of commodities; things as well as people were members of what one historian calls the system of "quasi-kinship relationships" that differentiated society after 1880.[5] Far from being an open market of commodities, the consumer culture of the late nineteenth century was marked by the *restricted* circulation of goods and honorific status, based on codes of taste, conduct, and class. James's contemporaries may have had no developed vocabulary to describe the new bonds of affinity between people and things, but they recognized a sea change. Durkheim described the "crisis" of social ordering that could follow "an abrupt growth of power and wealth." Writing in 1897, the same year that James's *Spoils of Poynton* appeared, Durkheim argued that such dramatic swelling of wealth created the need for a new classification of people and things:

Then, truly, as the conditions of life are changed, the standard according to which needs were regulated can no longer remain the
same; for it varies with social resources, since it largely determines
the share of each class of producers. The scale is upset; but a new
scale cannot be immediately improvised. Time is required for the
public consciousness to reclassify men and things. So long as the
social forces thus freed have not regained equilibrium, their respective values are unknown and so all regulation is lacking for a time.[6]

For the educated classes of a transatlantic society, it was precisely
this sense of disequilibrium that prompted efforts to describe a new
"scale" of social life. "Needs" seemed uncertain, boundaries of desire ungoverned. As the career of Durkheim himself illustrates,
many who set out to "reclassify men and things" – and the relation
of men *to* things – turned to ethnographic materials and terms. In
naming and explaining social relations in a new commodity culture, writers shared a language of rich description with studies of
primitive kinship and totemism, "the barbaric idea that confuses
persons and things."[7] Durkheim, for instance, would find the fundamental image of society itself in the bonds linking Australian
tribes to their totemic objects. From Marx's description of the commodity as a "fetish" to William Graham Sumner's treatment of the
modern "cult" of home decoration or Veblen's analysis of leisure-
class "animism," writers borrowed an exotic tribal vocabulary to
describe the new webs connecting people and property. When Weber came to write the definitive analysis of modern status groups, or
"castes," he wrote an ethnographic description of social stratifica-
tion that construed monopolized goods as class gods: "Individual
castes develop quite distinct cults and gods." Caste is now the
result of a "stylization of life."[8]
     Alongside a sense that "regulation is lacking," that boundaries
were shifting and unstable in modern societies, then, scholars introduced a vocabulary of new social castes whose terms were modeled
after a displaced tribal world. The exotic language is a sign of the
anxiety that modern consumption could evoke; Veblen's ethnographic descriptions expose what he called the "vague and shifting" line between "the inert and the animate" in contemporary
culture.[9] But notably, a sense of modern disorder and a language of
an emergent caste order appear together. Just as the language of
commodity fetishism encodes cultural anxiety, so is the same idiom
a means to articulate a "new scale" of culture.

Scholars were not the only ones to represent modern social life this way. Large printings of major ethnographic works and frequent review articles in leading journals (like the 1868 *Nation* essay "The Progress of Anthropology," by William James, edited by Henry James) helped to popularize a primitivism that in turn circulated in descriptions of modern social life. In Wharton's *Age of Innocence,* the "books on Primitive Man that people of advanced culture were beginning to read" become a lens for family and property relations: Newland Archer finds "inscrutable totem terrors" where he used to see "simple and natural demonstration of family feeling."[10] In *The Spoils of Poynton,* James does not expressly use the vocabulary of totemic kinship (as he does in *The American Scene,* for instance, when he describes Philadelphia society as the product of a "scheme of consanguinity" that produces "security"). But James's portrait of an intimate affinity between the rich and their property, in *The Spoils of Poynton,* belongs with the larger fin-de-siècle effort to "reclassify men and things." The "subject," as James put it in his preface, "residing in somebody's excited and concentrated feeling about something," was the germ of a whole "social and psychological picture."[11] This narrative method, fastening on a seemingly excessive human desire for things as the key to a larger social order, is the same technique writers used to analyze primitive totemism on the one hand and modern consumption on the other. The literature of primitivism made the new commodity culture conceivable, capable of being imagined and written: it was the image of aberrant desire that writers saw in totemism that allowed them to describe an essential "fetishism" behind civilized fashions and commodities.

Certainly there is evidence that James shared contemporary apprehensions about a "disproportionate passion" for things in his era. Supplanting a traditional picture of Victorian domesticity, James presents a warring household in which law and possession are the real forces within family life. At Poynton, "all regulation is lacking": the powers of law are in the hands of the vulgar and the powers of taste on the wrong side of the law. Yet in *The Spoils of Poynton* the excesses of desire, even as they are exotically enlarged, become the medium of real and powerful social bonds. Out of the "crisis," as Durkheim called it, of the disorder between people and things, the novel fashions a new kind of kinship, not of blood but of culture, a "community of taste." As in anthropology, the irrational paths of desire reveal the hidden workings of culture. But to do so, the novel relies on the tension between ethnographic and humanistic notions of culture. Even as the novel reinscribes key distinctions of high culture – taste and vulgarity, refined feeling and will, honor and self-interest – it anatomizes the aggression and power that operate through the extralegal spheres of manners and aesthetic sensibility. Paradoxically, it is by exposing ethnographically the play of power and economic interest inherent in culture that James produces his own self-described "sublime economy of art."

PEOPLE AND THINGS

James's extensive notes for *The Spoils of Poynton* and the preface to the New York Edition of the novel show him intent on revising Victorian domesticity through questions of custom and customary power. James had observed English life as an urban fieldworker. In London "I took on board such an amount of human and social information," he wrote William, "I have very large accumulations . . . and I now simply want elbow-room for the exercise, as it were, of my art."[12] And like an ethnographer, he began his work on the novel with information he received from local gossip ("I obtained much of my material through their confidences," Malinowski informs us of the Trobrianders, "and especially from their mutual scandal-mongering").[13] The incident James hears from Mrs. Anstruther-Thompson ("my informant") at a Christmas Eve dinner – of a Scottish woman who loses legal possession of her cherished house and furnishings when her husband dies and is soon "at daggers" with her son, the legal heir – circulates among London natives as scandal, a transgression of what is right and natural in family sentiment. In his notes, however, James transforms the incident from a scandal to an example of the cruelty of native custom: it is "a situation in which, in England, there has always seemed to me to be a story – the situation of the mother deposed, by the ugly English custom, turned out of the big house on the son's marriage and relegated."[14] As a tale of the widow deposed, it is a story with a long past: "The story of the status of widows," Sumner writes, "is one of the saddest in the history of civilization." Yet the old story had found its way into a new genre in this era, the professional study of kinship. James's rewriting of the Scottish widow's story follows the template of the enthographer's view of the kinship system as a set of relations linking property and rights through consanguinity.[15] But though James examines the sphere of established custom, *The Spoils of Poynton* is about a new order of kinship; it presents neither the familiar Victorian domesticity nor any ancient tradition but a modern middle-class kinship with its new relations between people and things.

This was an order of kinship that James would "discover" and display in American society as well. What James observed in England, however, had its own particular contours. Somewhere around the year 1880, according to Max Beerbohm, there was felt "the primordia of a great change." The elite discovered it could "not live by good breeding alone," and "thus came it that the spheres of fashion and of art met, thus began the great social renascence."[16] When "good breeding," as Beerbohm notes, was no longer sufficient, the strict criterion of birth rank was supplemented with a new set of distinctions that included the discriminations of aesthetic style and perception. What emerged in these years, in fact, was a notion of status that *fused* birth and taste, as writers began to represent aesthetic sensibility as a kind of deep trait – Sumner explicitly calls it "racial taste" – that distinguished the social strata. In Veblen's formulation, "Canons of taste are race canons."[17]

In England, the "social renascence" that absorbed art to "breeding" corresponded to a new circuit of social life organized around villas and suburban mansions. These homes were easily reached by a new network of railways that enclosed individual families and their weekend guests and were detached from any responsibilities to tenants, parishes, or local governments. As Lawrence Stone writes, there was a transition to the concept of "a house in the country, as distinct from a country house."[18] The social universe of *The Spoils of Poynton* is limited almost entirely to this world of suburban villas joined by rail links to the city. Unlike most of James's earlier novels, *Poynton* has jettisoned all vestigial lords and expatriate princesses; the novel is wholly given over to the homes, habits, and conflicts of the ascendant middle classes. But despite the fact that the social spaces in *Poynton* are the familiar territories of the bourgeois novel, despite its familiar plot interests in marriage and inheritance, James's narrative consistently strikes readers as a perversion of the Victorian novel and its conventions. Whether or not we see the world of *Poynton* as pathological, it is clear that James has exoticized the marriage novel. Passion and domestic love are there in abundance, but love is as often attached to furniture and art objects as to people. "No account whatever had been taken of her relation to her treasures, of the passion with which she had waited for them, worked for them, picked them over, made them worthy of each other and the house, watched them, loved them, lived with them" (15–16). Mrs. Gereth's sentiments for her "treasures" are indistinguishable from Victorian family feeling. "Breeding" has indeed merged with the aesthetic "principle of taste" (37) that is the widow's deepest sensibility.

In this sense Mrs. Gereth is a near relative, we might say, of someone like Olive Chandler in *The Bostonians*, for whom taste is a physiological "nerve." Venturing into the parlors and chambers of Boston's social activists, Olive suffers "from the injury of her taste," though "she had tried to kill that nerve." Similarly, Mrs. Gereth knows she is "of the same family" with Fleda Vetch when they recognize a shared "esthetic misery" at Waterbath, a pain that is, like Olive's, a physical suffering: Mrs. Gereth confesses the drawing room had "caused her face to burn," and both women "had given way to tears" (7) in their private rooms. In these opening scenes, James introduces the topic of taste with a gentle humor. Yet as the real "relations" between Mrs. Gereth and her things gradually become more apparent ("The things themselves would form the very center of the novel," James writes in his preface), the novel offers up a series of increasingly outlandish figures. Mrs. Gereth is described as a "conjuror" (74) and a "wizard" (70). The archaic descriptions of the Poynton property as "spoils" and "plunder" (133) impose an analogy that is historically and culturally skewed. Like the overlay of exotic and epic images in Pope's "Rape of the Lock," James's metaphors are disfiguring, making a drawing-room "row" appear grotesque, humorous, and frightening all at once.

But unlike Pope's satire, James's stylistic distortion does not deflate his "spoils." Indeed, it is the wholesome "household art" (19) of Waterbath that is satirized, while the Poynton things take on a strange but charismatic halo. When in the 1908 preface James recollects the process of writing the novel, he mystifies the Poynton "Things" even further, representing them as powerful, animistic idols that had threatened to overthrow the novel's civilized order of drawing-room dialogue. Had his form permitted it, James writes, the central characters of the novel would have been

> the Things, always the splendid Things, placed in the middle light, figured and constituted, with each identity made vivid, each character discriminated, and their common consciousness of their great

dramatic part established. The rendered tribute of these honours, however, no vigilant editor, as I have intimated, could be conceived as allowing room for; since, by so much as the general glittering presence should spread, by so much as it should suggest the gleam of brazen idols and precious metals and inserted gems in the tempered light of some arching place of worship, by just so much would the muse of "dialogue," most usurping influence of all the romancingly invoked, be routed without ceremony, to lay her grievance at the feet of her gods. (19)

This extravagant figure opens to our view an archaeological subtext, a buried language (the things "might have, and constantly did have, wondrous things to say") which was conjured up but necessarily cast out in favor of the more conventional idiom of the novel of manners. But though buried, this exotic language can be said to reappear in oblique forms of well-mannered worship and desire. Mrs. Gereth seems both to recognize and to defy a charge of heretical worship, for instance, when she affirms the power of the things: "When I know I'm right I go to the stake. Oh he may burn me alive!" (114). The excessive images conflate the refined, well-groomed image of Mrs. Gereth with an ancient record of women sacrificed at the stake, from witches to widows. Mrs. Gereth's forced dispossession of Poynton is an "amputation": "Her leg had come off" (69). She is compared to a "tropical bird, the creature of hot, dense forests, dropped on a frozen moor" (146). Later she is not the victim but the conqueror, expressing "the loud tactless joy of the explorer leaping upon the strand" to "take possession" of the island (131). In Mrs. Gereth's struggle to retain possession, Fleda is "sacrificed" (37) and "buried alive" (209). The novels' governing metaphors estrange this tale of middle-class manners and marriage. As if adding his own exotic design to an upholstery fabric or an architectural facade, James stamps his story with a repeating signature pattern. Rereading the novel for the New York Edition, James himself looks at the printed lines as at "barred seraglio-windows behind which, to the outsider in the glare of the Eastern street, forms indistinguishable seem to move and peer; 'association' in fine bears upon them with its infinite magic" (x).

The Spoils of Poynton is identified as one of the first works James wrote in his late style, and we might be tempted to overlook these images as mere examples of the hyperbolic conceits that appear so frequently in the later novels and prefaces. But the novel's mannered style, I am suggesting, shares a historical resonance with its subject. A contemporary reviewer confirmed as much, writing that *The Spoils of Poynton* has a style "as exquisite as the things which it describes." Yet the same reader was critical of the novel's characters – of Mrs. Gereth with her "malady" and the "over-sensitive perversity" of Fleda. This mingling of praise and condemnation of specialized tastes is historically telling as well, for as the wealthier classes began collecting art and "exquisite" furnishings with an unparalleled enthusiasm during this era, the same moment produced a systematic critique of commodity consumption, especially in its most luxurious forms. Yet virtually all of the cultural critics fashion their prose in a highly stylized manner, a manner, I think, not unfairly called "luxurious." James was only one of many writers in this era exotically to redescribe Victorian furnishings and art objects and the desire that adhered to them. Thorstein Veblen pointed to "household furniture" as leading commodities in the current cult of "pecuniary beauty" and compared them to Hawaiian feather mantles and ceremonial adzes of the Polynesian islands. In his *Folkways*, Sumner identified the "new gospel of furniture and house decoration" as one of the most pronounced forms of modern object worship. Charlotte Perkins Gilman, lamenting the "savage" dependency forced upon women, described the modern "consuming female" as "the priestess of the temple of consumption," who creates an exotic "market for sensuous decoration and personal ornament, for all that is luxurious and enervating."[19]

Primitive totemism supplied a flexible discourse for describing and analyzing what has been called "one of the central concerns of the American novel in this period: a concern about the status of persons, as subjects and as living property, and, collaterally, a concern about the status of material things."[20] Gilman's "consuming female" cast as a modern priestess illustrates this concern. For Gilman, the modern appetite for things seemed to change the very nature of women – and therefore "the race" – through the ingestion of things: "To consume food, to consume clothes, to consume houses and furniture and decoration and ornaments and amusements . . . is the enforced condition of the mothers of the race." In the same era, Durkheim invokes totemism as a *contrast* to the wildly unregulated desire in the modern consumer society: the "liberation of desires has been made worse by the . . . development of industry and the almost infinite extension of the market." Unlike the savage practicing totemism, the modern subject "can no longer figure out to himself its limits, since it is, so to speak, unlimited." In the work of these theorists, the image of the totemic object is explicitly matched with its modern homology, the commodity, and the themes of desire and social order are recast from a theology of need and avarice to a sociology of culture and anarchy.[21]

Is James, like Durkheim, alarmed by this "infinite extension of the market" into every sphere of life? Mrs. Gereth is clearly stamped as a figure of excess, with "her strange, almost maniacal disposition to thrust in everywhere the question of 'things,' to read all behavior in the light of some fancied relation to them"(24). Certainly James acknowledges the central place of desire in his narrative; in the preface he writes that the widow's story illuminates "the most modern of our current passions, the fierce appetites for the upholsterer's and joiner's and brazier's work, the chairs and tables, the cabinets and presses, the material odds and ends, of the more labouring ages" (ix). But this modern passion, as James conceives it, is a "mark of our manners" that, because it is shared, is "full of suggestion, clearly, as to their possible influence on other passions and other relations." As a matter of *manners*, the desire is not individual but cultural. If Mrs. Gereth's passion for antique furniture is "warped," it follows the warp in the fabric of a shared social system. *The Spoils of Poynton* is aptly called a book of fetishism only if we understand "fetish" in an ethnographic sense that is social rather than individual or pathological.[22] Mrs. Gereth's passion signifies an irrational value from the point of view of political economy, but it represents a powerful, effective form of social capital when it is considered in a lived cultural context. Mona thinks that Mrs. Gereth's attachment to her furnishings is irrational and overblown until she glimpses the power that is at stake in controlling them. Then, with good reason, she joins the struggle for their possession: "Whether or not she felt the charm she felt the challenge" (28).

That Mona comes to desire things she does not find particularly beautiful tells us that the value of the Poynton objects is not aesthetic. Money or mere property is not really at issue, either. The battle between Mrs. Gereth and Mona is a sign that the property contains some other undefined but highly prized quantity of value. It is possession itself that is the source of the value, because possession will signify a triumph over a rival. In portraying an open struggle between the two women, James presents in an exaggerated, literalized form the tacit social competition that generates prestige, a value-added quantity that adheres to the owner through selected objects. Like Veblen and Sumner, James presents a narrative of modern fetishes, deliberately exoticizing objects and their attraction in order to display species of value and social force that are invisible to the economist or art historian. Beauty and "charm" may indeed contain a "challenge."

But although Mrs. Gereth's powers of taste include a hidden – and later, an all too open – aggression (eventually she attempts Veblen's "pantomime of mastery" without the pantomime), her powers are set against the even stronger forces of the law. The threat to "send down the police" (142) is a ritualistically repeated warning. Mona's "rights" to Poynton are supported by an invisible but all-powerful machinery that lies in reserve outside the view of the novel. The property rights in marriage and inheritance, James knew, were a primary structure of the English kinship system. "The right of inheritance is the test of kinship," McLennan announces in *Primitive Marriage* (a copy of which was owned by James). Mrs. Gereth's dispossession "according to English custom" makes visible the social construction of the Victorian family; the novel could be said to rewrite domesticity through the kind of kinship analysis recently invented by Morgan and McLennan. But the story of Mrs. Gereth's dispossession, we have seen, also describes a kind of domestic kinship, or family feeling, between the widow and her property. For Mrs. Gereth, the Poynton things contain the deepest human relations: "They were our religion, they were our life, they were *us!* And now they're only me – expect that they're also *you*" (30–1), she exclaims to Fleda.

Both dimensions of kinship in the novel – legal rights and filial ties to property – represent a significant departure from the domesticity of the earlier Victorian novel. By underwriting an intimate family relation between Mrs. Gereth and her property, *Poynton* violates a sovereign principle of the genre: the strict opposition between people and things, between human and property relations. Literary historians such as Nancy Armstrong have shown that one of the crucial tasks of the early novel was to purify the space of the family from the economic relations openly recognized in the aristocratic-governed regime, as indicated by sumptuary laws, marriage dowries, and customary signatures of wealth and rank in the visual environment of the household. Overturning these signs as superficial and corrupt, the novel and the domestic ideology it helped bring to ascendancy replaced them with other sentimentalized measures of family value. Property, of course, was a fundamental condition for middle-class domesticity. But the genre's implicit codes ruled that the essential value of any individual or family was defined only by the measures of moral character and sentiment. For the domestic novel, the integration of family and property relations visible in the aristocratic home had confused the oppositional categories of persons and things.[23]

By rewriting the family this way, the domestic novel achieved "the destruction of a much older concept of the household," Armstrong writes, most significantly by setting in place the new domestic woman, whose identity was defined as natural rather than economic and political, as it had been understood in the earlier regime. "By the 1840s, norms inscribed in the domestic woman had already cut across the categories of status" maintained in the earlier model of hierarchical households and had changed "the entire surface of social experience."[24] Icons of the true household were now those objects that gave evidence of natural nurturance and virtue – a mother's kitchen, a cradle, a father's chair – rather than the family crest or ancestral jewels, which had incarnated an earlier hierarchical family status. In the face of this tradition, James's novel flaunts the relations between people and things that the domestic novel had outlawed. And it does so in precisely the terms of sentiment – tenderness, jealousy, desire, virtue – that the genre had traditionally reserved for human relations, especially for domestic relations. "They're living things," Mrs. Gereth says of her possessions, "they know me, they return the touch of my hand" (31). James refashions a new kind of household in which Victorian sentiments of domestic love are political and economic. If it was a household that surprised and unnerved novel readers, outside of the pages of fiction it was recognized as a real though troubling phenomenon.

"Why men want so many things is a great subject fit for inquiry."[25] Certainly moralists warned in this moment of the corrupt bonds possible between humans and their property: "It is a folly to suppose when a man amasses a quantity of furniture that it belongs to him. On the contrary, it is he who belongs to his furniture."[26] But even in decrying such bonds, these voices were further witnesses to a new sense of *belonging*, operative if immoral, a current of attraction between people and things so strong that it could confuse the hierarchy between owner and owned. What can it mean to imagine the reversal of ownership and belonging in this way? In what sense could objects have social agency or a social life of their own?

The historian Asa Briggs has argued that the notion of things – and even the word "thing" itself – acquired a new and distinctly ethnological valence in the Victorian era. Books with titles like *Things Japanese* (1888) and *Things Chinese* (1892) helped to give the word a "peculiarly Victorian sound" and usage.[27] James similarly intoned the word in his novel's first working title, *The Old Things*, before he exoticized the image as "spoils," though the syllable "things" rings out as a talisman throughout both the novel and the preface. Just as the word acquired a particular semantic density during this time, the *category* of things simultaneously acquired the status of what we now call "material culture." Pitt Rivers's "universal collection" of ordinary things from around the world ("any ponderable object produced or used at home") explicitly displayed the paraphernalia of everyday life as cultural artifacts, linking, for example, a European crucifix with a Chinese geometric compass and Nigerian divining bones. The collection was not the cabinet of curiosities popular in earlier centuries but a realized, emblematic taxonomy of meaning; Pitt Rivers classified and displayed the objects according to an evolutionary scheme that would reveal the "succession of ideas" in the progressive course of civilization. In fact the early institutions of British anthropology are closely bound up with this important collection of artifacts (originally begun as an amateur collection of firearms). In 1883 the collection was established in its own building at Oxford, where E. B. Tylor became the first museum lecturer, preaching to a large university audience the new sciences of ethnology and archaeology.[28]

The fetishizing descriptions of furniture and art that we see in the pages of James or Veblen, I am arguing, have their material counterpart in the Pitt Rivers ethnographic museum and in the popularizing lectures Tylor delivered there. The uncanny relations binding people to their possessions were mirrored in the ancient or exotic objects that were receiving new public prominence in institutions of culture. A whole way of seeing, displaying, and speaking about things was bound up both historically and theoretically with an ethnological concept of culture then being organized into a professional discipline. Exotic objects set side by side with familiar ones, on the shelf or on the page, exchanged their respective auras of the strange and the ordinary. Objects were more than clumps of substance or mere tools or curiosities; they became vessels of meaning. They acquired "value," as Marcel Mauss puts it, "in the full magical and economical sense." The "material" and the "magical" (Pitt Rivers's terms) belonged to a single social order. Such animistic notions, it was presumed, were originally the crude superstitions of savages, but in the cross-cultural display of objects in an ethnographic collection, animism was placed on a continuum with the "spiritual," or cultural, meaning adhering to modern things. The fetish was a sign for the unreal or irrational value, but the sign itself had acquired a new reality from the museum and from the shared public discourse through which a solid world of commodities was named. For Mauss, the ethnographic study of tribal objects – "magical property," as he called it – revealed "one of the bases of social life."[29]

What appeared to be a cultural problem or even a "crisis" – a modern fetishism of commodities – was also the problem scientifically addressed in the ethnological museum, where fetishism helped explain the foundation of culture. Do anxieties about commodities help to foster the authority of museums? If so, it would not be surprising that some homes (like Poynton) began to look like museums preserving rare and exotic objects, while some museums (the Isabella Stewart Gardner Museum, for instance)now resembled homes displaying antique aesthetic treasures.[30] The transformation of the Victorian home had aroused a range of unsettling feelings at the same time as the aura of authenticity from museum culture began to reach into the domestic sphere.

Thorstein Veblen offers one of the most richly drawn portraits of a new household of "magical property." His *Theory of the Leisure Class* sets forth a totemic economy yoking people and property through "ethnological generalization." What emerges from this book, part comedy of manners and part ethnographic museum, is a startling revision of domesticity that both critiques and draws cultural authority from its own scientific refashioning. Modeled explicitly after "savage" tribes, Veblen's leisure-class household reckons goods, quite as much as people, as vital members of the family. Indeed, the "physiognomy of goods" could be said to be the more distinguishing feature of the domestic body. In Veblen's account, the "apparatus of living" – patent leather shoes, spoons, cast-iron trellises, corsets, close-cropped lawns – have greater specificity and character than any human inhabitants. Leisure-class wives are classified unequivocally with household property as a species of honorific "trophy." Husbands, for their part, are hardly less reified. Despite their identity as owners and masters, they appear in Veblen's portrait as another set of objects belonging to a larger entity, the total household establishment. Personal servants are needed, for instance, because the "master's person" is "the embodiment of worth and honour." If the human beings in Veblen's family portrait are rather like the commodities they buy and display, it is similarly true that the center of animated life is an exotic composite family, embracing people and things, that Veblen calls the "quasi-personal corporate household." The energies of desire, which traditional religious imagery located in the individual soul, have spilled over to animate the objects themselves.[31]

It is this provocative totemic household that James has created in *The Spoils of Poynton*. Though his human characters are not the faceless figures of Veblen's sociology, they share what Frazer calls the "intimate and altogether special relation" to "material objects" elaborated in the literature of totemism. "They're living things to me," Mrs. Gereth claims (53). As in Veblen's household, at Poynton people appear to draw their life from the life of their property: "The mind's eye could indeed see Mrs. Gereth only in her thick, coloured air; it took all the light of her treasures to make her concrete and distinct" (146). When Mauss surveyed a mass of nineteenth-century ethnographic literature, at every turn he found kinship economies "in which persons and things become indistinguishable": "Originally, things had a personality and a virtue of their own. . . . Things are not the inert objects which the laws of Justinian and ourselves imply. They are part of the family: the Roman *familia* comprises *res* as well as *personae*." At James's Poynton estate, *res* and *personae* dwell as kindred inhabitants of an exotic but ordered family. "She knew them each by every inch of their character – knew them by the personal name their distinctive sign or story had given them" (73). The *vaygua*s or precious objects of the Trobrianders are similarly recognized and named: "Each of these precious objects and tokens of wealth has its name, quality and power."[32]

The Spoils of Poynton gives the "shifting line" between the animate and the inanimate a dramatic immediacy. Critics have tended to reconstitute that line by dismissing Mrs. Gereth as a figure of satire, finding all of Victorian fetishism embodied in one "warped" woman. Interestingly, even the Victorian theorists of totemism were tempted to locate its origins in the natural wandering of female desire. Frazer speculated that totemism began when pregnant women became fixated on a special object at the time of the first fetal stirrings, and Freud, it will not surprise us, found this suggestion persuasive: "Such maternal fancies, so natural and so universal, appear to be the root of totemism."[33] But if James means to condemn the "ruling passion" (37) of the widow, the same species of desire is also shared by the more sympathetic Fleda – indeed, it is heightened and eroticized in Fleda. The "rapture of that first walk through the house" is explicitly marked as physical "initiation." Entering Poynton brings on a "soft gasp" and a "roll of dilated eyes," eventually tears, and a "submission" (21) to the beauty that "throbbed out like music" (26). Through Fleda, the passion for things is made erotic, aesthetic, almost sacred. In *The Spoils of Poynton* desire is a palpable ether, a spirit not residing in the human subjects but suffusing the household itself. It is no wonder, then, that to Mona Bridgstock, Poynton has "an air almost of indecency; so that the house became uncanny to her by the very appeal in its name – an appeal that . . . Mona thanked heaven she *was* the girl stiffly to draw back from" (27).

Philistines may stiffly draw back, yet James's "uncanny" household seems designed to provoke anxiety in even the most sophisticated readers. As with the household in "The Turn of the Screw," the Poynton estate forces readers to ponder aberrant desire, a spreading of longing and passionate interests beyond their customary boundaries. Fleda's curious aesthetic-erotic desire is displayed dramatically in one of the novels' most lyrical passages. After the climactic revelation that Mrs. Gereth has sent back the Poynton furniture before Owen manages to break with Mona, Fleda has a vision of the spoils. Under the pressure of James's style, the scene unsettles the foundational categories of person, place, and thing, casting the Poynton furniture first as stages of a "journey," then as an abstract quality, "beauty" (which, though abstract, can be measured in "tons"), and finally as living creatures. These metamorphoses effect a reversal of ownership and belonging, turning Poynton into precisely the kind of "quasi-personal," animated household presented to us in Veblen's ethnological description:

> The time seemed not long, for what were the stages of the journey but the very items of Mrs. Gereth's surrender? The detail of that performance, which filled the scene, was what Fleda had now before her eyes. The part of her loss that she could think of was the reconstituted splendour of Poynton. It was the beauty she was most touched by that, in tons, she had lost – the beauty that, charged upon big wagons, had safely crept to its home. . . . She equally, she felt, was of the religion, and like any other of the passionately pious she could worship even now in the desert. . . . They were nobody's at all – too proud, unlike base animals and humans, to be reducible to anything so narrow. It was Poynton that was theirs; they had simply recovered their own. The joy of that for them was the source of the strange peace that had descended like a charm. (234–5)

This vision has seemed one of the most unaccountable things about the novel; one recent critic writes that "it is difficult to decide whether this flight of fancy is sublime or ridiculous." Yet the uneasiness aroused by this scene, I would argue, is as telling as anything else about it. For when critics describe the uncanny quality of this passage, they reproduce the late nineteenth-century anxiety about aberrant desire as well as the language of fetishism that expressed it. The novel arouses anxiety about the arousal of desire, another instance in which the style enacts its own theme.[34]

Partly for that reason, to dismiss Fleda as somehow delusional is to follow a path of diminishing returns; it can only lead to the old story (as old as Genesis) of the errors – the *errare*, or wandering – of female desire. The novel, in contrast, rather than diminishing Fleda's "worship," inflates it, enlarges it to a new lyrical realism. Fleda's response to Poynton is the model for what the preface calls a "sublime economy of art": though Mrs. Gereth's extravagant actions arouse her alarm, her worship relays that anxiety into an exotic but recognized form of culture. Her distress at Mrs. Gereth's aggression, for instance, becomes Fleda's fantasy of Poynton as her own "museum," with the widow in attendance as a "custodian versed beyond any one anywhere in the mysteries of ministration to rare pieces" (147). Fleda's extravagant daydreams and visions have not restored the boundary between people and things; desire remains an ambiguous "female energy," as Gilman would call it. But the novel locates an unbounded desire for things at the site of a temple of culture.

The preface identifies this narrative method as "the rule of an exquisite economy":

Yes, it is a story of cabinets and chairs and tables; they formed the bone of contention, but what would merely "become" of them, magnificently passive, seemed to represent a comparatively vulgar issue. The passions, the faculties, the forces their beauty would, like that of antique Helen of Troy, set in motion, was what, as a painter, one had really wanted of them, was the power in them that one had from the first appreciated. (30)

"Appreciation" is a primary critical term here.[35] It returns in a later description of Fleda's special sensibility: "The thing is to lodge somewhere at the heart of one's complexity an irrepressible *appreciation*" (xiv). As much as the novel provokes our anxiety by exoticizing a desire for things, it simultaneously invests that desire and its objects with heightened significance, cathecting both the social force and the personal intimacy in bourgeois objects of consumption – "the power in them." The narrative "germ," as James calls it, of this excessive or errant desire eventually yields a whole "social and psychological picture," a middle-class epic he compares to a domesticated Homeric myth, with household antiques transposed into an "antique Helen." The novel appreciates or magnifies the question of unfixed desire even as it associates that desire with "power" – social, legal, and cultural.

Totemism, Freud believed, was "inadequately appreciated." Once we remove our prejudices against animism, "which like a screen conceal understanding," the savage's animistic desire, which is the power of wishes and thoughts over objects, explains not only modern neuroses but "the great social productions of art, religion and philosophy" – in short, culture. *Totem and Taboo* is Freud's *appreciation* of savage animism as culture. As would become clear in *Civilization and Its Discontents*, this economy of appreciation was ambiguous: culture partakes of neurosis as much as neurosis is endowed with the dignities of culture. It was an ambiguity that Freud in part inherited from the ethnological literature he read. As Christopher Herbert and others have argued, anthropology contained its own "exquisite economy" linking the themes of desire and culture, which in turn reflected a social logic that relied upon anxiety about desire to affirm the authority of culture. With its central categories of culture and custom, anthropology effected a complex "reconfiguring of moral and religious ideas about sin and human passions." The theology of boundless human passion is banished, but "one of the paramount functions of anthropology in its early

modern stage was in effect to validate scientifically this very myth
[through the savage] and thus the theory of social control with
which it has always been inseparably connected." The sublime
appreciation of animism as culture, Herbert suggests, supports a
practical social economy, that is, an intense cultivation of desire"
in tandem with its "vigilant repression" in a society that seemed to
thrive on the tension between the two poles. The governing notions
of free desire and culture as restraint are "two reciprocal elements
of a single pattern."[36] The same pattern governs *The Spoils of Poynton,* in which an unsettling passion and a cultural power are located
in a single set of "idols." Just as the Poynton treasures are associated with the erotic and the illicit ("mixed up with a theft" [80]),
they also evoke "an origin, a sort of atmosphere for relics and
rarities" (68) that purifies the desires of ownership.

   The conjunction, though, means that, however rarefied the emblems of culture, they can never break free from disruptive desires
and cultural conflicts. In James's novel, those features that the
domestic ideology found most disturbing about the premodern
household – an intimate identification with family property, and a
status for women distressingly like property – are discovered inside
the bourgeois home.[37] Fleda is "advertised and offered" to Owen in
Mrs. Gereth's attempt to keep control of Poynton, and the widow is
open about trading on male desire: "Don't you know a little more
. . . what men are, the brutes?" (141). An archaic kinship banished
from the traditional domestic novel returns in full force, turning
mother and son into "intimate adversaries" (83), women into commodities, and marriage into what the Tlingit Indians call a "war of
property." At the same time, though, the Poynton war will disclose
new boundaries of culture that mark a "community of taste."

THE WAR OF PROPERTY AND THE WEAPONS OF TASTE

The Spoils of Poynton places taste at the center of the rules for bourgeois marriage. From the opening chapter, in which Mrs. Gereth is
"straightway able to classify" Fleda as the only non-Philistine at
Waterbath, the narrative contains principles of classification for
marriage that are based on relations of taste. Mrs. Gereth was
"always looking at girls with reference, apprehensive or speculative, to her son" (36), and the plot hinges on whether her tacit
marriage rules, which define an ideal match with Fleda in opposi-

tion to the "abomination" of marriage to Mona Bridgstock, will be upheld or transgressed. The novel comes to ratify Mrs. Gereth's rules, if not to fulfill them: Owen eventually finds Fleda the most desirable mate, and any potential story of Mona and Owen as star-crossed lovers blocked by a disapproving parent is quickly dropped. His awakening to Mona's Philistinism – "She's so different, so ugly and vulgar, in the light of this squabble" (99) – corresponds to his awakening of aesthetic taste: "I never knew how much I cared for [the things]. They're awfully valuable, aren't they?" (88). Desire and sentiment in this marriage story are inseparable from the governing relations of taste and ownership. Fleda's love for Owen, for instance, is from the start linked to her desire for a life at Poynton, described as "a future full of the things she particularly loved" (11): "She thought of him perpetually and her eyes had come to rejoice in his manly magnificence more even than they rejoiced in the royal cabinets of the red saloon" (58). When anticipating a marriage between Owen and Mona, the novel gives less emphasis to Owen's future misery than to the "desecration" of Poynton falling into the hands of a Philistine. James's novel gives a fictional exposition of a system of marriage and inheritance wedded to categories of culture and taste. That system includes an affinity that James in his notebook calls a "community of taste," a bond that makes Fleda and Mrs. Gereth "of the same family" (11).[38] The bond is not a tie of blood or even of class; glimpses into the homes of Fleda's father and sister reveal that the Vetches are barely this side of middle-class respectability. But a community of taste, as James presents it, is still a tie that is crucial to questions of property and family, and the kindred sensibilities of the two women become the central bond in the novel's complex system of inheritance, law, courtship, and marriage.

Because James's "principle" of taste is bound up with the intrinsic relation between people and property, it could never be one of the rules of marriage recognized in the traditional domestic novel. A commonality of taste and sensibility was certainly one of the strands that determined a suitable marriage match in the novel tradition. But in *Poynton*, taste carries the weight of taboo-enforced laws of incest. Owen's marriage to "the maiden of Waterbath" will be an "abomination" (19). There is certainly a comic quality to the extravagant importance of taste in the novel. But the hyperbole serves the more fundamental purpose of opening to view the tacit laws that structure middle-class status, juxtaposing Mrs. Gereth's "principle" of taste with the "ugliness fundamental and systematic" of Waterbath (6). *Poynton* is an anatomy of taste – its social power, its strategies, and its limits. Whereas Arnold had categorized Philistines by the "furniture of their minds," James represents the Philistine mind through its furniture. Fleda finds Mrs. Bridgstock herself an utter blank ("she had the face of which it was impossible to say anything but that it was pink, and a mind it would be possible to describe only had one been able to mark it in a similar fashion" [172]). But with the meticulousness with which Lewis Morgan lays out the "houses and house-life of the American aborigines,"[39] James catalogues the rooms and landscaping of the Bridgstock home through metonymic symbols of the Philistine ethos: the "relics of Waterbath, the little brackets and pink vases, the sweepings of bazaars, the family photographs and illuminated texts, the 'household art' and household piety" (19) of the Bridgstock house help to construct a typology of taste in British middle-class culture. James surveys the rooms at Poynton and at Mr. Vetch's quarters as well, charting cultural boundaries that are not recognized by any code of law or official public discourse.

Contemporary readers found this sustained analysis of taste a strange and distorting departure from the conventions they expected in a marriage novel. Even those reviewers who most admired the novel found James's central focus on the Poynton property a puzzling, if not disturbing, anomaly. An 1897 *New York Times* review expressed surprise at the novel's abrupt turn away from the expected "romantic" treatment of courtship and marriage:

> Speaking broadly, the mother wants the son to marry one of the young women, and he intends to marry the other, and does. There, with another deserving hero, or even without one, would be material enough and to spare for the sentimental novelist. But Mr. James makes nothing at all of the situation that he might be expected to make . . . He allows nothing for the romantic taste that is in us all.

Instead he allows everything for aesthetic taste, the reviewer notes, but "not one novel reader in ten thousand probably, will be able to comprehend his and Mrs. Gereth's and Fleda Vetch's views of life, art, and conduct." After these oblique laments, however, the *Times* author is quick to include himself or herself in that chosen number: "counting all the tens of thousands of novel readers in the English-speaking world, one from each of the tens of thousands will make up a company that is worth while." The novel itself, it would seem, performs an operation of taste, separating the aesthetic sheep from the goats. Like the Poynton treasures, the novel is an object of discriminating beauty, "as exquisite as the things which it describes." As James began to refine his late style in *Poynton*, the curious, rarefied quality of the novel's subject and narrative method created a species of specialized beauty and – at least as perceived by readers – an implicit aesthetic challenge. James deliberately violates the expectations of the middle-brow novel reader when he refashions a novel of courtship into a complex "social and psychological picture." Its beauty is uncanny, not unlike the way that "the house became uncanny" (27) to Mona when she is challenged to appreciate the Poynton things and a "dim instinct" tells her that there are questions of power at stake. The perceived aesthetic value of James's novel, I am suggesting, is tied to particular departures from the novel tradition. Through his portrait of highly cultivated and even perverse relations of taste, James has "come into possession," one reviewer argued, "of a field completely his own."[40]

It is accurate, I think, to say that James's focus on taste and property creates a new "field" for the novelist. His swerving from the conventions of the marriage novel adds to the special authority that critics were beginning to award to James as a preeminent artist of high culture. But the "deep lucidity" James achieved in this "field" was matched by similarly penetrating analyses of taste and manners by contemporary social theorists, analyses that follow closely the contours of the novel James created when he made a story of courtship into a story of "spoils." In the work of Veblen, Mauss, Georg Simmel, and others, the forces of fashion and taste were recognized as powerful, agonistic social weapons in the tacit war of property that was fought vicariously through consumption, ownership, and display. Out of these writings we can see a new field of taste ordered around anxieties about commodity desire and social boundaries. Like James's narrative, the war of property that theorists uncover in bourgeois society is made visible by exotically recasting customs and manners as aggressive, even coercive, rituals and strategies.

"To refuse to give," Mauss writes, is "the equivalent of a declaration of war." The kinship economy of gift exchange and inheritance is "in theory voluntary, disinterested," but is in fact "strictly obligatory and the sanction is private or open warfare."[41] James recognized a similar disguised coercion in bourgeois kinship and discovered there a "drama-quality" for the novelist. Mrs. Gereth's refusal to accept the dispossession of "the mother" threatens to unveil the presence of force behind the natural sentiment of family relations. She must choose to give – she is expected to *want* to give – or inheritance will resemble nothing so much as piracy and the family a form of despotism. The collective denial of any coercion within family relations is necessary to preserve the identity of the family from what it is not: a social institution policed by the law and its reserves of force. Hence when Mrs. Gereth's resentment becomes an "active force" that prompts her rebellion, it makes visible all of the usually concealed forces that regulate English kinship.[42] Ethnographers likewise analyzed incidents of kinship crisis, episodes in which a transmission of family property threatened to reveal social coercion behind the structure of natural rights and propriety. Malinowski found that although the matrilineal descent so counterintuitive to Westerners was the foundation of the Trobrianders' sense of reality, it nevertheless produced "frequent tensions and difficulties, and not seldom [gave] rise to violent breaks in the continuity of tribal life." By granting illicit gifts and privileges to his son, rather than to his heir (a nephew), the chief of the Omarakana village had fostered in his kinsmen (his sister's relatives) a resentment at once economic and emotional. Narrating an episode he calls "one of the most dramatic I have ever witnessed in the Trobriands," Malinowski describes the night when the "tense equilibrium" broke out into open hostility, bringing accusations of adultery, visits to the White Resident Magistrate some miles away, a midnight "driving-away" ceremony, and the exile of the chief's son to another village. The son's greatest crime had been to call in the magistrate, violating the tribal fiction of their independence from external rule. Acting on "outraged tribal law and feeling," the chief's kinsmen used the most powerful force short of physical violence: "Once the words "Go away" – *bukula*, "we drive thee away" – *kayabaim*, had been pronounced, the man had to go. These words, very rarely uttered in earnest, have a binding force and an almost ritual power." Transgressions of the rules of kinship created "a deep rift in the whole social life of Kiriwina," providing Malinowski with a glimpse of the powers of law and ritual enforcement that hold kinship in place.[43]

Like the absent but ominous authority Malinowski attributes to the White Resident Magistrate in Kiriwina, the power of the civil authority always hovers at the margins of *The Spoils of Poynton*. The coercive power of the state is in theory so incongruous a presence in the (civilized) family that the first allusion to it is farcical: "Fleda asked Mrs. Gereth if she literally meant to shut herself up and stand a siege, or if it might be her idea to expose herself, more informally, to be dragged out of the house by constables" (48). But after Mrs. Gereth has transported the Poynton treasures to Ricks, the intervention of the law becomes a direct and regularly repeated threat. At the urging of the Bridgstocks, Owen is ready to bring in his solicitors in order to ensure Mona the "enjoyment of her rights" (43). The open invocation of the law – "what he calls setting the lawyers at you," as Fleda puts it (111) – exposes the social power that is the foundation for what is supposed to be an autonomous sphere of sentiment and natural family identity.

But though police authority is the story's ultimate horizon of force, all-powerful but nowhere visible, there is a different order of power at play in the novel. This is the force that, like the Trobriand driving-away ceremony, operates only through the pressure of customary authority and manners in an extralegal struggle for domination that Pierre Bourdieu calls "symbolic violence."[44] Just before Mrs. Gereth steals away with the Poynton things, Fleda senses the terrific conflict that is about to erupt, a hostility that will be expressed less through the actual removal of the treasures than in the violence done to the kinship order, the double blow consisting of Mrs. Gereth's revolt against the widow's customary dispossession and her usurpation of Mona's legal claim to be mistress of Poynton: "It was absurd to pretend that any violence was probable – a tussle, dishevelment, pushes, scratches, shrieks; yet Fleda had an imagination of drama, of a great scene, a thing, somehow, of indignity and misery, of wounds inflicted and received (56)." Fleda, with her "high lucidity" and special Jamesian "appreciation," translates the acts of symbolic violence encoded in this novel of manners. The "drama" that unfolds makes visible the kinds of force that can be wielded with the weapons of manners and polite usage. If the Bridgstocks are ready to call in the constables, Mrs. Gereth and, more subtly, Fleda herself, make use of the potentially devastating forms of social force available to them. In essence these are the weapons of inclusion and exclusion: acts of formal recognition of social status and their opposite, acts of "slighting," or "cutting."

Ultimately the symbolic "wounds inflicted and received" in the novel are these acts of cutting. By withholding the Poynton property from Mona, Mrs. Gereth refuses to recognize the status that Mona inherits upon marrying Owen. She refuses to recognize, in other words, that Mona can replace her and become the next Mrs. Gereth of Poynton. From her attempts to "offer up" Fleda in exchange for Mona to the threshold "sting" that she delivers as the Bridgstocks depart from a Poynton luncheon and the "strange dim bravado" with which she "kidnaps" the precious things from "their danger," Mrs. Gereth performs an escalating series of formal refusals to recognize Mona. Fleda's sensibility registers for us the true violence of these acts, as when "white and terrible," she lets fly her horror at Mrs. Gereth's viciously polite dismissal of Mona after the luncheon – "Great God, how *could* you?" (36). (Mrs. Gereth's speech to Mona is a masterpiece of cutting, taking as it does the very question of whether Mrs. Gereth *has* cut her as both its theme and most wickedly sharpened edge.) Like the word "cutting" itself, this metaphorical violence expresses the real damage done to the social status or ambitions of the receiver, whether that victim is thin-skinned and "feels" keenly the slight or is more like the thick-skinned Bridgstocks.

In anthropology, writers had begun to transpose these questions of manners into issues of social power. In fact, when Tylor surveyed the tribal "customs of avoidance" that governed the tense relations between new spouses and their in-laws, it reminded him of nothing so much as the civilized practiced of cutting. He argued that these well-documented customs, in which the mother- and father-in-law refuse to acknowledge their child's spouse in any way, served to navigate the dangerous passage by which a "stranger" becomes a family member. "The ceremony of not speaking to and pretending not to see some well-known person close by," Tylor writes, "is familiar to ourselves in the social rite which we call cutting":

> As the husband is initially a "stranger," and has intruded himself among a family which is not his own, and into a house where he has no right, it seems not difficult to understand their marking the difference between him and themselves by treating him formally as a stranger. So like is the working of the human mind in all stages of civilisation, that our own language conveys in a familiar idiom the same train of thought; in describing the already mentioned case of the Assineboin marrying and taking up his abode with his wife's

parents who pretend not to see him when he comes in, we have only to say that they do not *recognize* him, and we shall have condensed the whole proceeding into a single word.[45]

In this kind of custom we have an example of formalized – and hence culturally controlled – hostility toward those outsiders who through marriage can claim kinship privileges and property. By ritualizing in-law aversion, avoidance customs defuse it.

In bourgeois kinship, on the other hand, refusing to recognize a family member is an aggression much too blatant to be sanctioned. For the middle class, it would seem, in-law aversion is formalized only in the uneasy, illicit language of jokes ("The fact that the witticisms of civilized races show such a preference for this very mother-in-law theme," Freud writes, points to something similar to the "sacred loathing" observed in tribal avoidance customs). As Karen Haltunnen has shown, "the subtle art of the 'cut'" was a practice intended to regulate the social distance between classes, especially in public spaces outside the home, where the vulgar had free access to make claims of familiarity ("If you meet a rich *parvenu*, whose consequence you wish to reprove," one etiquette manual pronounced, "look somewhat surprised and say 'Mister – eh – eh?'").[46] Part of what makes Mrs. Gereth's response to Mona so stinging an assault is that she refuses to ignore social distinctions, a blindness required of her when a class "stranger" becomes a daughter-in-law. Her extravagant acts go far beyond the permitted forms of expressing aversion: by so radically cutting Mona, she openly admits the hostility that Freud argues is allowed only oblique expression in jokes. As we have seen, Mrs. Gereth's antagonism leads to a full-scale kinship crisis. Though illicit, her refusal to accept Mona is a real and potent power; eventually even Mona and Mrs. Bridgstock feel the cut that she has given them, as they begin to recognize the symbolic power of the Poynton property and the full significance of Mrs. Gereth's refusal to relinquish it. But because Mrs. Gereth's acts are sanctioned neither by law nor official custom, they necessarily function as an unauthorized, transgressive power. Potent but illicit, Mrs. Gereth's machinations appear sinister to onlookers – even to Fleda, in her more frightened moments.

In a tribal society, Mrs. Gereth would be called a witch. Without the male-sponsored power of the law on her side, her strategies could only be recognized as a dangerous and unregulated species of magic. Through the ethnographic record of magic, writers presented a revealing pattern of the gendered nature of power. Among the kinds of occult power practiced by Trobrianders, for instance, Malinowski found "its character changes entirely with the sex of the practitioner." Whereas male sorcery is "concrete, and its methods can be stated clearly, almost as a rational system," the black magic of the witch is secretive, uncontrolled, and often more violent and deadly. In cultures the world over, female power is by definition illicit or occult when official authority is monopolized by men:

> Competition for official power can be set up only between men, while the women may enter into competition for a power which is by definition condemned to remain unofficial or even clandestine and occult. We find in fact in the political sphere the same division of labour which entrusts religion – public, official, solemn, and collective – to the men, and magic – secret, clandestine, and private – to the women.[47]

James's novel traces the same hierarchy in bourgeois society. A modern English witch is precisely what Mrs. Gereth becomes after she interferes with the kinship laws. When, "in spite of all her spells," (36) Owen determines to marry Mona, Mrs. Gereth turns to stronger, more clandestine powers. Fleda, stunned but impressed after she sees the widow's spoliation of Poynton, exclaims, "I take you simply for the greatest of all conjurors": "'You've operated with a quickness – and with a quietness!' Her voice just trembled as she spoke, for the plain meaning of her words was that what her friend had done belonged to the class of operations essentially involving the protection of darkness" (74).

Yet, according to Malinowski anyway, being a witch is better than being a mere mortal woman. A witch is the first one suspected when there is a death or theft, but at the same time this transgressive magic gives her respect and unofficial power. "She is surrounded by a halo of glory due to her personal power," Malinowski writes of the Trobriand witch, "and usually she has also that strong individuality which seems to accompany the reputation for witchcraft."[48] Fleda recognizes the same kind of charismatic force in Mrs. Gereth. She is distressed at the widow's open and easy violation of social taboos. (Fleda's greater reverence for official codes of honor, we will see, governs her own attempts to win possession of Poynton.) But through Fleda's eyes, Mrs. Gereth eventually emerges with all the glamor of the heroic outlaw: "Her fanaticism gave her a new distinction, and Fleda remarked almost with awe that she had never carried herself so well. She trod the place like a reigning queen or a proud usurper" (46).

But how does James mean for us to read Mrs. Gereth's usurpation? Is Fleda's heroic view of it distorted by her own desire for Owen and his property? Some critics have been quick to write off Mrs. Gereth as a thief, even a "bawd"; but these are, we might say, legal judgments.[49] Instead of this juridical interpretation, James's analysis, figured as it is through exotic terms, presents Mrs. Gereth's power as a cultural force, as the power of illicit but "brilliant" (75) strategies at play within the broader structure of the laws of the English kinship system. Certainly she is a "conjuror" or a witch, but ethnographically this label simply means that she is a powerful woman who operates wide of the law. Mrs. Gereth draws upon sources of cultural power that, though not officially authorized, nevertheless have a profound effect in shaping social life. Her "exquisite tastes," and the personal boldness it inspires, locate for us a certain middle-class power that can never be openly identified as such. Manners and taste have no legal recognition; their effectiveness depends on their acceptance as the only proper behavior and sensibility of civilized people. Mrs. Gereth, it follows, does not use the vocabulary of power but of morality. Although she recognizes that absconding with the Poynton things is illegal, Mrs. Gereth does not regard her actions as evil or immoral. In fact she describes Mona's legal possession of Poynton in the standard middle-class language of outraged moral feeling: it is "perverse," a "violation of decency" (16) and a stain on what is "true and pure" (32). When Fleda sees the spoils displayed at Ricks, Mrs. Gereth presumes that the young woman's visible response is one of approval, "and there was nothing she could so love you for as for doing justice to her deep morality" (73). In point of fact, however, Fleda responds to the sight not with any sense of Mrs. Gereth's morality but rather of that woman's supreme power of taste. From a cultural perspective, Mrs. Gereth's "higher," or extralegal, principles do not belong to a moral code but to the mystified economic code that is fashionable taste:

> In the soft lamplight, with one fine feature after another looming up into sombre richness, it defied her not to pronounce it a triumph of taste. [Fleda's] passion for beauty leaped back into life; and was not

what now most appealed to it a certain gorgeous audacity? Mrs.
Gereth's high hand was, as mere great effect, the climax of the
impression. (72)

Mrs. Gereth's power is really her mastery of the unofficial, un-
coded, but profoundly influential system of elite taste. Her passionate convictions of taste, what Fleda unironically calls her "principle
of property" (246), belongs to the invisible social forces that govern
the distribution of prestige and status in a middle-class world.
Though she finds herself at odds with the law, Mrs. Gereth's fierce
sense of beauty and *worthy* ownership are another source of power,
in the same manner that the "mystical aggression" of African
LoDagaba magic was seen as a "potent supplement to judicial
proceedings" in property disputes.[50] The "gorgeous audacity" –
the highbrow witchcraft, we might say – through which she tries to
intervene in the laws of inheritance comes from a particular cultural source: the mystical, discriminating force of manners, which
operate independently of the official regulatory powers of the law.
Taste is middle-class magic.

This is more than a figure of speech. At the turn of the century,
theorists discovered a symbolic economy, operating within the larger marketplace, in which social value and power circulated in the
disguised form of aestheticized commodities like art, antiques, fashionable clothing, and other distinctive luxuries. This mystified
economy, as we have begun to see, was distinguished theoretically
by way of analogy with primitive economies and their "irrational"
features – ritual consumption and display, gift exchange, sumptuary customs, the magical value of fetish objects. Like the mythic
beliefs that governed tribal economies, the invisible forces operating in this bourgeois sphere were the elusive, ever-changing dictates
of taste, what William James called the "mystery" of the refined
judgment and sensibility by which the genteel distinguish themselves. As theorized by Veblen, taste, or "aesthetic proficiency," was
the competence necessary for converting wealth to prestige in the
competitive arena of conspicuous consumption. Along with conspicuous leisure – "spending" one's time in those activities that will
bring the proper return in status – fashionable consumption produced the rarefied values that untutored money could not buy.
Presided over by women, the economy of prestige that emerged in
modern bourgeois culture regulated, as one etiquette author put it,
the conduct "that 'law' cannot touch" and articulated social dis-

tinctions that were formerly measured by birth.[51] Through an ethnographic lens, taste emerged as a refined species of social power.

To Veblen, luxurious household furnishings were leading examples of the economic value he called "pecuniary beauty": the "blending and confusion of the elements of expensiveness and of beauty is, perhaps, best exemplified in articles of dress and of household furniture." Like manners generally, the reigning canons of taste and beauty have an "ulterior economic ground" and strategically display wealth and status in a mystified form. Whoever possesses taste possesses the exclusionary honor that garners recognition of high status. But this quantum of aesthetic-economic value, Veblen noted, could never be rationally analyzed by the "classical doctrines" of economics, which hold that the end of acquisition is utility. The economist cannot see that "the motive that lies at the root of ownership" is not consumption itself but "emulation," the competitive drive for esteem, honorific status, and social power. To calculate the emulative value of an object requires a cultural analysis, an understanding of the arbitrary, irrational ways of acquiring prestige in a given society. With a keen eye for the details of social life, Veblen describes a symbolic economy that regulates the competition for status in modern Anglo-American culture.[52]

But significantly, to authorize his cultural analysis Veblen turns from economics to the "irrational" phenomena of anthropology. He argues that the "traditions, usages, and habits of thought" that foster prestige belong to an "archaic cultural plane." Veblen makes a quite literal identification, linking kinds of leisure-class consumption, from gambling to art, with primitive animism. Like the heroines of *The Spoils of Poynton*, the "modern barbarian" of the leisure class perceives "an animistic propensity in material things." The "sense of status" itself, as Veblen explains it, is an animistic belief. Like an explorer who happens upon a pristine tribe, Veblen "discovered" a system of barbaric magic at the highest echelon of civilized society: "So far as concerns the communities of the Western culture, this phase of economic development probably lies in the past; except for a numerically small though very conspicuous fraction of the community in whom the habits of thought peculiar to the barbarian culture have suffered but a relatively slight disintegration."

Veblen's evolutionary framework is now discredited, of course, and his claim that leisure-class culture is a product of fossilized instincts now a recognized fiction. In fact what is most striking today is the book's unintentional prophetic quality: the analysis of supposedly "archaic" leisure-class consumption reads like a first-draft description of the economy of spectacle now thriving in late capitalism. Veblen was not describing a primitive survival but an emergent phenomenon that would come to dominate at every class level. Whatever affinities it might have with real tribal economies, conspicuous consumption is a distinctly new feature of modernity that has multiplied with the twentieth-century perfection of mass communication. But for that reason, the ethnographic dimension of Veblen's discovery provided a crucial, if often satirical, lens. It is the *otherness* of an anthropological discourse – the aggression it is willing to see in family and social life, the blurring it allows between people and things, the picture of culturally patterned desire and culturally sanctioned, if shocking, cruelties – that underwrites Veblen's enterprise and makes it possible to represent the competitive practices that were everywhere visible but denied. The discourse of savagery had become the canonical frame of reference for all human behavior that diverged from rational bourgeois behavior – crime, religion, sexual behavior, and desire. For Veblen, the "irrational" economy of prestige could be presented scientifically only in ethnographic terms: the leisure class is the racial past of modern civilization. This temporalizing leads him to the "dolichocephalic blond" ethnic type – like Arnold's "Philistine," a tribal name for a modern social type.[53] But in these images of otherness, the ethnographic idiom provided a medium through which Veblen created his analysis of culture. As with Arnold and James, it is an ethnographic lens that allows Veblen to represent modern society and its heterogeneity in a way that is now very familiar to us: as a world in which socioeconomic groups, of sometimes even quite subtle gradation of class, emerge as distinct cultures, distinguished not by inherited rank but just as explicitly by styles of sensibility and consumption. Sumner's label of "racial taste," though a misnomer, announces a new system of human kinds. Taste is not genetic, as his language seems to present it; rather, taste and style become the boundaries – and enforce the boundaries – of social types and identities.

In 1904, Georg Simmel argued that the "field of fashion" – clothing, aesthetic judgment, social amusements, and conduct – reveals the usually hidden relations of a peculiarly middle-class totemism. These "externals" make up a zone of intersection where the human subject has merged with the world of objects: "We encounter here a close connection between the consciousness of personality and that of the material forms of life, a connection that runs all through history." Simmel located the origins of the twin principles of caste cohesion and segregation in primitive habits of fashion: "Among primitive peoples we often find that closely connected groups living under exactly similar conditions develop sharply differentiated fashions, by means of which each group established uniformity within, as well as difference without, the prescribed set." But if these social functions are rooted in primitivism, the boundary-making task of fashion takes on a new importance in bourgeois society, where the fashion system unofficially but definitely maps the complicated topography of status:

> Fashion plays a more conspicuous role in modern times, because the differences in our standards of life have become so much more strongly accentuated, for the more numerous and the more sharply drawn these differences are, the greater the opportunities for emphasizing them at every turn. In innumerable instances this cannot be accomplished by passive inactivity; but only the development of forms established by fashion; and this has become all the more pronounced since legal restrictions prescribing various forms of apparel and modes of life for different classes have been removed.[54]

Fashion replaces the sumptuary laws of the premodern world. The social forms and styles that emerge through the fashion system constitute a new mythology of status that replaces what Jeremy Bentham explicitly called the "fictions" of monarchical rank. Fashionable household furniture and objets d'art had become some of the most powerful totemic idols in the bourgeois field of fashion. But unlike aristocratic family relics – Lawrence Stone mentions "deeds and patents of nobility, portraits of ancestors, family plate and jewels, and personal gifts from kings or queens," the symbolic capital that was an intrinsic part of the inherited family "seat" – the household gods of the bourgeois have to be acquired through the power of taste. Taste must be backed by wealth, of course, though money by itself is not at all a sufficient substance. Acquiring the new symbolic capital requires the skills that allow one to maneuver in a field of fluctuating values and forms. In the aristocratic regime, a claim to status was essentially complete in a single moment at birth. But in the restless bourgeois social world, where status cannot be permanently monopolized; where, as Simmel notes, "the danger of absorption and obliteration exists"; where the maid could imitate the dress and manners of her mistress; and where "social rites" such as cutting could defeat efforts to rise – in this world the condensed social value Veblen calls the "immaterial goods" of prestige must be perpetually won and retained in an agonistic struggle. The field of fashion and taste was, as Simmel called it, a "battlefield." When the veil is lifted, all prestige property can be called "spoils"; all such objects are trophies acquired on the battleground of status competition.[55]

Like Veblen and Simmel, James uncovers a battlefield hidden in plain sight in the manners and consumption of bourgeois social life. He shows the competition for symbolic values that adhere in fashionable objects and dramatically illustrates the social stakes in possessing them. Despite the fact that he is writing in the medium of fiction, James's method for revealing this symbolic economy is in essence the same method as the social theorists': he frames a social reality in which agents and objects, people and things, are joined in a single cultural nexus. The novel's fetishistic language and its insistent, almost overwritten analysis of taste and the passions of ownership make "beautiful things" into a special locus for interpreting social identity. In Simmel's words, objects of fashion furnish "a combination of relations to things and men, which under ordinary circumstances appear more divided."[56] By representing the English family through the lens of kinship – sentiment entwined with questions of property and power – James allows a suppressed otherness to transform his picture of social life. Like Veblen's defamiliarizing images, James's language brushes against the grain to reveal the profound cultural identities that are defined by taste and lifestyle and traces a symbolic economy that regulates them. Veblen explains this economy as "archaic," but, as exotically as James presents it, he knows that the battle between Philistines and their more "cultured" counterparts is, distinctively, a social drama that belongs to modernity. Marcel Mauss, in a brilliant synthesis of the ethnographic data about forms of tribal exchange, made the same discovery: that the bourgeois prestige economy was not a relic of the past but a new incarnation of the always antagonistic, always mythic distribution of status. In the tribal systems of magical property, Mauss explained, "wealth is, in every aspect, as much a thing of prestige as a thing of utility": "But are we certain that our own position is different and that wealth with us is not first and foremost a means of controlling others?"[57]

THE EXQUISITE ECONOMY OF ART

In surveying the multifarious record of social life in tribal societies, Mauss draws out particular "economic" activities – modes of exchange and destruction and transfer of wealth – that seem to contradict Western notions of rational economic behavior. Central examples are the ritual systems of gift exchange, such as the Trobrianders' *kula,* and the ceremonious destruction of property most familiar in the potlatch of the Native Americans of the Northwest. At first sight these institutions are unintelligible; there is no sign of profit making in any part of the often elaborate activity. In the potlatch, for instance, there appears to be only the extravagant waste of great accumulations of wealth. The idea of property itself is made uncertain in tribal exchange, for it is not just goods that change possession but also "courtesies, entertainments, ritual, military assistance, women, children, dances, and feasts." But these irrational expenditures made it possible for Mauss to see a specifically social dimension to wealth and ownership. What emerges from these forms of "wasteful" gift giving and transfer of ownership is the creation of bonds of obligation and social identity: "Food, women, children, possessions, charms, land, labour, services, religious offices, rank – everything is stuff to be given away and repaid. In perpetual interchange of what we may call spiritual matter, comprising men and things, these elements pass and repass between clans and individuals, ranks, sexes and generations." The spending and giving of things creates identities and relations between people. Things are the carriers of social meaning. As "spiritual matter," property is the paradoxical medium of an intangible social order.[58]

This strange sphere, embracing both objects and persons, seems at odds with the modern commodities markets. But Mauss insists that the same symbolic economy exists within the otherwise rationalized societies of the West. "Things sold have their personality even nowadays," he writes, and not all buying and selling can be measured by notions of scarcity and utility: "Make a thorough statistical analysis . . . of the consumption and expenditure of our middle classes and how many needs are found satisfied? Does not the rich man's expenditure on luxury, art, servants and extravagances recall the expenditure of the nobleman of former times or the savage chiefs whose customs we have been describing?" In the "rich man's" consumption, Mauss finds the same seemingly useless expenditure of wealth that characterizes tribal exchange. Like Simmel and Veblen, Mauss points to the "magical property" of art and luxuries. As in tribal societies, money and time are "wasted" on these valuables with the aim of securing social power and strengthening a hierarchy of relations; art objects carry the surplus value produced in the expenditure.[59]

By recasting this feature of middle-class life in ethnographic images, Mauss turns aesthetic and prestige values into a particular form of social and economic power. The accumulation of art and other kinds of "noble expenditure" – Mauss mentions corporate gifts to workers – are examples of social rivalry that disguises itself in the form of beauty or polite largesse: "But the motives of such excessive gifts and reckless consumption . . . are in no way disinterested. Between vassals and chiefs, between vassals and their henchmen, the hierarchy is established by means of these gifts. To give [to spend] is to show one's superiority, to show that one is something more and higher, that one is *magister*." Mauss stresses the aggression in these forms of "magical property." The potlatch is the "monster child" of tribal economy: "rivalry and antagonism are basic."[60] Theorists after Mauss have tended to gloss over this strong note of aggression, presenting the tribal economy as a system of "erotic" bonds that foster group cohesion.[61] But in keeping with the vision of power that ethnographic texts held for early writers, Mauss sees a world of barely suppressed force and hostility. The antagonism is greatest in the potlatch, where the wasted wealth appears to be pure extravagance. Tribal moieties meet, in their phrase, "to show respect to each other," and yet these festivals contain a "spirit of rivalry and antagonism which dominates all their activities." Spending is a sublimated warfare: "Essentially usurious and extravagant, it is above all a struggle among nobles to determine their position in the hierarchy to the ultimate benefit, if they are successful, of their own clans." Traditionally it is the wealthy tribes that practice the potlatch. Ritually destroying vast amounts of surplus wealth, the rich fight without weapons for honor and political power. Interest takes the form of expenditure. Fear and ambition are expressed as gifts and friendship. "Nothing better expresses how close together lie festival and warfare." The symbolic value acquired through ritual spending *contains* the domination that would otherwise be purchased with blood and death.[62]

In Boas's field reports on Kwakiutl and Tsimshian potlatch; in Westermark's history of alms giving and Tylor's speculations on tribal gambling; in Lévy-Bruhl's description of the confusion of things and people in the primitive mind; in Maori dictionaries and Melanesian travelogues, Mauss discovers a cultural logic that explains the mystified power hidden in the civilized rich woman's beautiful objects. Bourdieu describes this power as the product of "social alchemy," the magic that converts wasted wealth into the social power called "honor":

> The gift, generosity, conspicuous distribution – the extreme case of which is the potlatch – are operations of social alchemy which may be observed whenever the direct application of overt physical or economic violence is negatively sanctioned, and which tend to bring about the transmutation of economic capital into symbolic capital. Wastage of money, energy, time and ingenuity is the very essence of the social alchemy through which an interested relationship is transmuted into a disinterested, gratuitous relationship.[63]

In the "beautiful things" of Poynton, we have James's portrait of what were perhaps the most powerful – because most aestheticized – form of symbolic capital in turn-of-the-century society. The objects carry in their beauty a disguised, domesticated social conquest won not through violence (that could be done only in the colonial world) but through what Bourdieu calls the "cultural competence" of taste. The dominance of the middle class is displayed, tranquil and composed, in the aristocratic beauty that its members had come to literally and materially possess – they may now "finger fondly," in James's words, "the brasses that Louis Quinze might have thumbed": "Poynton was the record of a life. It was written in great syllables of colour and form, the tongues of other countries and the hands of rare artists. It was all France and Italy with their ages composed to rest. For England you looked out of old windows – it was England that was the wide embrace" (22).

Gazing at the Poynton things, Fleda registers for us in personal and principled terms the class power of Mrs. Gereth's ownership: "What struck Fleda most in it was the high pride of her friend's taste, a fine arrogance, a sense of style which, however amused and amusing, never compromised nor stooped." But when symbolic capital is exercised as overt social power, as Mrs. Gereth tries to exercise it on the strength of the "high pride" of her taste, at that moment the force of aesthetic taste loses its efficacy. When the social power lodged in beauty and taste shows its hand, the game is up, for the force of manners lies in not being recognized as power. Here we reach the fatal limit of woman's power: the magic of manners and taste loses all potency when openly exerted as an aggression. The key to the social alchemy is the "collective misrecognition" that allows interest to be sublimated in the disinterested form of honor and competition to be expressed as manners. In her scandalous "revolution," Mrs. Gereth removes the veil from the social antagonism that underlies the mystery of taste. So dishonored, her sense of beauty appears to operate as a blunt violence: "In the watches of the night [Fleda] saw Poynton dishonoured; she had cherished it as a happy whole, she reasoned, and the parts of it now around her seemed to suffer like chopped limbs. To lie there in the stillness was partly to listen to some soft low plaint from them" (78).

In Poynton's full-blown kinship war, with all relations suddenly re-presented as relations of interest and power, Fleda Vetch is the novel's only hope to mediate the crisis. This is true most obviously in her role as the "sole messenger and mediator" (47) between Mrs. Gereth and her son. But more fundamentally, Fleda is the one character who can bring back the social misrecognition that allows exposed interest to recede in favor of an economy of honor. She is no less interested – socially, aesthetically, and materially – in the Poynton treasures than anyone else. But to "save" Poynton she must restore to the kinship system the values of honor and disinterestedness, the necessary fiction that veils power in the discourse of duty, rights, propriety, etiquette, and graciousness. To accomplish this, the narrative turns to what anthropologists imagined as the most primitive method of social mediation: the traffic in women. Mrs. Gereth serves up Fleda to Owen in a frank exchange – the spoils in return for Fleda's marriage – and James presents Fleda as a *tonga*, a piece of "feminine property," that creates the desired alliances.[64] Owen, who acts rather more discreetly at this point than his mother, appears to accept the offer by hinting at a "more wonderful exchange – the restoration to the great house not only of its tables and chairs but of its alienated mistress" in return for "the installation of his own life at Ricks" with Fleda (101). In the anthropological imagination, the shocking but fascinating practice of bartering for wives represented the foundation of civilization and its sublimation (not elimination) of violence. Through wife exchange, the threat of war is made an occasion for social bonding, and the sexual forces of nature – male desire – are harnessed to the arts of culture. Mauss describes this as a moment, balanced in an equipoise of festival and warfare, when conflict recasts itself into solidarity: "One lays down one's arms, renounces magic and gives everything away, from casual hospitality to one's daughter or one's property."[65] James's undisguised bartering follows the same logic. For Mrs. Gereth, Fleda represents an ideal solution to the "abomination" of Mona Bridgstock's inheritance: since Fleda belongs to her own "community of taste," a marriage between Owen and Fleda will ensure that Poynton remains her spiritual possession. In ethnographic terms, a match between Owen and Fleda is akin to a cross-cousin marriage, an alliance, selected by the parents, that is just endogamous enough to keep the property in the family and just exogamous enough to avoid incest (although not in the eyes of the Bridgstocks, who think the relation between Owen and Fleda is "jolly unnatural" [185]).[66]

As a bourgeois marriage, however, the transaction is to be accomplished under the sign of love. In representing the unlikely attraction between Fleda and Owen, James includes passages that many readers – Edith Wharton, for one, as we have noted – perceived as some of the most erotic in all of his fiction. Yet even the novel's images of sexual desire bear the trace of an *interest* that is unmistakably economic. When Fleda senses Owen's attraction, it is as if she feels her stock rise in value: "To know she had become to him an object of desire gave her wings that she felt herself flutter in the air: it was like the rush of a flood into her own accumulations" (105). Mrs. Gereth's repeated injunction to Fleda – "let yourself go" (142) – carries this same double meaning: the phrase is both sexual and commercial. Love and ownership are not exclusive kinds of interest. From the perspective of kinship, they are both forces of attraction at play in the same gravitational field that determines lines of cohesion and enmity in the larger society.

Though unnerved by being so blatantly put up for sale, Fleda is secretly "thrilled" by the idea of the exchange, for it means she will become mistress of both Owen and the treasures, the combined *res* and *persona* of Poynton. But even after Owen falls in love with her,

the kinship crisis remains. For to undertake a deliberate transaction
for Poynton would be to destroy the things as a "magical legacy," as
Mauss describes totemic property.[67] Removed from the mystified
relations of the kinship system, the Poynton treasures would be
reduced to the mere property that Mona perceives: "To have loved
Owen apparently, and yet to have loved him only so much, only to
the extent of a few tables and chairs, was not a thing she could so
much as try to grasp" (107). If Fleda openly transacted for the
property, she would *become* Mona: "It would seem intolerably vulgar to her to have 'ousted' the daughter of the Bridgstocks" (106).
The things, then, must be acquired without violating laws of sacred
duty and Mona's "rights," and to save Poynton from being recognized as property, Fleda must restore the customary codes whose
violation had turned the "beautiful things" into spoils: "She herself
at any rate – it was her own case that emerged – couldn't dream of
assisting him save in the sense of their common honour" (106).

The process by which Fleda restores a "common honour" is both
social and psychological. For she must not only recall all parties to
the imperatives of honorable action but must also bring back the
sense of honor, the cultural rules that, to have any efficacy in society,
must be ultimately lodged in consciousness as feelings and sensibility. In representing Fleda's closely held thoughts and emotions,
James has created a brilliant portrait of consciousness as it is socially informed. He presents the complex constellation of subjective
desire and culturally shaped patterns of thought and restraint that
anthropologists were attempting to represent under the label of
"social psychology." Fleda's mind is the locus of the social mystification that necessarily disguises interest and calculation in the
name of honor. In the "wondrous mixture" of Fleda's interior reflections, her agile operations of mind suspend the contradiction
between the bourgeois orders of interest and "sacred duty." Fleda's
recorded thoughts provide the novel's repository of the rules of
honor ("Nobody had a right to get off easily from pledges so deep
and sacred" [106]). But at the same time, the portrait of Fleda's
consciousness also shows the canny, suppressed, and yet acute calculations that coexist with her no less genuine commitment to principles of duty. In one passage, for instance, her magnanimous respect for Mona's rights modulates almost imperceptibly into a
mental comparison – unfavorable to Mona – between the two potential brides, and in her strict adherence to honor she obliquely

calculates the one honorable way that she could become mistress of Poynton:

> Fleda's emotion at this time was a wondrous mixture, in which Mona's permissions and Mona's beauty figured powerfully as aids to reflexion. She herself had no beauty, and *her* permissions were the stony stares she had just practised in the drawing-room – a consciousness of a kind appreciably to add to the strange sense of triumph that made her generous. We may not perhaps too much diminish the merit of that generosity if we mention that it could take the flight we are considering just because really, with the telescope of her long thought, Fleda saw what might bring her out of the wood. Mona herself would bring her out [by breaking with Owen over the spoils]. . . . This was a calculation that Fleda wouldn't have committed to paper, but it affected the total of her sentiments. She was meanwhile so remarkably constituted that while she refused to profit by Owen's mistake, even while she judged it and hastened to cover it up, she could drink a sweetness from it that consorted little with her wishing it mightn't have been made. (107–8)

"Remarkably" as Fleda is constituted, she is constituted from the same cultural materials as everyone else. That is to say, the "quality of inward life" (xiv) so personally and intimately displayed through Fleda's consciousness is articulated through the interplay of the bourgeois codes of honor and interest. By dramatizing the subtle tacking back and forth between a "refusal to profit" and the symbolic profit that accrues from refusing, between self-sacrifice and self-interested calculation, James shows the cultural conditioning of Fleda's intelligence and spirit even as he shows that spirit's "freedom and ease."

In this way, James, like leading social theorists of the time, places "habits of thought" (Veblen's term) in a cultural context that includes the distribution of real and symbolic capital. What James calls Fleda's "generosity," her carefully protected dignity and honor, he nevertheless presents as a possession or store of goods that, having been won through self-sacrifice, she resists giving up without getting something back in return. This is clearest when she tries to keep Owen and his mother from knowing her feelings for him. The narrator presents this process as a form of speculation on symbolic goods in which Fleda weighs the relative profits and risks of revealing her valuable knowledge. At her lowest point she despairs at "having given everything and got nothing" (129). And later: "it shouldn't really be for nothing she had given so much;

deep within her burned again the resolve to get something back"
(134). Her extreme reluctance to reveal her "secret" is not because
she is "pathologically fearful of sex," as some readers have charged.[68]
Rather it is because her knowledge represents the only thing that
she controls exclusively that others would find valuable to possess.
Far from being pathological, Fleda's desire to withhold her knowledge is in her best interest, an interest that is especially precarious
because Fleda herself is the "feminine property" that is the object of
exchange. Critics have been divided about whether Fleda's renunciation is noble or excessively prudish, whether it is driven by
selflessness or a neurotic self-regard. But if we consider the underlying structure of bourgeois exchange that James has clearly marked
in the text, this ambiguity is itself part of the cultural logic of the
English kinship system. For it is by renouncing her most obvious
chance for Owen and following the rules of honor that Fleda pro-
tects the measure of dignity that is her most valuable asset. We
might say her actions are both selfless and self-serving – though
these terms are still too individualistic to capture the play of the
larger cultural forces that are the real influences shaping Fleda's
choices. I have suggested, rather, that her actions are both honorable and interested; that is, they are bounded by a cultural code of
duty on one side and a submerged economy of cultural capital on
the other, and that her strategy establishes a communication between two spheres that must remain officially autonomous.

For Fleda to try to regain Poynton through honorable means,
however, turns the agreed-upon exchange into a gamble, a game of
risk that can be lost through second-guessing and mistiming. When
Mrs. Gereth returns the furniture to Poynton, she does so in the
hope that her sacrifice will "secure" Fleda and that Fleda in turn
will secure Owen and the treasures. She follows the logic of the
gambler, hoping to gain from a high-stakes act of giving: "To have
played such a card would be thus, for so grand a gambler, practically to have won the game" (214). Fleda is dazzled by the "noble
risk of it" (213), and Mrs. Gereth grows in "grandeur" in her eyes.
The "noble" quality Fleda sees in this risk is significant; the ceremonial gambling of magical property was also a feature of the tribal
nobility in ethnographic kinship. Gambling, along with sports like
hunting and wrestling, is one of the honorable forms of exchange,
which are able to disguise the economic nature of a transaction
while winning prestige for the clan. The more extravagant the gift

or wager, the more certain the player is of eclipsing a rival. In the stories of ritual gambling in Hindu legend, Mauss saw another version of the symbolic economy of the potlatch. The founding epic of Indian civilization places strategic gambling at the center of economic, military, and family institutions. A "senseless" risk of wealth is at the heart of the kinship order: "The *Mahabharata* is the story of a tremendous potlatch – there is a game of dice between the Dauravas and the Pandavas, and a military festival, while Draupadi, sister and polyandrous wife of the Pandavas, chooses husbands."[69] Seen through the eyes of strictest reason, this kind of game playing seems childish or superstitious. But institutions like the potlatch or gambling are necessary in a symbolic economy that trades in honor. There is a danger that comes from the fact that chance cannot be eliminated from the most crucial social transactions. Yet the ingredient of danger is essential: it is precisely danger and chance that are required to generate the "immaterial goods" of prestige and honor rather than the prosaic values of pure exchange. The bourgeois economy of honor that James makes visible in *Poynton* must likewise contain an element of risk. Mrs. Gereth does the *honorable* thing, outwardly renounces her revolt and returns the property to Poynton – all in hopes of winning back the spoils. But without the open calculations governing transactions in the marketplace, her strategy goes awry. Mystification exacts a price: Mrs. Gereth sends the things back too soon and loses Poynton.

To all appearances, the Waterbath barbarians win the game. If we can imagine *The Spoils of Poynton* as a book recording the founding myths and epic battles of the wealthy middle class, as a bourgeois *Mahabharata* or (as James glosses it in the preface) an Anglicized battle of Troy, then this conclusion to the plot would appear to predict the historical victory of Philistines. It would seem to emphasize the relative weakness of the powers of taste and manners in the face of the official power of law, a power that in this tale – as in Arnold's cautionary essay, *Culture and Anarchy* – is in the hands of rich Philistines. But are the forces of manners and culture really so vulnerable? Or does juxtaposing culture with barbarism disguise culture's power under a veil of threat? Is it possible to win for losing?

On the surface of the story, there seems to be no such redeeming gain. When Owen and Poynton are finally lost to them, the two friends are forced to face up to a painful demystification. Mrs.

Gereth is reduced to her crudest account ever of the bartering that has taken place: I "denude myself, in your interest, to that point that I've nothing left," and "you're not even able to produce him for me?" (218). She submits Fleda to the same treatment, dismissing her scrupulous observance of the rules of honor as "bugaboo barriers, hideous and monstrous sacrifices" (225). Ending in this way, the novel is a tale of loss — loss of possession, loss of love and social position, and, most painful to Fleda, the loss of the symbolic value of honor. James underscores the thematics of loss in his last dramatic gesture — and it is most properly *his* gesture, since in fiction an act of chance is of course attributable to the will of the author only — namely, the setting on fire of Poynton and the loss of the objects themselves. Yet this last loss stands apart. It is not a loss so much as a destruction — deliberate, final, almost ritualistic. That he chose to resolve the story by burning Poynton and all its furnishings has always struck readers as James's ultimate comment on the complex relations the novel presents between people and property. But it is an enigmatic comment. Because the "conflagration" is functionally a random act of chance, there is no plot motivation for it within the frame of the novel. The only motive lies outside of the story, in James's choice of an ending. We can perhaps get at the significance of this ending, then, by asking not what it means but what it does, what its effect is as an authorial gesture or act. The most obvious answer is that, for James, the burning of Poynton satisfies what Frank Kermode has called the "sense of an ending." In some of the earliest working notes for the novel, James searches for a denouement, something that will provide "a full roundness for the action — the completeness of the drama-quality," and hits upon "the horrible, the atrocious conflagration." Here we can say the Poynton spoils are sacrificed for narrative form. Poynton's loss is art's gain. The reason why a final burning provides a satisfying "roundness" is not explained; it belongs to the ineffable sphere of aesthetic form, the domain James also described in these notes as "the sacred mystery of structure."[70]

The particular context of this phrase is important if we are considering the question of loss, for it describes the artistic gain — James's mastering the "sacred mystery of structure" — that he believed he had acquired out of the painful loss he experienced in his failed ventures in the theater. The notes for *Poynton* show that throughout the composition of the novel James is thinking of his "theatrical trials," "the old problems and dimnesses – the old solutions and little findings of light. Is the beauty of all that effort – of all those unutterable hours – lost forever? Lost, lost, lost?" And as he composes *Poynton*, he fixes upon the idea that the wasted time and lost "beauty" have been repaid in an increased command of aesthetic form, a power that will now redouble the value of his novels:

> When I ask myself what there may have been to show for my long tribulation, my wasted years and patiences and pangs, of theatrical experiment, the answer, as I have already noted here, comes up as just possibly this: what I have gathered from it will perhaps have been exactly some such mastery of fundamental statement – of the art and secret of it, of expression, of the sacred mystery of structure.[71]

As one of James's first major fictions after his failure in the theater, *The Spoils of Poynton* represents the "sacred" aesthetic power that would emerge from his loss. James presents his novel as the fruits of a "noble expenditure," not unlike the tribal economies in the ethnographic record: the "wasted" work was not lost but sacrificed. Similarly, James does not destroy Poynton but sacrifices it; that is, he converts it into the authority he would increasingly be accorded as the Master of high culture. Through the aesthetic achievement of his narrative – the "drama of my spoils," he called it – Poynton passes, transvalued, into *his* possession, not as property or wealth but as authorial power. His "exquisite economy" of representation, where loss converts to aesthetic value, resurrects the logic of the potlatch; James achieves a profitable waste, both within the frame of the story and without. The burning of Poynton, completing the "structure" of the novel, signifies in a strangely literal way the loss of earlier work – the "wasted years" and "beauty" – now recognized as a transformed achievement. It also uncannily recalls the ritualistic destruction of tribal potlatch ceremonies: "Whole cases of candlefish or whale oil, houses, blankets by the thousand are burnt," Mauss reported of the Tsmishian potlatch; "the most valuable coppers are broken and thrown into the sea." To European eyes, this ritual pointed to an intriguing economy of sacrifice. Eventually anthropologists argued that the deliberate destruction of wealth was not an irrational contradiction of the tribal economy but its ultimate fulfillment, an extravagant expenditure that yielded tremendous prestige for the individual or family that

sacrificed it. To burn valuable goods ultimately converted them
into symbolic capital – honor – which in turn was crucial for
gaining more wealth: "Sacrificial destruction implies giving something that is to be repaid."[72] In an anthropological view, loss and
possession are not opposites; they are both stages in an economy
that converts waste and excess to wealth *in a different form.* This was
Veblen's crucial ethnographic claim about the wasteful – but ultimately profitable – economy of conspicuous consumption. Perhaps
more clearly than any other artist of the period, James extends this
exotic economy to the realm of art: for James, the loss of the work
and "beauty" of his plays allowed him to possess a transformed
aesthetic "mystery" of narrative form, which he converts to his
novel about the mysteries of taste and beauty. Moreover, we can
link this moment to his larger career. The excesses of James's late
style inaugurated here in *Poynton,* the complex discriminations and
multilayered meditations that are the signature of the major novels,
can be said to sacrifice a more broadly accessible beauty (not to
mention possible book sales) to the symbolic authority of James the
Master.[73]

James himself traces an economy of aesthetic conversion. In the
preface to *The Spoils of Poynton,* he writes that the "splendid waste" of
real life provides "the opportunity for the sublime economy of art,
which rescues, which saves and hoards and 'banks,' investing and
reinvesting these fruits of toil in wondrous useful 'works' and thus
making up for us, desperate spendthrifts that we all naturally are,
the most princely of incomes" (vi). A "sublime" economy indeed:
before our eyes, James's figure magically turns the crass hoarding
and banking of bourgeois investment into a "wondrous" and
"princely" wealth of art. The income from art is princely not because of an increased quantity but because of its transformed quality. Art, James tell us, is the economy that is not one. Bourdieu
identifies art as the last sacred, mystified economy to survive the
eroding mythologies of a market society: "The world of art, a sacred
island systematically and ostentatiously opposed to the profane,
everyday world of production, a sanctuary for gratuitous, disinterested activity in a universe given over to money and self-interest,
offers, like a theology in a past epoch, an imaginary anthropology
obtained by denial of all the negations really brought about by the
economy."[74] Art and culture, Bourdieu argues, derive their power
from their denial of any economic exchange. The urge toward deni-

al is everywhere in James. At the same time, though, James's "sublime economy of art," so often self-described in the language of money, property, and exchange, never rests with any easy repose in the sphere of the aesthetic. Like so much of James's fiction, *The Spoils of Poynton* both acknowledges and disguises an economic dimension in high culture. With Veblen, he speaks a language of "pecuniary beauty," translating art into economic terms and wealth into aesthetic terms. Yet he not only links beauty with economy – art as "spoils" – but practices the alchemy that turns the profane substance of bourgeois life into a "sacred" power of art. James refines – wholly redefines, really – the edifying value that literature and culture had for middle-class life into the exotic, discriminating ironies of modernism, a sphere of art that, not coincidentally, would soon acknowledge the energies of primitivism and commodity consumption as its two strongest influences.[75]

The theme of ritualistic loss in *Poynton* also points to a second discriminating power of art. If James wins through his losses, we might also ask who in fact loses through the novels' final act of burning. The most direct answer, of course, is the Bridgstocks. James's gesture of burning keeps the Poynton things out of the hands of the Philistines. Like Mrs. Gereth, James intervenes in the laws of inheritance; his gesture, in fact, carries out her vow that she would "deface them with my own hands" (31) rather than let the objects pass to the Bridgstocks. The Bridgstocks' property is lost, but taste is redeemed. In the end, then, the threat of anarchy to the kinship system confirms the power of culture. Our anxiety at seeing force and desire so exotically exposed finally consecrates the boundary between Philistinism and culture, the boundary James describes in the preface as the line separating "those who appreciate" from "those who don't" (xiv) and later as the distinction between "taste" and "will." The line is most starkly visible in the opposition between the "thriftily constructed" Mona Bridgstock, who is "all will, without the smallest leak of force into taste or tenderness or vision," and Fleda Vetch, whose "passion is wasted" in "the perception of incongruities" (xvii) – wasted, but not lost, for Fleda's wasted passion has an extravagant payoff: "she sees and feels but in acres and expanses" (xvii). These are not Poynton's acres but the assets of the exquisite economy in which splendid waste can be converted into the magical property of art and the symbolic capital of perception.

CHAPTER 5

Edith Wharton and the alienation of divorce

Marriage is a form of sex-union recognized and sanctioned by society. It is a relation between two or more persons, according to the custom of the country.
                              —Charlotte Perkins Gilman, *Women and Economics*

Surveying the "fantastic" spectacle of international social life at a Paris restaurant, in Wharton's *Custom of the Country*, the Frenchman Raymond de Chelles is unable to properly classify American women. "Your young girls look so experienced, and your married women sometimes so – unmarried." His American companion, Charles Bowen, supplies the key to the puzzle: "Well, they often are – in these days of divorce."[1] Charles's description of the American divorcée as an "unmarried married" woman locates what will become an important kind of female identity or status in the novel. It is a status that is legally precise – she's either married or she's not – but socially far more complex: if divorced, she can be both. Charles's wordplay must be taken seriously, because Raymond's comment is prompted by the sight of the central protagonist in the novel, Undine Spragg. Though Charles assures Raymond that Undine is married, we will later learn that she is also already unmarried (divorced from Elmer Moffatt). What is more, she is at this moment about to embark with Peter Van Degen on a trip she chooses to call a "honeymoon," making her in a sense doubly married and waiting only for the law to "ratify the bond" (862). Van Degen will not turn out to be Undine's next acquired husband, but Raymond de Chelles will, as if self-selected by his blind perception of her status as divorcée. In *The Custom of the Country*, divorce is not the termination of marriage so much as its overdetermination. According to the logic of the plot, divorce produces marriage, or rather a new condition of marriage that is inseparable from being

160

divorced. Undine begins her marital "career" in New York already a divorcée and accumulates husbands without fully detaching herself from any of them. Divorce enables and multiplies marriage, and the seemingly "obsolete institution" of marriage survives in America, Charles jokes, because " one couldn't be divorced without it" (806).

What is true of Wharton's novel – that with divorce comes a proliferation of marriage – was also true of American society. Government studies in the 1880s and 1890s reported that the number of divorces was climbing at a dizzying pace, about five times the rate of population increase by the end of the century. Between 1867 and 1929 – close to the span of Wharton's lifetime – the divorce rate rose 2,000 percent. These numbers made the United States the preeminent nation of divorce; throughout the nineteenth century, more divorces were granted annually there than in all of Europe. Two-thirds of all suits, moreover, were filed by women, just one token of the way that American divorce was formalized as a feminine institution.[2] "She's an American – she's divorced," one of Wharton's French duchesses announces, "as if she were merely stating the same fact in two different ways" (879). To most Americans, these trends were ominous. Concern about divorce mills in lenient states such as North Dakota and Nevada and about the "registered concubinage" that followed from remarriage prompted a wave of public debates, antidivorce crusades, and efforts at enacting more restrictive legislation. Even those radicals who welcomed the higher divorce rate as liberating shared their opponents' assumption that divorce meant the erosion of the institution of marriage. But in fact, amid the divorce revolution American marriage underwent its own less dramatic but no less significant period of growth. The number of marriages increased, the proportion of the population refusing or denied marriage shrank, and the marriage age declined for both men and women. Far from presaging the demise of marriage, the divorce rate in this period was a barometer for its rising popularity. If Horace Greely's 1860 warning that Americans would someday "get unmarried nearly at pleasure" had come true, it would seem there was an increased pleasure in getting married as well.[3]

Wharton's portrait of Undine Spragg presents this combined historical escalation of both American divorce and American marriage, with both pursued "at pleasure." *The Custom of the Country*

examines the unsettling social transformation through which marriage could disseminate sexual and domestic relations rather than
delimit them; in the eyes of her critics Undine has too many husbands, not too few. But unlike Charles Bowen, the novel does not
finally diagnose this transformation as the "monstrously perfect
result" of the American custom of excluding women from "the real
business of life" (757). Instead, Wharton's novel is striking for its
representation of marriage precisely as the "real business" of American life. In *The Custom of the Country*, marriage – or more properly
remarriage – has become the most visible form of exchange and
incorporation, a diverse institution through which rights, wealth,
and interests are traded and consolidated. For Undine, marriage is
a means of social circulation and accumulation, an expression of
her "inalienable right to 'go around'"(939). If such a version of
marriage is scandalous (Ralph Marvell's grandfather, for instance,
is disgusted when Undine's marriage to Ralph is "dissolved like a
business partnership"[843]), scandal in the novel nevertheless becomes one more way in which the private sphere of marriage enters
the public domain, as it is circulated in the press, regulated in the
courts, and legitimated (or rejected) through the machinery of public opinion. Through divorce the private "holdings" of marriage,
from a couple's sexual history to their children and assets, become
public "shares," that is, items in a social discourse circulated not
only for profit (newspaper sales, lawyers' fees, alimony) but for a
public consumption that would help to transform the domestic
sphere and what it meant.

Quite naturally, then, Undine's marital transactions appear to
be almost purely contractual, mirroring the Wall Street deals of her
father and (first and fourth) husband. As imagined in Wharton's
novel, commercial and social relations are finally indistinguishable,
and the modern state of things thus invokes an ethnographic world
in which the exchange of wives is at the heart of the tribal economy.
Hence Ralph's anthropological musings that "the daughters of his
own race sold themselves to the Invaders; the daughters of the
Invaders bought their husbands as they bought an operabox. It
ought to have been transacted on the Stock Exchange" (673). To
explore the altered nature of marriage in the "days of divorce,"
Wharton writes an ethnography of modern marriage, an account
that will recognize the new, strangely mobile relations of early
twentieth-century matrimony. But if this picture of modern mar-

riage recalls a premodern bartering, Ralph's gloss also points to a crucial distinction. In his account, women are no longer the objects of exchange but the agents, the buyers and sellers who control the transactions, even if the financiers remain the fathers and brothers. In Ralph's description, as in the novel as a whole, the new conditions of American marriage make possible a new kind of agency for women. The question of whether they "bought husbands" or "sold themselves" is an important indicator of changing relations of social power among the rich, but in either case it is "the daughters" who decide and transact, appropriating the role that virtually defined male power in the anthropological imagination. That daughters like Undine seem to have sovereignty over parents is a further transformation of the hierarchies of primitive kinship, refashioning the relations between the generations as well as genders.

In this sense, a definitive figure in Wharton's ethnography of modern manners is the divorcée, the unmarried married woman who not only directs her own marital exchange but has proven her power to repeat and extend it. Modern marriage, as an institution defined by divorce, is a female industry enjoying the kind of exhilarating but distressing expansion that was enlarging the scope of corporate capitalism. In *The Custom of the Country*, the unsettling surplus of marriage and the power of a new agency for women are figured in a portrait of the American divorcée as a quintessential "alien" (as Undine is repeatedly labeled). Like contemporary ethnographies of the era, Wharton's novel brings to life a suspiciously commercial circulation of women, made possible by divorce and remarriage. In doing so, Wharton both articulates and detaches herself from a powerful form of desire, a form that takes on the intriguing outlines of Undine Spragg. To understand the context and function of that form, we can look to the odd assortment of ethnographic forms found in contemporary museums.

WOMEN AND MUSEUMS

In times of heightened social change, watch the women. This principle informs early anthropology and its pronounced interest in women as the key to cultural reproduction. As scientist Paul Broca expressed it in 1868, any change in the sexual and social order "necessarily induces a perturbation in the evolution of races, and hence it follows that the condition of women in society must be most carefully studied by the anthropologist."[4] Women watching has more than one meaning here. It is not only a process of professional study and observation, implying scientific detachment, but a careful monitoring, implying political regulation. At one extreme, the anthropological vision of women is an early alarm system, a technology of observation and description that posits as its necessary corollary the atavistic power of women to disrupt – even to reverse – the advances of civilization. Such is the picture presented by James Weir, who ethnographically transcribes the anticipated progress of female suffrage into a disastrous cultural regress.

> The simple right to vote carries with it no immediate danger, the danger comes afterward . . . , when woman, owing to her increased degeneration, gives free rein to her atavistic tendencies, and hurries ever backward toward the savage state of her barbarian ancestors. I see, in the establishment of equal rights, the first step toward that abyss of immoral horrors so repugnant to our cultivated ethical tastes – the matriarchate. Sunk as low as this, civilized man will sink still lower – to the communal kachims of the Aleutian Islanders.[5]

Any change in the social status of women, according to Weir, will bring about a lapse from civilized monogamy. "Degeneration" is a feminine drive: given political agency, women become essentially barbaric and will pull modern American society back with them toward the "abyss" of prehistoric culture.

In contrast, scholar Elsie Clews Parsons saw in the changing conditions for women a sure path of cultural progress. The first female professor of anthropology at Columbia, Parsons mused in 1913 that the nation would soon have to build a Museum of Women just to prove "to a doubting posterity that once women were a distinct social class."[6] Like Weir, Parsons looks to women for an index of civilization, but her anthropology of womanhood equates sexual reform with the upward evolution of the race rather than its degeneration. Yet even Parson's meliorism contains an assumption about the backwardness of women, for in her scheme advanced civilization will bring about the elimination from history of women qua women. The social creature who marks sexual difference – sometimes referred to simply as "the sex," Charlotte Perkins Gilman noted – is on her way to extinction.[7] Woman will become a museum piece. Where Weir sees in women a threatening atavistic life, Parsons and Gilman see a beneficial evolutionary death.

These apparently opposite accounts of woman share an impor-

tant common context. Parsons's feminist view is free of the reactionary phobia that animates Weir's vision of indiscriminate "communal" coupling and matriarchal dominance, two ethnographic images that haunt the social imagination in the later nineteenth
century. But Parsons's project to make woman legible as an anthropological object – even as an object of progress – points to a shared
problem inherent in the ethnographic registers of the era. The hints
of morbidity in Parsons's image of a Museum of Women, for instance, invite closer scrutiny. For as Parsons wrote, there already
existed a long history of ethnographic museums of women, exhibits
both professional and popular, that were inseparable from a complex poetics of reproduction and death. Parsons's trope, in other
words, evokes an aesthetics of what could be called "museum realism," in which the power of lifelike representation is dependent
upon the mimetic power of death, a mastery ranging from the arts
of vivisection to wax modeling and taxidermy. The effort by pro-
gressives to represent Victorian womanhood as a primitive relic
(Parsons's playfully calls her book on tribal women's customs *The
Old-fashioned Woman*) shares a complex kinship with its own opposition. As we will see, in debating the agency of women both sides run
the risk of reifying her status as a natural object and of distorting
(either denying or exaggerating) her powers as a historical subject.
Weir's model of atavism and Parsons's museum realism are the
discursive poles structuring the representation of women not only
in ethnography but in the fiction of Edith Wharton.

Throughout the nineteenth century, one of the most conventional
– certainly the most literal – examples of a Museum of Women was
the scientific presentation of the female body, replicated whole or in
exhibits of the genitalia and other isolated parts. The rising interest
in racial typologies was easily adapted to the display techniques of
both natural history museums (as early as 1797, Charles Peale
of Philadelphia offered wax figures of "a group of contrasting races
of mankind") and museums of anatomy (a conjunction announced
openly, for instance, in Reimer's Anatomical and Ethnological Museum of London). Within this symbolic domain, curators constructed visual accounts of the feminine parsed through a syntax of
anatomy and ethnicity, accounts that were among the most vivid,
popular, and authoritative in the century.[8] The live traveling exhibition of the South African woman Sarah Bartmann, known as the
"Hottentot Venus," for instance, had a second life in the wide

circulation of published reports of her autopsy (one of which was authored by Cuvier) and found a permanent life when Cuvier presented the dissected "genital organs of this woman" to the French Academy. The transition from living spectacle to scientific artifact reveals a stark logic of classification: Bartmann's sexual parts were the defining features of the African woman, and the black woman's sex was representative of the primitive nature of female sexuality in general.[9] So displayed, the primitivism was safely confined to the premodern (and postmortem) body of the female savage. Confirming this logic, the real body of Sarah Bartmann became the forerunner to a number of key genres of the representation of women: a medical vogue for the autopsies of Hottentot women, an army of life-size wax "Venuses," or models of women with removable parts (a "Moorish" woman divisible into seventy-five pieces, a "Greek Venus" whose face and chest could be removed), and populations of wax mannequins arranged in tableaux of "folklife pictures" and tribal "group life" installations. Such figures could be found variously in popular waxworks galleries, in medical exhibitions, and in museums of ethnology (Bartmann's dissected buttocks and genitalia are still on view in the Musee de l'Homme in Paris). Strange brides of quietness, these stilled museum objects together captured, tamed, and declared historically dead the dangerous force that Weir insisted was alive in modern women's "atavistic tendencies." They allowed a supervision of gender in a manner coded quite differently from the conventional representations of primitive man, for whom depictions of genitalia, for instance, were often notably absent.[10] Viewed a century later, these figures also disclose the sometimes aggressive power of mimesis, as painstaking arts of plastic reproduction master the chaotic sexual reproduction imagined in Weir's primitive "abyss." Culture conquers nature in the very act of preserving it.

The wax Venus and the exhibited female body belong to a larger aesthetic of nineteenth-century realism that asks every image to make transparent its own place in the social or natural order. It is a realism that seeks to unveil the perfect specimen – in the realist novel, the specimen (as Mark Seltzer argues) that will secure a full "social legibility of character"; in realist science and natural history, those specimens (as Donna Haraway argues) designed by the "politics of eugenics and the art of taxidermy" to stand witness to racial purity and nature's hierarchy.[11] At one extreme of this mode of realism, the arts of taxidermy, dissection, and embalming allow realist representation of achieve its aim with an alarming precision, making corpses into permanent, self-evident embodiments of the essential orders of life. Within this context of realist aesthetics, the enterprise of watching women – which is to say, the enterprise of re-presenting women to watch – has a built-in advantage. Woman is a perfect realist specimen because her real identity is her species identity; as Georg Simmel writes in a 1907 essay on prostitution, "women in general are more deeply embedded in the species type than are men, who emerge from the species type more differenti-ated and individualized." Hence a productive realist paradox: arti-ficially reproduced in art, woman naturally reveals her nature as the baseline nature of the species.[12]

Yet as naturally as mannequins and other reproductions might stand for the real, the mimetic perfection itself could provoke a queasiness in some spectators. The necro-realism of certain dis-plays of women had its attractions ("we see what seems to be the corpse of a handsome female who has just expired"), yet something about the popular wax Venuses could also be viewed as an "inde-cent" exposure or "imposture" ("a large disgusting Doll"). Precise-ly because of the "absolutely lifelike" reproduction possible in mu-seum displays, Franz Boas worried about the use of mannequins in ethnographic installations, citing "the ghastly impression such as we notice in wax-figures." Today an undercurrent of feeling about the morbidity or exploitation of such re-creations is not hard to understand – scholar James Boon builds a whole essay around it, entitled "Why museums make me sad." But during the "museum age," as this period has been called, when the realist ethos was not only fully persuasive but highly productive, the eeriness described by Boas and others is a telling by-product of some of the internal fissures of realism. The traces of ghastliness in an otherwise "per-fect picture" signify not only the theatricality of this mode of exhibit realism (which never really veiled its staginess anyway) but, more importantly, the conditions of death and dissection that underwrite the re-creation of life, conditions of a necro-spection in which iden-tity emerges through arrested motion, wax and plaster modeling, and inanimate posing. The residual uneasiness at these conditions, I want to suggest, is primarily the result not of guilt about the will to power in mimesis but rather a complex response to an image of life evoked through the medium of death.[13]

The response is a discomfort at viewing a lifeless form that visually contains – molds and makes present – life, a sight that is as much a resurrection as an entombment. Boas, for instance, was not disturbed by the attempt at a lifelike illusion but rather at the conspicuous suspension of movement and gesture in realistically posed mannequins; to counter the "ghastly" impression of arrested life, he wanted to see models arranged instead in naturally occurring postures of rest. Like the nineteenth-century versions of the vampire and the ghost, the museum model literally poses an intriguing ambiguity about human agency (an ambiguity raised more kinetically in our time, for instance, in endless cinematic nights of the living dead). Ethnographic mannequins hint at the atavistic force they seem otherwise so serenely to deny. They bring to life the races that science has pronounced historically dead, disclosing in museum colonies all the troubling resonances of a people *preserved*, perhaps unnaturally. As one historian of museums notes, human exhibits are "semiotic seesaws," characterized by "reciprocities between exhibiting the dead as if they are alive and the living as if they are dead."[14]

The same semiotic conversions are at play in the practice of collecting ethnographic materials of all kinds, as revered scientific relics – skulls and tattooed heads as well as tribal rituals, customs, and lexicons – compensate for the seemingly grotesque forms of life rejected by bourgeois civilization. As Peter Stallybrass and Allon White suggest, these excluded forms of life include domestic class practices, the renounced appetites and bodily excesses of the urban masses that are so easily transcoded to "savage" traits. The traces such exclusions leave on the middle-class psyche thus constitute an internalized anthropology of disavowed desires and energies, and the disease of bourgeois neurosis is capable of seeing and reanimating the vivid forms of life that lie behind the still and placid representations of ethnography. "Frau Emmy von N.," in Freud's *Studies on Hysteria*, thus sees the nearness of a primitivism that ethnographic representation located far away: glancing at "an ethnological atlas . . . some of the pictures in it of American Indians dressed up as animals had given her a great shock. 'Only think, if they came to life' (she shuddered)."[15] What becomes visible in this moment of fright, and in the shudder of Boas and others viewing ethnographic mannequins, is the fact that the perfection of museum realism is a direct result of the flickering play between animate and

inanimate images, an operative ambiguity that gives lifeless forms
their embodied authority. But to recognize as much – as Frau von
N. did, and as Boas did, to his personal and professional distress –
is to recognize that the scientific mastery bears within it an amalgam of anxiety, desire, and loathing about the uncertain line between life and death, between human agency and historical determination, and between civilized subjects and the vanished races
that haunt civilization in the form of perfect museum corpses.

If momentary recognitions such as these posed distressing questions about civilized men and their presumed autonomy, they posed
even more vexing questions about women and their presumed species identity. Such questions about the agency of women motivate
the fiction of Edith Wharton, for whom the ideology of women's
species identity is especially provocative because it is an identity
Wharton both repeats and resists. Like Boas, Wharton recognized
a quotient of eeriness in human models – indeed, in human representations in general – and she made the wax mannequin and its
visual effects into one of the key metaphors of *The Custom of the
Country*. Although the novel's first sentence consists of the animated
words of Mrs. Spragg (" 'Undine Spragg – how *can* you?' "), this live
voice is juxtaposed with her "prematurely-wrinkled hand," an image of unnatural flesh that is soon enlarged to full scale when the
mother is presented as "a wax figure in a show-window." The description may suggest a department-store mannequin, an appropriate enough allusion in a novel that will map expertly the emerging
culture of consumption. At the same time, the larger narrative
context for the image suggests the type of ethnographic human
model that is the scientific cousin of the commercial mannequin.
(Both types appeared behind plate-glass windows, for instance; the
windows for the Northwest Coast Hall organized by Boas at the
American Museum of Natural History were donated by Theodore
Roosevelt, Sr., who was both a founder-trustee and the owner of a
plate-glass company.)[16] The description of Mrs. Spragg as a "wax
figure" appears in an inventory of carefully arranged objects in the
drawing room of the family's hotel suite, a scene designed to convey
what Boas called the "condensed culture" of the ethnographic
"group life" display ("a family or several members of a tribe,
dressed in native costume and engaged in some characteristic work
or art illustrative of their life"). Wharton, like Boas, found that
selected house furnishings could provide a "synoptic collection of

specimens" to convey the condensed culture of hotel-dwellers like the Spraggs.[17]

> The Spragg rooms were known as one of the Looey suites, and the drawing-room walls, above their wainscoting of highly-varnished mahogany, were hung with salmon-pink damask and adorned with oval portraits of Marie Antoinette and the Princess de Lamballe. In the centre of the florid carpet a gilt table with a top of Mexican onyx sustained a palm in a gilt basket tied with a pink bow. But for this ornament, and a copy of the "Hound of Baskervilles," which lay beside it, the room showed no traces of human use, and Mrs. Spragg herself wore as complete an air of detachment as if she had been a wax figure in a show-window. (623)

The scene is at once busy and lifeless, the crowded objects bearing "no traces of human use." Listed as one more object, Mrs. Spragg is sealed within the same hermetic aura, and the added details of her physiognomy only heighten the air of inanimate "detachment." The finely wrought features of Mrs. Spragg's face are derived not from her flesh but from her metaphorical identity as a wax woman: "Her pale soft-cheeked face, with puffy eye-lids and drooping mouth, suggested a partially-melted wax figure which had run to double-chin." Wharton's realism here is established by courting the same interchangeability between real features and life-like reproductions that characterizes the ethnological models in museum exhibits: the wax mannequins in the Oriental and Turkish Museum of London, for instance, are "rough with real hair, most delicately applied – actual drops of perspiration are on the brows of the porters."[18] Posted at the entrance to the novel, the waxen Mrs. Spragg establishes a link between fictional characters and realist specimens, with all the uncanniness that such modeling can produce. Idol-like, the image reigns over the novel's exploration of women's status, a status that appears alternatively as a fixed taxonomic identity and a powerful agency, now a social death and now an ineffable life. But rather than seek to eliminate these tensions as Boas did, Wharton's novel exploits them, making the occult uncertainties about agency into the very subjectivity of the modern woman.

As a marked ethnographic object, the "wax figure" conducts us into the museum world of *The Custom of the Country* (the title itself is an ethnographic label), a world in which a controlling realist authority will present and decode the practices, objects, and idioms of the "clans" (639) of New York and Europe. The wax model image indicates the utterly objective nature of Mrs. Spragg's character; she is as socially specific and decipherable (to the knowing eye) as the gilded portraits and furnishings that tautologically date the scene: circa Gilded Age. A molded model, Mrs. Spragg stands for her own social identity with the same perfect referentiality: she is fashioned "fashionably," which is to say, "destined to swell the ranks of the cheaply fashionable" (675). The objective nature of these narrative signs, an objectivism I have called "museum realism," produces the constitutive gap between the novel's fixed orders of cultural identity and the narrator's expansive authority to read cultural codes. The "labyrinth of social distinctions" (684) so mystifying to Undine and her mother are wholly transparent to the narrator. Even the subtlest cultural artifacts – "shades of conduct, turns of speech, tricks of attitude" (991), the manners Malinowski called cultural *imponderabilia* – are certain to fall within the narrator's expertise.[19]

Yet crucially, the novel never rests with this superior narrative perspective – indeed, this kind of expert vision is itself objectified and unmistakably critiqued. Ralph Marvell practices precisely this brand of supervision, "surveying the march of civilization from a loftier angle" (673) and quickly decoding the "rites and customs" of the hotel "Invaders." For Ralph, then, Mrs. Spragg is a perfect model of her species: "Ralph had never seen them actually in the making, before they had acquired the speech of the conquered race. But Mrs. Spragg still used the dialect of her people" (673).[20] Yet for all his powers of sight, in the end Ralph is undone by the "sick intensity" of his own desire and vision, and the novel's ethnographic expert is converted into the novel's most grotesque museum artifact, figured as "some vivisected animal deprived of the power of discrimination" (933). In Ralph's story, the "loftier angle" of his ethnographic sight also makes him vulnerable to an incalculable alterity that emerges suddenly to exact a fatal compensation. He becomes the very kind of reified object he had produced when he habitually classified others. In the end Ralph becomes a corpse. If the image of the museum mannequin teaches us to read for fixed representative specimens, the morbid uncanniness that adheres to the figure spreads its own counter-energies in Wharton's novel. "Only think," as Frau von N. warned, "if they came to life."

It is Undine, of course, who comes to life most dramatically for

Ralph and ruptures his imposed cultural vision ("the clearness with which he judged the girl" [676]). In this respect, it is significant that Undine is also associated with the uncertain status of the realist mannequin. At the point in her adventures when she has been most codified, when she is surrounded and regulated by the "immemorial customs" (963) at the Chelles estate, Undine is forced into the role of social specimen and made to stand for a "group life": the "fetish they called The Family" (960). The status of specimen is glossed in this episode as a restrictive and lifeless existence, with "the dead leagued to defeat her, plotting under gravestones" (984), and, when she met Elmer Moffatt during this period, "she felt, under his cool eye, no more compelling than a woman of wax in a show-case" (1001–2). Wharton here emphasizes the deadening effect of this kind of real and symbolic confinement, at least for a woman like Undine ("her complexion was less animated, her hair less shining" [966]). The practice of representing women as figures "embedded in species type," though internal to Wharton's own realism, is subject to a counterpressure from its moribund implications. The consequences of the woman-as-specimen are clear: with a character that is essentially generic or representational, a woman has no real agency, no independent capacity to act. Species-determined, she has no self-determination. When Undine wants to divorce Chelles and break away, Moffatt's response is an appropriate one for a woman of wax: "you haven't got the nerve." But of course the larger plot of *The Custom of the Country* reveals that Undine has nerve enough for anything. Indeed, she is viewed from the beginning as excessively, dangerously "nervous" (648), which is to say, capable of unpredictable, uncontrollable action. With her "constitutional restlessness" (966), Undine could never share her mother's passive fate. Yet Undine's capacity for taking action does not amount to the self-determination of traditional bourgeois individualism; it is neither the "self-possession" (643) she first sees in Ralph nor the speculative self-brokering of Elmer. Undine's agency is the obverse side of the wax woman's immobility, an energy informed by the inert "species identity" it denies. It is, in other words, an atavistic identity, fully alive and powerful but inherently alien to what Weir calls the civilization of "cultivated ethical tastes."

In calling Undine an "atavism," I mean not only that her character displays the "atavistic tendencies" that Weir feared in modern women, namely, an indifference to monogamy and a relish for dominion over men; I mean also that a historical notion of atavism is part of the conditions of representation for Wharton's portrait, that the idea of a woman as an essential and unchanging identity suddenly transformed or *come to life* governs Wharton's fictional practice as it does certain contemporary ethnographic representations of women. The atavistic woman is a back-formation, as it were, of the species identity of women: she is both a lapse toward a more "savage state," and, at the level of representation, an image recast from static specimen ("beings who have not wandered so far as [men] have from the typical life of earth's creatures") to active agent. A fictional atavism, then, is a way of imagining a new agency for women that nevertheless retains the structural assumption of her "passive" nature as a "storehouse filled with the instincts, habits, intuitions, and laws of conduct" inherited in the history of the race. Weir's warning against female suffrage offers a clue about what may motivate an atavistic portrait of women's agency: his description of a modern "barbarian" is an attempt to give form to the strange creature that is the new woman, a being who by entering politics and the marketplace has seized the "progressive and divergent energies of men" though she remains by nature a "human embodiment" of the conservative principle of race reproduction.[21] Though rendered with far more complexity and ambivalence, Undine is similarly a new barbarian who has broken out of the domestic sphere and whose "constitutional restlessness" is not an independent will but an awakening and mutation of the traits conserved in female identity.

Thus it is that Undine is a wax woman alarmingly come to life. She is introduced, like her mother, as an abstract "form": "I never met with a lovelier form" is the pronouncement of Mrs. Heeny, the "society" masseuse who has the "double role" of fashioning the two women for New York as she manipulates their flesh. Yet in the first extended description of Undine, we witness a strange animation of her static pose: "The young girl whose 'form' had won Mrs. Heeny's professional commendation suddenly shifted its lovely lines" (624). The mention of a human actor, the "girl," is eclipsed by an eerily active form moving "its" own outline. Throughout the novel, Undine is similarly "reanimated" (652) and "revived" (990) and "restored" (877), after finding herself an "oddly brittle and transparent" form (661). The novel never separates Undine's energy and initiative from its almost impersonal embodiment in forms – including her own body – seemingly not under her complete control or possession. Undine's agency, her impressive "nerve," is neither an independent self-determination nor a passive social conditioning, though in the course of the story it alternately resembles both.

But just what is Undine's power of "nerve"? Critics have stressed the kinetic energy that characterizes Undine and seems to many her strongest redeeming quality: "Insofar as we are drawn to Undine and incline to be sympathetic with her . . . it is the splendid animal vigor in the nature that attracts us" – or, as Henry Adams might have put it, she's no virgin, but she's a dynamo. In this way, feminists anxious to rescue Undine from appearing as a mere satire on female avarice have traced a "delicate sorting process" in the novel that distinguishes her admirable drive and determination from a "mutilated" social selfhood produced by an exploitative patriarchy.[22] Certainly the novel gives a mixed account of Undine's "monstrous" personality, hinting at social causes as well as inherent traits. But the significance of Undine's atavistic character, I want to argue, is precisely that it unsettles the opposition between social fashioning and authentic selfhood. Undine's agency of "nerve" represents a cathexis of social forces and personal disposition: the two are never collapsed, but neither can they be "sorted." In her account of a new womanhood, Wharton relies on the models of both museum specimen and atavistic will, and the uncertain oscillation between the two – the shifting, eerie transposition between static forms and incalculable actions – constitutes the novel's Picasso-like portrait of female identity.

In this conflicted portrait, the essential nature of women is no essence at all but the uncanny or improvisational identity of a *living model,* a creature who reproduces life not genetically but mimetically. Accordingly, Undine's defining trait is her capacity for imitation: "Undine was fiercely independent and yet passionately imitative. She wanted to surprise every one by her dash and originality, but she could not help modelling herself on the last person she met (633)." The oxymoron here – an independent will to imitate – embraces the poles of incalculable agency and generic identity that make up Wharton's composite picture of the modern woman. The narrator makes visible the processes of "secret pantomime" (635) through which Undine becomes an inimitable figure on both sides of the Atlantic. In Undine's powers of imitation we can see more fully the wavering uncertainties at play in this account of womanhood: through pantomime she fashions her own identity by her own will but does so after the manners of others – others' bodies, others' language, others' habits and tastes. A self-made woman, her success is her lack of a consistent self. Hence the impossibility of saying exactly who does the self-making: "she could not help modelling herself." Based on imitation, Undine's identity is internally alien, an identity-through-otherness. It is as distant from the "transcendent femininity" of the nineteenth-century domestic woman, a spiritualized selfhood invulnerable to the contaminations of the marketplace, as it is from the status sought by turn-of-the-century feminists, a "realized" selfhood "of flesh and blood and brain, feeling, seeing, judging and directing equally with men, all the great social forces."[23] Both of these alternatives presume a self that is integrated and autonomous, though one derives its wholeness from its exclusion from the world of economic and social forces while the other depends on its active supervision of that world. Undine's mimetic atavism, in contrast, is produced in the world rather than against it. She neither transcends nor directs the social world but is created through an intimate transaction with it, an exchange with fragments of worldly identity – gestures, phrases, a repertoire of alienable manners – reproduced through her arts of pantomime.

But why create a protagonist who is this kind of living mannequin? An earlier Wharton heroine, Lily Bart, appears to forsake her authentic personality for similar powers of pantomime but with tragic results. We could say that Lily was sacrificed in order to exorcise the kind of imitative identity that so animates Undine; why does it then return with new force and even splendor in Undine? And why does Undine seem so much more lively, more genuinely lifelike, than the legions of "transcendent," spiritualized heroines of an earlier era of domestic fiction? A way to pose the question in ethnographic terms is to ask why Wharton invents an atavistic character, a woman whose display of life can be as distressing (though exciting) as the image of Lily's death is melancholy (though satisfying). To begin to answer these questions, we need to recognize the operative ambivalence in the novel's portrait of Undine, an affective structure that evokes repugnance at her crass artifice even as it elicits a fascinated identification with her mimetic energy and what she makes of it – her manifold self and her remarkable ability to "go round." This internal play of disgust and desire provides the symbolic animation of the atavistic woman, the wax woman come to life. As peculiar as this form of life appears to be, it brings into focus the central dynamics of a realism governed by an expert authority that is never wholly immune to its own uncertainties and destabilizing desires. The atavistic woman is one embodiment of the uncanny life of realist representation, and to trace its narrative contours is to explore the operative ambivalence in Wharton's own realism and in the alien form of life – neither private nor public, neither domestic nor commercial – that is the American divorcée.

<h2 style="text-align:center">IMITATION VERSUS PRODUCTION</h2>

Ralph Marvell reluctantly – and hence more authoritatively – delivers a key interpretation of Undine's mimetic character when he decides that "her pliancy and variety were imitative rather than spontaneous" (718). Until this damning judgment, he had mistaken her malleability for the rich liberality of a "flexible soul" (675), a spiritual self to be cultivated by his own marvellous sensibility, "the fugitive flash of consciousness he called self" (676). Put another way, he had fondly seen in her native "adaptabilities" (725) a potential for full assimilation to the ranks of what he calls the "subject race": the old-money race in subjection to the parvenu Invaders but also, we might say, the race of *subjects,* of fulsome interior selves. Logically enough, the testing ground that distinguishes such subjects is Europe, where a romantic responsiveness to art and the landscape confirms authentic subjectivity: in Ralph's words, "one felt one's self a mere wave on the wild stream of being, yet thrilled with a sharper sense of individuality" (714). And it is in Europe that Undine's "flexibility" is revealed to be not a "wave" of the undulating, vital self but the commercially constructed and regulated movements of the marketplace, of which she is almost literally a product: "we called her after the hair-waver father put on the market the week she was born – ," Mrs. Spragg explains, "It's from *un*doolay, you know, the French for crimping" (674).

For all her energy, then, Undine is colored by a stigma that is attached to the very word "imitation": she is seen as "soulless" and "devoid of interiority" at the same time as she has a profound social presence.[24] She is all that must be excluded in order to confer upon women the full individuality accorded men, just as the same essential imitative nature of the savage and his cognates – the black, the child, the idiot – are excluded from (and thereby constitutive of) the civilized self. In *The Golden Bough,* Sir James Frazer draws this boundary with his explanation of the mimetic principle of primitive magic: the savage imitates the world; civilized man acts upon and transforms it. In the "false science" of "Imitative or Mimetic Magic," the primitive "infers that he can produce any effect he desires merely by imitating it." Thus the Dyak wizard attempts to facilitate a woman's labor and birth through a "simulation": "He, in fact, pretends to be the expectant mother." This example of the couvade rite, a favorite of ethnographers, made obvious the inferior nature of a form of agency based on the "principle of make-believe, so dear to children."[25]

Behind this crucial opposition between imitation and civilized agency is the testimony of Charles Darwin, describing his momentous first encounter with the natives of Tierra del Fuego, a scene in which he marvels at "how entire the difference between savage & civilized man is." Seeming to lack any tools or inventions, with a language that "does not deserve to be called articulate," the Fuegians are most striking as "excellent mimics," intuitive and capable of great fidelity: "as often as we coughed or yawned or made any odd motion, they immediately imitated us . . . . They could repeat with perfect correctness each word in any sentence we addressed them, and they remembered such words for some time." Darwin extends his observation into a general principle: "All savages appear to possess, to an uncommon degree, this power of mimicry," which he attributes to the keener animal senses of men "in a savage state." The same opposition between primitive imitation and civilized agency leads Charlotte Perkins Gilman to lament the "savage" condition of "the consuming female, debarred from any free production" and forever "pouring the rising tide of racial power into the same old channels that were allowed her primitive ancestors," though Gilman insists, unlike most male theorists, that this archaic lack of agency is "the enforced condition of the mothers of the race." Like Veblen, Gilman classifies the mimetic or "emulative" passion of modern consumption as a primitive stage of culture that stands in contrast to the one truly progressive force in civilization: the creative drive to produce.[26]

The Custom of the Country can be said to perform a similar marking of boundaries as it anatomizes Undine's "passionately imitative" character, classifying it as the antitype to the creative and "flexible soul." Set down amid the landscapes of Europe, Undine is tellingly rigid and unresponsive – "her beautiful back could not adapt itself to the irregularities of the tree-trunk" (714) – and these litmus settings provoke an uncivilized "wail of rebellion": "I don't like Europe" (722). At the same time, she adapts herself perfectly to the "phantom 'society'" of the European luxury hotels, a world where "the type was always the same even if the individual was not" (802). Undine thus *classes* herself, both socially and typologically, with the transparent hotel types and their many "duplicates," such as the instantly readable Mrs. Shallum, "as open to inspection as a shop-window," (726), and her "wax-featured husband" (724). Undine belongs with the community of "the factitious" (802), and her skill at refashioning herself, a mimesis through consumption, is placed in opposition to creative production, the highest form of which is, for Ralph as for Gilman, the art of writing ("You're not going to write a book *here*?", she exclaims in dismay, when told of the "vision of a book" [721] that has appeared before Ralph in the Siena moonlight). Aligned with fashion as opposed to art, with commercial reproduction as opposed to Gilman's "free production," Undine is cast as a dazzling but objectified social type, the creature Gilman labels "the consuming female," or, in the more ethnographic image she employs, "the priestess of the temple of consumption."[27]

A a stylized modern type, Undine is thus "open to inspection": through a kind of narrative dissection we are made to see the processes that fashion her tastes, appearance, and body, revealing a genesis of character driven by her "instinct" of "copying 'the others' in speech and gesture as closely as she reflected them in dress" (727). By disclosing the almost mechanical principle behind her chameleonlike transformations, the novel secures an explanatory knowledge of what had appeared to be a capricious personality. The novel thus fulfills the "realist imperative of making everything, including interior states, visible, legible, and governable."[28] Yet, as we have begun to see, the same narrative process that classifies Undine as a static type also articulates a figure with an unstable and uncanny semiotic life. Precisely because she assimilates so perfectly to other social identities, Undine blurs the boundary between agent and type, between identity and mimicry. If the novel is a realist museum featuring fixed specimens of an American consumer culture, it is also a world in which its carefully fashioned models come to life in incalculable ways and evoke conflicted desires as much as objective detachment. As such, we could say that the novel is also a kind of narrative theater and that it desublimates the odd theatricality inherent in all museums – and in all realism.

The uncertain status of Undine's mimetic nature, for instance, is emblematized in the image of her "face" as "a theatre with all the lustres blazing" (736), a conceit that straddles both the productions of high art and the low reproductions of consumer society. The simile occurs to Ralph just after he has returned from an enthrall-ing afternoon of classical drama, staged in the "vanishing grand manner" (735) at the Francais. But the light illuminating Undine's face turns out to be generated by the prospects of a group excursion to the *petit théâtre* of the Folies Bergère with the shallow Shallums and a proposed trip on Van Degen's boat, where, Ralph informs her, she would "succeed to half the chorus-world of New York" (739). What we might call Undine's "face value" in this scene, then, shifts from the beauty of classical representation, historically and aesthetically legitimized, to the spectacles of the lowest commercial theater, erotically and commercially suspect. Ralph quickly recasts his impression: "Undine was no longer beautiful – she seemed to have the face of her thoughts" (738). The power of beauty located in the theater of Undine's face become a means of her containment, as it is met and mastered by Ralph's own desire, turned to "disgust" and "odious" exposure – he "fled for solace to museums and galler-ies" (741). Ralph's repugnance is a thematic version of the novel's own supervision of Undine's force and value, a cultural work that is extended by the critics who are compelled to label and explain her "grotesquely perverted" character and its social origins.[29] By de-claring her a "monstrously perfect result" of the American social system, Undine's observers (both the characters inside of the novel and the critics outside of it) put in place the critical distance that Ralph secures by his flight to museums and galleries. Undine is rendered knowable and explicable, if not harmless: her almost oc-cult beauty and powers are finally no greater than the debased attractions of *The Sorceress* (as Van Degen's boat is called), with its shoddy values of "the chorus-world of New York."

Yet Ralph is never able to sustain either his disgust or his distance. To the end, "Undine's moods still infected him" (741), and he is presented as dying of this contaminated desire. Significantly, this desire can infect him as much through mimetic images as through her physical presence: even after Undine requests a divorce, he is unable to remove the reproductions of her likeness – the "effigies of all shapes and sizes, expressing every possible sentiment dear to the photographic tradition" (844) – that have "throned over" his home. The very "factitious" quality in Undine is her most potent. She wields her influence through a wide variety of "effigies" or reproductions: not only photographs and oil portraits (746) but the "newspaper portraits" (653) and gossip items of the mass press, a medium Ralph cannot escape despite his disdain (846–7). Moreover, Undine and her many effigies erode the aesthetic distinctions between art and commodities, and between galleries and mass markets: she reinvents herself as one of the "ornaments of the Society Column" (642) but possess an equal facility – a "surprising quickness" (992) – at appreciating and placing herself among the "rare things" of private art collections. Undine is the one object common to "inaccessible" galleries of Ingres, private collections of aristocratic heirlooms, and the public pages of *Town Talk,* and she forges a circuit of commercial exchange that unites all three. The melodrama of Ralph's marriage – his eventual disdain for Undine and its failure to protect him from the desire ignited by her many reproductions – enacts thematically the critical drama performed by the novel as a whole, an operation whereby Undine is repeatedly displayed as a monstrous commercial product, even as her mimetic identity multiplies both in force and aesthetic range.

There is no question that Wharton intends a satirical condemnation of this promiscuous intermingling of art and the marketplace, of deep-rooted manners and phantom imitations, of "actual beauty" and capacity (a distinctly American skill, according to Chelles) for "producing the effect without having the features" (805). The novel's realism, not to mention its humor, relies on our distinguishing the imitative, market-driven culture of the "new class of world-compellers" (803) – what Wharton was to call in one of her letters "Fordian culture" – from the indigenous culture of "subject races."[30] At a climactic moment, for instance, the novel assumes our recognition of the scandal of mistaking the ancient Chelles tapestries for commodities. Yet in this case, as in so many others, Undine's mistaking of the tapestries becomes an all too real taking;

the tapestries do indeed become commodities, and a satire on the cultural blindness of a "priestess" of consumption becomes a record of her power to restage culture. With a mixture of horror and wonder, the novel chronicles the ability of an "unbounded material power" (802) distilled in Undine and her effigies to make over the real, from her upward displacements into the sphere of aristocratic titles, rare paintings, and objets d'art, which embody a surrogate "rareness and distinction" (984), to her mass incarnations in the press, where representations have a virtual life of their own. Though a continent away, Undine appears before Ralph in the New York subway, "on the first page of the heavily head-lined paper which the unshaved occupant of the next seat held between his grimy fists": " 'Society Leader Gets Decree', and beneath it the subordinate clause: 'Says Husband Too Absorbed in Business to Make Home Happy.' " The paragraph reporting their divorce "continued on its way through the press" in a series of shifting reincarnations:

> [it] called forth excited letters from similarly situated victims, was commented on in humorous editorials and served as a text for pulpit denunciations of the growing craze for wealth; and finally, at his dentist's, Ralph came across it in a Family Weekly, as one of the "Heart problems" propounded to subscribers, with a Gramaphone, a Straight-front Corset and a Vanity-box among the prizes offered for its solution. (847)

Like his graphic position in the article's subtitle, Ralph is subordinated to a chain of material texts whose real purpose is not reporting facts but reproducing stories that facilitate commercial and social transactions. The other side of Wharton's satire on the transatlantic "nomads" (853) and their "habit of imitating" (802) is a fascinated recognition of the real and unprecedented effects of their powers of exchange, mobility, and reproduction, powers inseparable from the very "passion for the factitious" (802) that officially invites contempt.

At one level, the novel tries to contain these powers through the ethnographic categories of custom and country. This effort is most explicit in the chapter midway through the novel in which Charles Bowen and Raymond de Chelles serve as participant observers of the symbolic performances on display at the Nouveau Luxe restaurant. Through their eyes, the energies of the extravagant spectacle become a "social order" that is the invention of a single "original race," leisure-class Americans. In the same way, a disingenuous code of post-Victorian sexual and social mores becomes the sole creation of "the American woman," and the rituals of "slavish imitation," ethnographically understood, provide "satisfying proof of human permanence" (802–3). Framed in this manner, the unnerving capacity of early twentieth-century capitalism for producing and reproducing a new, highly spectacular reality is reduced to a more comprehensible and finite masquerade, a grotesque yet colorful set of images and gestures observed just as Darwin observed the "ludicrous" mimicry of the Fuegians or Durkheim dissected "the essentially imitative nature of Arunta rites."[31] It is a perspective that affords not only a "special titillation" (802) at the estranged theatricality but a twin feeling of detached melancholy at the "social upheavals" (803) that accompany it. Viewing the dazzling Nouveau Luxe spectacle and, at its center, a display of Undine's mimetic "arts" (807), Bowen anticipates the destruction they will bring to more traditional forms of marriage and manners. He feels "the pang of the sociologist over the individual havoc wrought by every social readjustment: it had so long been clear to him that poor Ralph was a survival, and destined, as such, to go down in any conflict with the rising forces" (807).

The ethnographic lens in this scene offers us a figure for Wharton's ideal of fictional realism. For Wharton, serious and successful fiction, a discourse she associated with science, should provide a "direct grasp of reality."[32] Both the detached pleasure and the scientific "pang" that Chelles and Bowen experience are secondary reflections that accompany a clear-eyed view of an objective "social order" and a "destined" cultural history. But at the same time, these marginal emotions contain hints of energies in the novel that ultimately will undercut the ethnographic containment of this brand of realism. The "pang of the sociologist" that Bowen feels, for instance, describes remarkably well the phenomenon that Renato Rosaldo has called "imperialist nostalgia," a structure of feeling common in both colonial regimes and anthropology, "where people mourn the passing of what they themselves have transformed."[33] Bowen fancies himself an outside observer indulging in an inverse slumming among a collection of exotic bodies – "plumed and jewelled heads" and "shoulders bare or black-coated" (802). He laments the destruction of "survivals" like Ralph that will go down in their wake. Yet the engraved stationery sheet on which he sets out to compose his social "impressions" records for us his position within that community and its "fantastic" powers: its heading reads "The Parisian Diamond Company – Anglo-American branch." Bowen is an agent for the economic circuit that joins American capital with Parisian culture – and, in all likelihood, with the raw materials and labor of colonial Africa – to produce the spectacular social order he views with such wry detachment. The "jewelled heads" under his gaze are incarnations of the diamond capital he serves. His superior wistfulness at the social damage that follows from these "rising forces" obscures – but also marks – his own role in the exhibition before him. Like the array of jewels, imported commodities, and stylized gestures on display in the restaurant, Bowen's letter and his very impressions are themselves products in a new global system of representations, a system staging those conspicuous identities, both personal and cultural, that owe their existence to a rising international economy. Though Bowen's products take the form of private letters and intimate conversations, rather than theatrical fashions and leisure pursuits, they follow the same geographic and social channels as the "drifting hordes" (849) of the international rich. If we follow the path of exchanged "impressions" mentioned in the chapter, for instance, it joins the colonial territory of the Nile to aristocratic strongholds in the French countryside, to Paris playgrounds for the international elite, to more somber New York bourgeois neighborhoods and back again to Paris, in a relay of private correspondence underwritten by a public corporation. Like professional ethnographies, Bowen's reflections on Nouveau Luxe manners and fragile Victorian survivals are extracted through the same work of modernity that brings about the damage he elegiacally mourns. Like early anthropologists, he is permitted what Stephen Greenblatt has called a "luxury of forgetting" often granted privileged institutions and their agents: the erasure of his own concrete interests in the world of public ritual and appearance, and a sublimation of what is theatrical – culturally staged – in his own representations.[34]

We could say that the same luxury of forgetting is enjoyed by Wharton's fiction of manners. With its critical distance from the "sham" world of conspicuous leisure it portrays, the novel would seem to elide its own relation to the new market-driven sphere of self-display and high visibility. In fact, though, Wharton's fiction draws upon the same energies of stylized exhibition they critique. It is not merely that the novel makes visible the glamorous rituals of the new elite; Wharton also extracts an æsthetic intensity for her novel from the low mimetic "arts" of Undine and her duplicates. Wharton's most striking narrative scenes are often of exactly those events that are the most striking social scenes – the *tableau vivant* episode in *House of Mirth*, the crucial theater and opera-house scenes that structure the plots of *The Custom of the Country* and *The Age of Innocence*, the series of "showy" performances that Undine enacts whether she is before a gazing crowd, in a private dining room, or alone in front of "an imaginary circle of admirers" (635). The novels profit from reproducing on the page the spectacularity of a Nouveau Luxe social world, and this close parallel of interest breaks down Wharton's careful division between Undine's mimesis and an ethnographic realism: both are fueled by energies of exhibition and a fascination with staged identities.[35] But Wharton's financial and aesthetic interests in the conspicuous performances of the new capitalists at times are veiled in her lament for the loss of the "moral treasures" of the Victorian culture they overran. The denial-through-elegy is particularly notable in her memoir *A Backward Glance*, where memory is allowed the luxury of forgetting almost as a privilege of the genre of memoir. Here Wharton expresses an ethnographic nostalgia for "old manners and customs" made as powerless and "quaintly arbitrary as the domestic rites of the Pharaohs" and now facing "sudden and total extinction." The memoir is an archaeological re-membering of relics of the past – "its smallest fragments begin to be worth collecting and putting together before the last of those who knew the live structure are swept away with it" – that almost entirely obscures what could be called Wharton's fictional miming of Nouveau Luxe mimesis.[36]

But to focus on this denial alone is to miss the remarkable, if oblique, recognition in *The Custom of the Country* of its own mimetic interest in the new theatrics of capitalism, a recognition that coexists with the novel's sharp critical disdain. In this regard, Bowen's "special titillation" at viewing the Paris spectacle is even more telling than his ethnographic "pang." His pleasure comes from an erotics of detached observation, an "exercise of his perceptions" that is visual and intellectual only: observation yields a cognitive thrill from "the sense of putting his hand on human nature's passion for the factitious, its incorrigible habit of imitating the imitation" (802). The language of titillation here acknowledges the notable eroticization of vision in realist fiction as analyzed by recent critics – the controlled pleasure in overseeing what one would never touch, the privileged observation that differentiates the gazer from the object that is thrillingly exposed.[37] Yet because it is a form of desire, the appeal of this kind of realist supervision – enacted for us by Bowen and Chelles – is never wholly stable. The very pleasure produced through a privileged gazing "always also implicitly calls forth its opposite: the dangers and vulnerabilities inherent in that desire."[38] The men's bemused enjoyment at the society of imitators has as its obverse side the risk of their own absorption in the mimetic spectacle. Bowen and Chelles are not so much deceived as absorbed or *taken in* by the Nouveau Luxe colony, or rather by its most artful member, Undine. For Chelles this absorption will take the form of a bad marriage and an even more disastrous divorce. That outcome is predicted in the very first instance of "Chelles' gaze" (805) at what he calls the exceptional "case" of Undine Spragg, when, despite his superior social perceptions, he is unable to see – and hence unable to *fore*see – the divorcée in Undine. In *The Custom of the Country*, ethnographic supervision has a special blind spot: the American divorcée. She is the one social type who exceeds realist vision despite – or, more accurately, because of – her dazzling mimetic visibility. But for the same reason she is the figure who calls forth a continued, more urgent supervision. Undine is a catalyst for a compulsive circuit of interest and disinterest in her observers. The urbane "titillation" that is the proof of Bowen and Chelles's cultural difference from the "sham" society contains – albeit in an altered or refined form – the desire they must deny to uphold that difference. More broadly, the erotics of detachment in realism, by denying its full interest in mimetic spectacles, makes the realist vision vulnerable to being taken in by its own desire – a desire that prompts the detachment in the first place.

The same dynamic can be found in the realist discourse that is a model for Wharton's fiction: professional ethnography. Thanks to his diary, the dynamic is easily traced in the writings of Bronislaw Malinowski, the ethnographer acknowledged to be the discipline's master realist. Malinowski exercised his own brand of ethnographic titillation in observing and representing the "fantastic spectacle" of tribal life in the Trobriand Islands. The tactic is most obvious in his writings about the natives' sexual practices, where he promises to make visible a doubly hidden phenomenon – not just sex, but "savage" sex – even as he insists on his scientific detachment in recognizing sex as "rather a sociological and cultural force than a mere bodily relation." His cool pose in writing about such a provocative subject provides a running proof of his ethnographic authority. Like a realist novel, the ethnographies self-consciously dispense with either moralizing or idealizing. They examine the sensational only as a guide to the cultural, the "organic unity" of a society. Above all, his professional writing bears witness to the realist faith in the powers of sight, the "ethnographer's magic" grasped through the special fieldwork observation that alone is able to disclose "the true picture of tribal life."[39] In Malinowski's fieldwork diary, however, the scientific composure of the ethnographies is supplanted by a remarkable volatility of the writing ego – instead of objective authority, a ferocious insecurity about virtually all things professional or personal; instead of intellectual detachment, a dramatic sense of his being engulfed by native sights, sounds, and stares in a kind of cognitive cannibalism; instead of a controlling erotics of sight, a sense of being blindly seduced by objects that also disgust him. In marked contrast to the equanimity of the ethnographies, the diary portrays a mix of anxiety and enthrallment at what seemed to be a possibility of the release of his own unchecked, infinite desire in the Trobriand environment.

When it was published posthumously, the record of this desire seemed to challenge scandalously the authority of Malinowksi's realism: scientific detachment, it seemed, was a mask for desire and aversion after all. But in an important sense, this is to get it backward; the impression of the *Diary* as a belated revelation – realism is desire *after all* – was an accident of chronology. For although the *Diary* was published decades after the ethnographies, it was of course written before any of the books that established Malinowski's scientific fame. In a sense, this "obsessional document," as one reviewer called it, can be read as a workbook for ethnographic realism. By calling up and writing a narrative of errant desire, the diarist embodied the kind of unconstrained passions that the ethnographer was at pains to demystify. The Malinowski of the *Diary* is closer to the mythic primitive type – impulsive, superstitious, without sexual self-control – than are the Trobrianders of *The Sexual Lives of Savages,* where natives resemble class-conscious "burghers" who prize respectability and marital fidelity above all else. The compulsive, repetitive, and self-damning "moral evaluation" carried out in the *Diary* represents a perverse cultivation of desire, just as the ethnography represents its successful repression. "I must devote myself to my work, to being faithful to my fiancée, and to the goal of adding depth to my life as well as my work": these disciplinary edicts, always transgressed in the record of the *Diary*, were realized in the professional authority Malinowski secured for the role of ethnographer, a liberal hero for most of the twentieth century. As a diarist, Malinowski internalized the myth of the savage as one step in a process of achieving the supervisory authority of a new species of realist ethnography. In this way, the *Diary*'s obsessions can be said to be productive of realism and its powerful detachments.[40]

I have suggested that Wharton's novel of manners has as a source of its own productive obsessions the figure of the divorcée. The myth of the savage is the myth of unbounded eros; Undine, as a divorcée, represents the myth of free and unregulated desire in the mimetic marketplace. Hers is not an erotic desire, though it operates through channels of pleasure. It is instead an undisguised appetite for mobility, recognition, social status, and domination at once fundamental to the formation of bourgeois identity and at the same time a threat to the very social discriminations necessary for that identity. Asked playfully what she expects from marriage to Ralph, Undine announces, "Why, *everything!*" Foolishly, she makes an open avowal of her unlimited desire and of her belief that "everything" can be possessed, if not through marriage then through divorce. (Her declaration comes after she tells the Marvells that her acquaintance Mabel Lipscomb will "never really get anywhere till she gets rid of" her husband [684].) So exposed, her drive to remake herself after the "very best" society dooms her from ever doing so, as does her mistake in openly ratifying divorce as a means of the remaking. Here Undine's thirst to imitate becomes a form of self-containment, unwittingly displaying her vulgarity while at the same time paying homage to the values of the elite.

Instinctively, though, she simultaneously conceals from the Marvells her own status as a divorcée, a tactic that is in keeping with the uncanny – *unheimlich*, literally un-homelike – identity of the American divorcée as it is presented in the novel. She re-creates herself as a marriageable young woman and makes that status real by marrying. She repeats the process with each new husband by further transforming the role of divorcée, refining it into the more decorous figure of widow, in one instance, and refashioning it to that of the aggrieved wife in another. (Historically, this last was the divorcée's most successful public role and was emphasized by proponents of liberal divorce laws.)[41] If in Undine these personae never strike us as wholly authentic, they nevertheless become social facts. From this angle, her mimetic desire represents a power for the successful remaking of identity, a power able to override the social boundaries that exclude and thus define the vulgar, the low, the undesirable. It is the source of this mimetic power that makes Undine so uncanny as a divorcée: the sanctioned domestic identities of new bride, widowed mother, and wronged wife are all achieved outside of the domestic sphere, through the "unbounded material power" that underwrites her mimetic transformations. At one level this material power is the power of capital: the novel charts with some precision the particular Wall Street transactions that make possible Undine's divorces and marriages. But more pertinent is her power to materially transform herself, to assimilate in tone, posture, and attitude the appropriate domestic manners through public pantomime rather than through private inculcation in the home. Her changing series of domestic poses have their perfect analogue in the multiple photographs – the effigies "expressing every sentiment dear to the photographic tradition" – through which Undine makes some of her most striking appearances in the home. However ironically, in *The Custom of the Country* domestic "sentiment" can be produced – produced in objects like photographs, in other people, and, after a fashion, in Undine herself, since she has feelings for her parents, her husbands, and her child that always follow belatedly her construction of a new role for herself. In this regard the novel's exposure of Undine's mimetic desire discloses something quite different from vulgarity: it displays an ability to socially and materially refashion the self, an ability that draws a fascinated scrutiny from the agents of realism in the novel – Bowen and Chelles, the narrator, and Wharton herself. Their scrutiny of the divorcée is demanded by the realist imperative to see through posturing and performance to the real, but their fascination is prompted by her ability to make a new reality out of a performance.

The ability to trade upon a represented self makes the divorcée akin to the actress and the prostitute, two female figures that garner obsessive inspection in realist fiction. Like them, the divorcée has stepped from the domestic sphere into a public and commercial

world, there to offer herself as a means for the intimacy and eroti-
cism that are sanctioned only in the home. The attempt to fathom
the true nature of the divorcée – not only in fiction but in a growing
volume of religious tracts, feminist publications, statistical studies,
and social science – belongs with a wide effort to represent the
emergence of women from domesticity and to imagine the forms of
female agency that appeared to be succeeding what Gilman called
the "amiable but abortive agent" that is the Victorian wife.[42] In
fiction, the actress and the prostitute embody a powerful but compromised agency: the actress commands public attention but is
only miming a fictive self; the prostitute, though starkly visible, is
selling and thus losing a self. By focusing on the provisional or
corrupt conditions that surround the public appearances of these
two types, realist fiction delimits the force of their identities even as
it explores their intriguing resemblance to domestic womanhood.
The divorcée, however, poses a more difficult case: she turns a
resemblance to a domestic role into reality and through remarriage
makes the status of wife a way to legitimately "go around" in public
society. Through the story of the divorcée, Wharton's novel presents a new kind of domestic economy operating both inside and
outside of the home. Almost in spite of itself, the novel also exposes
a new female agency that is impossible to fully supervise as a realist
artifact, a female power that, to borrow Ralph's words, could be
called "the thrill of the agent." Before tracing this power in more
detail, however, it is instructive to examine Wharton's earlier portrait of agency in her heroine Lily Bart of *The House of Mirth*, a
woman who wards off a dangerous resemblance to both the actress
and the prostitute – even to the "abortive" agency of the traditional
wife – but only at the cost of a representative death.[43]

A DEAD SURE THING: REPRESENTATION AND EXTINCTION

The problem of realism in *The House of Mirth* is cast as the problem
of "the real Lily Bart."[44] The quoted phrase first appears at the
unlikely moment when Lily is imitating Reynold's painting *Mrs.
Lloyd* as the model in a *tableau vivant*. Though the fashionable *tableaux vivants* were liable to be "only a superior kind of wax-works"
(140), it seems Lily's true self is visible for the first time only
through the "spectacular effects" (139) of this kind of moneyed
production. Rather than resembling a wax model or mannequin,

she becomes visible in her fullest "flesh and blood" beauty, and the
novel's consummate observer, Lawrence Selden, "for the first time
seemed to see before him the real Lily Bart" (142). But this Keat-
sian moment, in which the *tableau,* like a "splendid frieze" (141),
allows representation to disclose truth, proves a fleeting one. For
rather than secure her real identity and value, the staged appearance subjects Lily to the speculations of a circle of wealthy men,
speculations that Wharton pointedly links to both commercial and
moral registers. Lily's spectacular visibility prompts rumors of sexual impropriety – to the men, she is "a girl standing there as if she
was up at auction" (166) – and the rumors, like stocks or commodities at auction, have value not according to their truth but according to the shifting, collective evaluations of the privileged specula-
tors. Thereafter, Lily undergoes fluctuations of social identity that
her mimetic genius ("her vivid plastic sense" [138]), unlike Undine
Spragg's, is unable to counter or control. The novel records the rise
and fall of Lily's social position as dictated by the unstable currency
of gossip. Whereas Undine thrives in this medium, Lily is eventually caught and framed, as it were, by the forces of social speculation, forces that are ultimately fatal.[45]

But the novel offers some recompense: in death, "the real Lily"
(343) is revealed for good. Against the fluctuations of value in this
commercial society the novel deploys the perspective of a "drawing-
room naturalist" (121) who seeks to affix permanent identity. The
final chapters strip away commercial theatrics to preserve the root
"tentacles of self" (336) of Lily's character. Acknowledging her love
for Selden, destroying the letter through which she could extort a
renewed social value, ridding herself of all "taint" of commercial
"transaction" (347) with men: with these acts Lily throws off the
masks she had cultivated in her attempts at social ascendance.
Wharton's realism is thus set in opposition to the "debasing" mimetic spectacles of New York leisure society.[46] But we should recall
that the drawing-room naturalist, like the museum curator or the
botanist, secures knowledge of the real order of things through
mimetic arts of her own. Strikingly, the final, definitive appearance
of "the real Lily" (344) is achieved through an eerie self-
embalming, the work of a chemist's drug that allows a calm "semblance of Lily Bart," posed as a "motionless sleeper" with a perfect
"tranquil face" (343–4), to supplant the frantic woman who was
vulnerable to what Selden calls "ugly uncertainties" (345). The

novel offers a production of permanence against social decadence, a "victory" over "atrophy and extinction" in which an authentic self is "saved whole" in a striking image, though not in life. Strangely, then, this tragic victory is not really the antithesis of the *tableau vivant* episode it seems designed to counter. The death scene in fact replaces Lily's earlier "triumph" of exhibition, albeit in an elegiac mode. As had occurred with the *tableau*, Selden's gaze perceives Lily's "real self" in a carefully posed representation, though her flesh now evokes an ironic death mask: "the sleeping face which seemed to lie like a delicate impalpable mask over the living lineaments" (344). As before, Lily's arrested figures allows Selden an epiphany, "all that his heart craved to find there" (347). But death now provides a superior form of representation: Lily's corpse is the one perfect "semblance" of the real Lily Bart. The realism of the drawing-room naturalist here recalls nothing so much as the specialized realism of the taxidermist. As Donna Haraway has argued, the new arts of taxidermy developed to perfection in natural history museums during this period deployed methods of scientific spectacle to offset the decadent spectacles of the rich and the sight of the menacing, ungoverned bodies of the poor. Displaying an exact image of the real served as "a prophylaxis for an endangered body politic." The aesthetic of taxidermy is "a technology providing a transfusion for a steadily depleted sense of reality. The image and the real mutually define each other, as all of reality in late capitalist culture lusts to become an image for its own security."[47] Like the art of the taxidermist, Wharton's novel represents the real by displaying a scientific fetish object, a corpse endowed paradoxically with the ability to signify real life. Against both the imitative, "spectacular" surface of leisure-class social life and the "shrieking mob" (339) of the masses in the streets, the novel interposes Lily's dead body. Lily is no longer "human merchandise" (268); she is restored to a natural identity, though at the cost of death. Lily becomes what Elmer Moffatt would call a "dead sure thing" (710).[48]

The iconography of Lily's death illuminates a tendency in works of realism – even in novels with feminist sympathies – to gravitate toward the image of the female corpse. What is gained from representing woman as a "dead sure thing"? Edna Pointellier, Anna Karenina, Emma Bovary, Strindberg's Miss Julie, Tess D'Urbervilles: in their stories the body of the dead young woman, especially when it is the product of suicide, replaces the chaotic subjectivity of the modern woman with a social or medical artifact. Their deaths, only apparently self-chosen, are recast as either an external victimization, a "virtually involuntary surrender to social forces," as one critic has described it, or an inherent pathology, such as a fatal hysteria or a woman's "primitive capacity," as Strindberg said, "for succumbing to illusions and responding hypnotically" to the will of others.[49] In the realist novel the corpse is an explanation, a sign of certainty that issues from the volatile uncertainties surrounding the status of the modern woman. For Selden they were "ugly uncertainties," the transactions between unmarried women and men that seemed worryingly like prostitution. But against such troubling ambiguities, Lily's "mute lips" and still body express a tragic silence that the narrative insists (perhaps too emphatically) had at last "made all clear" (347).

Framed through the perspective of victimization or pathology, the possibility of women's full agency or heroic self-will dissolves into the figure of the corpse; at the same time, though, the corpse becomes a guarantor of professional knowledge or expertise for the author who exhibits that body as an object of social or medical meaning. For this reason there exist feminist versions of the what I have called the "aesthetic of taxidermy" just as there are misogynist brands. Gilman's anthropology of women, for instance, almost cheerfully embraces a motif of morbidity. No one is more concerned to decry the imposed "primitive condition" of women than Gilman, but no one surpasses her for vivid illustrations of that moribund status. Because of their economic dependence on their sexual attraction, modern women have the "economic grade of many thousands of years ago." Modern wives share the status of the infamous "girls of Babylon," thought to have been bought and sold at auction. The "ugly uncertainties" that Selden feared in Lily are to Gilman the "socio-sexual" realities for wives and prostitutes alike: what we see "with horror" in the "open market of vice" is in marriage the "same economic relation made permanent, established by law" and "sanctioned by religion." But with her faith in social evolution, Gilman foresees the birth of a new "economic free agent" out of the death of the "starved and thwarted class" of women, for the simple reason that "all morbid conditions tend to extinction." The title of drawing-room naturalist fits Gilman well, devoted as she is to uncovering "the natural cause of our unnatural conduct" and to offering emblems of its destined extinction. Accordingly, her book shares something of the naturalist's aesthetic attraction to the fossil, the preserved specimen, the neatly dissected body – that is, to objects that symbolize in reified, inanimate form the mastery and knowledge of the expert observer. For Gilman, as for the naturalist and the ethnographer, there is a professional advantage in the "morbid conditions" that allows for a powerful vision of woman as a social specimen. The beauty of the exhibited specimen is an opposite counterpart to the aesthetic of the romantic sublime: where the object of the sublime moves the spectator to an exhilarating evacuation of self, the realist specimen inspires an elevation from mere spectator to expert. This aesthetic effect, I suggest, can account for the conviction and seeming pleasure with which Gilman displays the "savage condition" of women in innumerable concrete forms, even as she establishes her own professional expertise through the act of writing *Women and Economics*.[50]

Wharton won a similar professional authority from writing Lily's death. According to her own account, composing *The House of Mirth* transformed Wharton's career. The "discipline of the daily task" of writing required to meet the publisher's deadlines developed in her, she said, a "mastery over my tools" and effected a change "from a drifting amateur into a professional." Wharton here emphasizes her formal methods of self-discipline, but feminist critics have linked her new mastery to the novel's central aesthetic object as well: the dead Lily. In her essay "The Death of the Lady (Novelist)," Elaine Showalter explains the novel's final death scene as a function of Wharton's "transition to a more serious artistic professionalism, craftsmanship, and control." But interestingly, this reading relies upon an evolutionary narrative of Edith Wharton's "death" as well: "In choosing to have Lily die, Wharton was judging and rejecting the infantile aspects of her own self, the part that lacked confidence as a working writer, that longed for the escapism of the lady's world and feared the sexual consequences of creating rather than becoming art."[51] From ornamental lady to professional working writer – with this interpretation, feminist analysis has itself mirrored the narrative of a happy extinction: "The death of the lady is thus also the death of the lady novelist." Like Gilman's analysis of women, critics have sought to unveil the natural cause – and thus natural death – of the "unnatural conduct" of the early Wharton, the leisure-class lady who was a priestess of consumption. To do so yields a satisfying narrative of organic growth, one that Wharton herself at times endorses. Yet the critics' narrative repeats the structural opposition we have traced in Wharton's fiction and in the anthropological paradigm that informs it; that is, an opposition between a mature and civilized agency associated with writing and a primitive or "infantile" mimetic instinct associated with the world of leisure-class fashion: in short, an opposition between production and imitation.

There is good reason to question this opposition, not least because Wharton herself does so. In *The Custom of the Country*, we have seen, the binarism is on one level even more pronounced. Undine Spragg appears to be a creature of pure imitation, utterly mismatched with the novel's figure of creative production, Ralph Marvell. Moreover, with the novel's sometimes devastating satire, there would appear to be no confusing Undine, the lady manqué, with Wharton, the working novelist. Yet I have also suggested that a countercurrent in this novel begins to expose a coincidence of opposites, a new agency *in* imitation. In mapping a new world of "unbounded material power," *The Custom of the Country* describes mimetic transactions that operate through actors like Undine, transforming both the social reality and the subjects that inhabit it. The position or role that embodies this material power in the novel is the divorcée, a figure who risks (rather than resists, as Lily did) the dangerous proximity to compromised subjects such as the actress or the prostitute – or, as I later show, the atavistic "Amazon." In *The House of Mirth*, Lily's death seals her away from the "taint" of these social and sexual transactions, but of course it removes her as well from any effective agency at all. Writing *The Custom of the Country* over a decade later, Wharton relinquishes the narrative mastery that was gained from writing a death to take up a far more equivocal exploration of an unbounded material life. For Wharton, now both a professional writer and soon-to-be divorcée, Undine was no "dead sure thing."

THE THRILL OF AGENCY

It is not as though Undine, in her manifold appearances, never resembles the icon of the "beautiful corpse," however.[52] For her fashionable oil portrait, Undine casts herself in a "dead white" Pre-Raphaelite glamour, after the manner of Millais's Ophelia: "She was dressed for the sitting in something faint and shining, above which the long curves of her neck looked dead white in the cold light of the studio; and her hair, all a shadowless rosy gold, was starred with a hard glitter of diamonds" (746). The aesthetic methods behind this style of drawing-room portrait – techniques for "idealizing flesh and realizing dress-fabrics" (750) – are not unlike those of the preservation aesthetic that produces specimens of museum realism. The result is a mannequinlike figure of seeming life that appears on the verge of human action: "the full-length portrait of Mrs. Ralph Marvell, who, from her lofty easel and her heavily garlanded frame, faced the doorway with the air of having been invited to 'receive' for Mr. Popple" (785). But an important difference obtains: the genre of the society portrait is designed to publicize new wealth and status rather than expose, as the realist specimen is fashioned to do, a fixed order of natural identity. Thus Van Degen makes a direct contrast between leisure-class portraits and realism, distinguishing the commodified art of New York society from the art of the realist novel that depicts it. Although portraits should be to some degree "life-like," Van Degen proclaims that "a woman's picture has got to be pleasing": "Who wants it about if it isn't? Those big chaps who can blow about what they call realism – how do their portraits look in a drawing-room? . . . They don't care – they're not going to live with the things. . . . That's where old Popp has the pull over 'em – he knows how we live and what we want" (750)."

Scorning realism, Van Degen's speech elevates it by contrast, for the "pleasing" ethos of art he defends would produce little more than drawing-room furnishings. But just as we have seen that the wax woman or realist specimen is never predictably lifeless or obedient to realist authority in this novel, so the commodified portrait is not wholly commercial. In her incarnation as a portrait, Undine does not become a passive object of "human merchandise" in the way Lily had been; the painting does not signify a woman "captured" and "subdued to the conventions of the drawing-room" (13). Instead, her canvas effigy is a form through which Undine moves out of the home and drawing room and into a public circulation for which she is the controlling authority. "She saw herself throning in a central panel at the spring exhibition, with the crowd pushing about the picture, repeating her name; and she decided to stop on the way home and telephone her press-agent to do a paragraph about Popple's tea" (752). Undine is able to recognize and exploit the erotic interest that animates her "dead white" representation, and she harnesses the powers of (male) speculation – in its double sense of both the gaze at an "exhibition" and the swirl of talk "repeating her name" – that had controlled Lily. Objectification makes Undine powerful. Rather than trapping her, the male gaze only extends her range of influence and mobility – and Undine herself extends it even further through the technologies of the telephone and the mass press when she calls her agent to authorize a tabloid paragraph about her debut appearance as a portrait, a paragraph that in turn will be an advertisement for her later appearance at the spring exhibition. Emblematic of this dynamic economy of representation, Van Degen's "bulging stare" at Undine's portrait is described as an active transference "from the counterfeit to the original" (746); the phrase condenses a larger pattern in the novel in which the erotic interest generated by her likeness is shown to circulate back to Undine herself, whereupon she launches new replications of herself. In *The Custom of the Country,* there is no status comparable to "the real Lily Bart." No single image could capture an authentic self. Instead, Undine derives her identity from an erotic current that moves between "counterfeit" and "original" embodiments of an always changing self, in a mimetic rivalry that she encourages and profits from: "Undine, radiantly challenging comparison with her portrait, glanced up at it with a smile of conscious merit" (750).

Shown here in its full dynamism, the figure of Undine exceeds the realist categories the novel has elsewhere set in place. Undine is nothing if not artifactual, but she has neither the taxonomic identity of the realist specimen nor the reified status of the commodity. She is both the object and the controlling subject for her own "dead white" *tableau,* and she thus unties what is, in its final and most exaggerated form, the polarity in the realist novel between expert and corpse. We could say that Undine makes the realist desire for the female corpse serve her own desire for social mobility. As long as observers want to see her in still-life form – as a "woman of wax," a domestic photograph, an oil portrait, a newspaper clipping, the "rare and sensitive object" of the connoisseur (997) – Undine will have, in her words, the power to "go around." Moreover, in the face of Undine's inexhaustible self-representations, the opposition between realism and drawing-room mimesis becomes tenuous at best. Both the "pleasing" portraits of rich women and the authoritative representations from those "big chaps who blow about . . . realism" are products of desire, as well as carefully staged replications. We also glimpse this fact in Ralph's telling gloss on his own fondness for ethnographic analysis. When he describes his family as inhabitants of a "Reservation," destined to be "exhibited at ethnological shows, pathetically engaged in the exercise of their primitive industries" (669), the mode of ethnographic realism is for the moment more transparently theatrical (and notably less forceful) than the spectacles of the Nouveau Lux society.

In creating Undine, Wharton seized upon the dynamic possibilities of a mimetic character who draws power from what Walter Benjamin termed "exhibition value."[53] Undine's images have been severed from any demand for authentic identity; they are instead markers of new paths of desire, social energy, technology, and capital – in Van Degen's words, a map of "how we live and what we want." Undine's "career" in the private sphere of marriage is in fact a worldly progress through a series of interconnected sites of public representation: a global geography that reaches from the midwestern town of Apex to the Nile; a social labyrinth that joins Wall Street brokers with inhabitants of French estates and judges in western divorce towns; a series of material relays that move along telephone lines, ocean lines, and newspaper headlines; a chain of artifacts in Undine's likeness displayed in homes, galleries, trains, and exhibitions. By tracing the astonishing movements of Undine and her effigies, the novel discloses a rich, almost hyperbolic account of what Stephen Greenblatt has called "the reproduction and circulation of mimetic capital."[54] Her story points toward a vast network for generating and transmitting the most charged, and often most conflicted, images through which the culture renews and extends itself – centrally, in this case, images of the American woman, her body and her imputed selfhood.

Wharton's novel, of course, is itself one site in the collective circulation of the figure of the American woman. What seems most notable about the way this novel presents her is precisely the extraordinary mobility attributed to a figure who is at the same time a literal poseur, a factitious model self. With the curious capacity Undine has for directing and distributing her own self-production, the novel seems to sacrifice a measure of authorial control over its own realist project, namely, the project of securing a full social account of womanhood. In contrast with Undine's dynamic portrait, the taxonomic images of women produced and exchanged among those we have described as drawing-room naturalists and ethnographers offered a sense of expert mastery over this most valuable and potentially volatile of social objects. Contingent though not identical representations by feminists like Gilman and Parsons, theorists like Veblen and Simmel, scientists and museum curators from Cuvier to Boas, novelists of the sociological suicides of women (including the Wharton of *The House of Mirth*) – all of the images produced by this collection of odd realist bedfellows have as a common virtue the promise of rendering a fixed and knowable identity for women and thus a fulcrum for limiting or, alternatively, liberating her "morbid" imitative nature. Undine, on the other hand, makes her very "passion for imitation" into a means for if not liberating then at least transforming and multiplying her personal force and presence. In Undine, productive agency and imitation have become impossible to tell apart. She thus embodies those uncertainties about women's agency that we have traced in the museum age, anxieties that the ethnological binarism of production (civilized, progressive, rational) versus imitation (primitive, regressive, instinctual) was supposed to resolve. Lily Bart, we have seen, died to put to rest just such "ugly uncertainties"; why reanimate them in the "monstrous" figure of Undine? Why does Wharton seem to pose a choice between the alternatives of martyr and monster?

In turning from a tragic still-life heroine to the all too lively figure of Undine, we might say that Wharton took a greater risk in her exploration of the vexed question of women's agency, though it was a risk that was not without its greater potential for reward. Through Undine, Wharton gives at once a more open expression to and a more potent disavowal of the form of desire, particularly dangerous in women, that I have called "mimetic" – that is, a desire for direct and profitable transactions between self and world, an unfettered self-posing and self-selling that nevertheless could achieve complete self-possession and social domination. Behind this desire is a fantasy of freedom from all social constraints, a utopian self without customs and manners that is achieved, paradoxically, through the perfect refashioning of one's customs and manners. In other words, it is the impossible fantasy of absolute social mobility and absolute social distinction, which is at once the

dream of the bourgeoisie (when claimed for itself) and its night-
mare (when claimed by the Others necessary to bourgeois distinctions). These desires and fears had taken on a new force in an era of
"unbounded material power" and had a new focus in the debates
about the agency of women; the "woman question," as one historian writes, "crystallizes the issues of bourgeois individualism,"
and this is undeniably the case with the desires and hazards of
mimetic mobility.[55] In Undine, the fantasy of unlimited mobility is
both expressed and punished. It is expressed in the astonishing
success with which she enters and dominates virtually all social
spheres, a success she considers merely her "inalienable right to 'go
around.'" Undine thus dramatizes the restlessness that James Weir
singled out as one of dangerous symptoms of the atavistic woman
who "mixes freely with the world": "Not satisfied with the liberty
she now enjoys, and which is proving to be exceedingly harmful to
her in more ways than one, she longs for more freedom, a broader
field of action."[56] But, as Weir's description suggests, Undine's
success in a broader field of action is also what condemns her, for
her more expansive action is at the same time exposed as the inferi-
or or perverted agency of imitation. To "go around" (Gilman describes it as "the historic tendency of women to 'gad about'") is
cast as a transaction with the world that is a mere parody of pur-
posive action, like the Fuegians mimicking the crew of the *Beagle,*
or, as Weir diagnosed it, like a woman mimicking a man and thereby revealing her "psychic atavism." The women's desire for a
"broader field of action," Weir explains, is an imitative impulse that
is "essentially retrograde": "There are two kinds of genius; the first
is progressive genius, which always enunciates new and original
matter of material benefit to the human race and which is consequently healthy; the second is retrogressive genius, which is imitative and which always enunciates dead and obsolete matter long
since abandoned and thrown aside as being utterly useless."[57] Like
Weir's demarcation here of a defective kind of "genius," Wharton
credits Undine with a form of power but distinguishes it as imitative and pathological. The novel thus splits off or alienates the
personal force and ambition it allows Undine to exercise, though
this estrangement creates a doubling effect – much as Weir produces a doubling of "healthy" and "obsolete" forms of action – that
gives her power a weird attraction and familiarity. Though Undine
is never sentenced to the fate of the beautiful corpse, this process of

alienation provides a different kind of check on the cluster of anxieties evoked by a woman who "mixes freely" with the world.

The novel alienates Undine's desire rather than killing and aestheticizing it: since I argue that *The Custom of the Country* partakes of
ethnographic strategies and impulses, the notion of alienation here
is meant to carry a special semantic weight. "Alienation," in the
sense in which I am using the term, refers to both an operation in
the novel for disavowing desire and a practice in ethnographic discourse for classifying certain traits as exotic and inferior – as, literally, the traits of aliens. A poetics of ethnographic alienation allows
writers to recognize desire but to recognize it only as Other, a
process of estrangement that cultivates an object of perverse fascination and power. For instance, Weir's anthropology of women,
which appeared in *The American Naturalist,* alienates the aspirations
of women by representing them as the aspirations of aliens: "the
'New Woman' was born many thousands of years ago," and "her
autotype, in some respects, is to be found to-day in Mangalore"
among the Nair. Her claims for a larger sphere of action are recast
as the transactions of the coarse sexual economy that was the primitive family, or, more particularly, a distinct form of the primitive
family. For the powers women really want, Weir argues, are the
"prerogatives" of these savage women who practiced polyandry.
Under polyandry, the primitive woman rules by way of a "farcical
marriage" that is in fact a system of sexual and political domination.

> Once safely wedded, the girl becomes emancipated, and can receive
> the attentions of as many men as she may elect, though, I am
> informed, that it is not considered fashionable, at present, to have
> more than seven husbands, one for each day of the week. Of no
> importance, heretofore, after her farcical marriage, the Nair woman
> at once becomes a power in the councils of the nation; as a matter
> of course, the higher her lovers the higher her rank becomes and
> the greater her influence. Here is female suffrage in its primitive
> form. . . . As far as children are concerned, the power of the mother
> is absolute; for they know no father, the maternal uncle standing in
> his stead. Property, both personal and real, is vested in the woman;
> she is the mistress and the ruler.[58]

The archives of ethnography allow Weir to make what now
seems an outrageous equation: female suffrage is tantamount to
Nair polyandry. The rhetorical distortion is obvious. But it is the

same ethnographic rhetoric that allows Weir to publish and circulate his analysis of the American woman in a scientific journal like
The American Naturalist. Moreover, the extremity of Weir's claim is
also a sign of the high stakes in the anthropological history of the
family and in the alienation effect it employed. The early narratives
of anthropology contained a cosmology able to unite the spheres of
kinship, ownership, and government. Behind the "monogamian
family," according to Lewis Morgan and the theorists who followed
him, was a natural history of property relations. Once men began
to see wives and children as property to be exchanged and transmitted, they evolved beyond the earliest stages of "primitive promiscuity" and polyandry (in which any patrimony was impossible)
and ascended to polygamy and monogamy. The key to this evolution is the restriction of women to one sexual partner, allowing men
to imagine private property in the form of the wives they alone
owned and the children they knew they sired. It is this "growth in
the idea of property" in the womb of the family that eventually
"brought the Aryan and Semitic nations out of barbarism into
civilization."[59] Behind the civilized family and male suffrage, then,
is a natural history of sexual and economic relations, relations that
are natural only because they are now extinct or alien. Through the
lens of anthropology the family is recognized as a sexual economy
of property relations, while the built-in alienation of that lens, its
categorical otherness, ensures that such an economy is necessarily
primitive or, in Weir's language, "degenerative," if found among
the civilized.

This anthropological narrative of marriage, it can be argued,
gives us a form of Victorian patriarchy writ large. But this should
not obscure the fact that, because it is a narrative that admits a
worldly history of property and politics into the sphere of marriage,
it therefore also imagines with exceptional vividness a potent social
agency for women. Weir means for his reader to look upon women
as a clear and present danger. Far from bringing on the extinction
of old ways, social change, in Weir's view, is bringing obsolete
habits and hungers to life. In his obsession with her "atavistic
desires," then, Weir articulates for women a historical claim on the
control of property, children, and sexual relations – the control, in
other words, of economic and social reproduction. For all his mis-
ogyny, he presents woman as a more formidable figure than Gilman's priestess of consumption, an "abortive agent" on the verge of

sure extinction. Weir's atavistic woman – like Undine – is both a subject and an object of the material powers in the "age of luxury." She is a woman who "mixes" with the world and exercises power through channels that include mechanical and theatrical reproduction: "We see forms and phases of degeneration [of women] thickly scattered throughout all circles of society, in the plays which we see performed in our theatres, and in the books and papers published daily throughout the land." But Weir's apprehension of an immanent power in women is matched by his intense and literal savaging of women who advocate suffrage. According to Weir, such women express their atavistic desires in a range of abnormal physiologies and sexualities; he devotes much of the article to detailing what he calls "the *clientele* of the alienist," the "viragints, gynandrists, androgynes, and other female psycho-sexual aberrants" who are the modern aliens of American civilization. Weir's ethnographic imagination makes it possible for him both to recognize a woman's desire for the (male) powers of social reproduction and simultaneously to reduce that desire to "degenerative" sexual compulsions.[60]

In Wharton's novel, the alienating portrait of the woman who belongs to the "genus" of "homo sapiens, Americanus" (757) is prompted not by the prospect of female suffrage but by the "modern drama of divorce" (843). Wharton's divorcée, with her growing collection of husbands, shares the same alarming virility as Weir's Nair woman. Undine exercises "her father's business instinct" (778) through the transactions of divorce and remarriage and does so to profits that are as impressive as they are damning. As the novel diagnoses it, the "problem of American marriages" is the confusion of sexual and economic relations that undergirds American society, bringing to life the conditions made most vivid by the anthropologists of marriage. (One of the most famous, Edward Westermarck, was a favorite author of Wharton's.)[61] But unlike Weir, Wharton does not attribute this state of things to the sexual appetites of female "aberrants." Nor does she suggest, as Charles Bowen does (in agreement with Gilman), that wives are kept in a sexuo-economic subjection through "bribe[s]" (759) that amount to a system of private prostitution. Instead, Wharton's novel presents us with the prospect of an unparalleled social power and mobility – the prerogatives of wealthy men – in the body of a woman. Where Weir imagines woman as a voracious sexual agent (a would-be Nair polyandrist), and where Gilman imagines woman as an oppressed economic victim (a coerced Babylonian prostitute), Wharton imagines a powerful mimetic agent, a figure who gets the social recognition, mobility, and influence she craves by mastering the American system of "easy divorces" (758). The alien type Wharton sets forth, in other words, is the divorcée as "Amazon" (704), a woman who possesses a power that is both intriguing and threatening, and who derives that social power from her gender. In Undine we are confronted directly with the drive for an unlimited social agency; it is not deflected as either a sexual pathology or a social victimization. But I want to suggest that the very openness of the expression of bourgeois desire is the key to Wharton's own complex renunciation. Embodying desire in the divorcée, Wharton is able to alienate it.

We can examine this seeming paradox more closely by analyzing one of the divorce transactions that Wharton presents in some detail, a transaction that is less a matter of any legal action than it is a series of mimetic operations. It begins, appropriately enough, in the scene of portrait painting where Undine is posing for one of her more lavish reproductions. The painter Claud Walsingham Popple, we learn, is "the only man who could 'do pearls'" (745). This is not an insignificant fact, since a Popple portrait is not meant to represent a person – an individual's face, hair, clothing, a personal aura – so much as to display social prestige, and pearls are therefore one of a female portrait subject's most distinguishing features. To "do pearls" is not just to paint them, it is also to use an aesthetic image to convert an economic object into a conspicuous signature of status. In the case of Undine's portrait, however, this act of mimesis also reveals an economic deficit. Van Degen pronounces the painting "damn good" but tells Popple that "the pearls ain't big enough" (746). Mimesis acts in reverse here, turning attention from the semiotic to the economic: "But it's not *his* fault," Undine answers, "*he* didn't give them to me!" The allusion is to her current husband Ralph and his failure in a sentimental economy of male tribute that Undine professes as her creed, the belief that a "quick rise to affluence" was "man's natural tribute to woman's merits" (772). The painting becomes a representation of the commodities that, because they do not accrue magically as chivalric "tribute," have forced Undine into the quotidian world of prices and purchases:

"[Popple will] tell you he's giving me the picture – but what do you suppose this cost?" She laid a finger-tip on her shimmering dress.

Van Degen's eye rested on her with cold enjoyment. "Does the price come higher than the dress?"

She ignored the allusion. "Of course what they charge for is the cut – "

"What they cut away? That's what they ought to charge for, ain't it, Popp?" (746)

Van Degen's lascivious puns further transform the meaning of the portrait as he presents the dress as a figure for the body it covers, or rather, uncovers. In Van Degen's verbal portrait, it is Undine who has a "price," and it is her body she is pointing to when she asks, "What do you suppose this cost?" For Van Degen, the painting is an advertisement not of what has been purchased – a dress and pearls – but what could be purchased: a body that is the fleshly version of those "glimmering" objects.

As with the *tableaux vivant* scene in *The House of Mirth*, then, this episode of mimesis shows a woman's vulnerability to being made an object of exchange. Like Lily, Undine appears to be caught by her own self-display in a society that commodifies women. But in this novel Wharton has altered the terms of the social marketplace. Undine still shares Lily's dilemma: that (in Gilman's words) "woman's economic profit comes through the power of sex attraction."[62] But Undine is not forced to trade on her looks or else face starvation; this is not a story of scarcity but of excess. Where Lily renounces any exchange that would bring a "taint" of "transaction," Undine willingly exercises what Ralph calls the "thrill of the agent" (795), the novel sensation he relishes when he participates in his first big Wall Street deal. Taking a calculated risk, she gives herself to Van Degen, and in doing so Undine chooses to realize Van Degen's interpretation of the portrait as a woman up for auction and asking; "What do you suppose this costs?"

The answer, it would appear, is already on the canvas: the "cost" is the string of (bigger) pearls she owns after her "misadventure" with Van Degen. But are pearls her real object? Undine's father construes them as the "price of her shame" (869) and orders her to return them in order to protect her honor and his own position, weak though it is, as the controlling patriarch. The logic is clear: if she keeps the pearls she will prostitute herself and supplant her father as the familial and financial authority behind her marriages.

But characteristically, Undine defies this entire kinship structure (which Gilman pointedly characterized not as the modern kinship system of monogamy but as a system of "monogamy *plus* prostitution" available to husbands).[63] She refuses the idea that the pearls are a payment for sexual services and treats them as an investment in a new marriage: "she saw what they might be converted into, and what they might rescue her from" (871). Accepting the pearls does not make her a prostitute but a divorcée. Of course, in *The Custom of the Country* being a divorcée does not mean escape from the world of economic calculation – in this novel no role or status can so escape. Nor is the divorcée a figure who believes above all in finding romantic love in marriage, which is the argument of historians in recent interpretations of the turn-of-the-century escalation of divorce rates.[64] Rather, in Wharton's novel being a divorcée means being Gilman's "economic free agent," not in the marketplace, as Gilman prophesied, but within the sexuo-economic web that is modern marriage. Undine's object is not pearls but (re)marriage. It is Undine who speculates on Van Degen, rather than the other way around, betting that their "honeymoon" is a prelude to marriage: "It had been a bold move, but it had been as carefully calculated as the happiest Wall Street 'stroke'" (861). Her ultimate goal had not been economic but mimetic – she claimed, alas too soon, that she was "really his wife" – though by this time in Undine's story the spheres of economy and mimesis have become virtually indistinguishable. The gamble fails, but the pearls she retains and later sells finance her next transformation, circulation, and remarriage: they pay for a return to Europe, where, through carefully staged appearances before Chelles, she succeeds in becoming a new bride – now "really his wife" – and a whole new Undine, the Marquise de Chelles.

The "thrill of the agent" that Wharton describes in this novel, then, is enacted through the relations of the sexes but is not a sexual power per se, at least not the kind of pure erotic pathology that Weir imposes on the "additional desires and emotions" stirred in women who venture outside of the home. Instead, Wharton imagines a power for women by which the transactions of kinship – sex, marriage, childbirth, divorce, even adultery, all inseparable from economic relations – offer her an accumulation of social strength and the most public and far-reaching forms of self-representation. This power is, in one sense, the social power and protection afforded to men, as Simmel noted in his essay on prostitution: "The meaning and the consequences which society ascribes to the sexual contact of men and women are also based on the assumption that the woman contributes her entire self, with all of its worth, whereas the man contributes only part of his personality," with the result that a woman "gone astray" loses all social standing and "prostitutes become irredeemably declassé; but the worst rake can still rise" and "no social status is closed to him."[65] Undine embodies a fantasy in which these unequal restrictions on women have vanished. It is the fantasy that the one sphere of action then open to a woman – sex and the family – offers her the excitement of change, risk, and accumulation but with a secret immunity against any fatal loss of bourgeois identity, indeed with an unlimited potential for social ascendance. For that matter, the fantasy even offers the potential for a protected social descent, as when Undine and the other Paris visitors indulge in a "tumultuous progress through the midnight haunts where 'ladies' were not supposed to show themselves, and might consequently taste the thrill of being occasionally taken for their opposites" (809). For Undine, the ability to freely contract marriage and divorce means that women have the ability to "show themselves" in virtually any social territory, in almost any social role. Marriage brings women an unbounded mobility, which brings more marriage. In this world it is only husbands who live within an "archaic structure of . . . rites and sanctions" (932) and end up displayed as corpses.

I have called this picture of women's agency a fantasy, but as Ralph's fate reminds us, it is a construct that obviously includes a measure of viciousness and a grim critique of the Victorian ethos of marriage. Undine's life, its sheer velocity of change and sensation and its "rush of physical joy" (754), give expression to the desire for an alternative to Lily's starved immobility, however noble. But it is crucial to see the place of this energy of desire within the larger narrative operations of the novel and the cultural work they perform. The fantasy of total social mobility is never without the accompaniment of a darker phantasm of Undine's "monstrous" potential for inflicting social damage. The very openness with which she feeds her appetite for the "thrill" of mimetic agency calls into play the kinds of narrative alienation we have previously examined, devices for a formal disavowal through otherness.

For one thing, Wharton's divorcée is an American polyandrist.

Strictly speaking Undine practices what has come to be called "serial monogamy." But Wharton, like Weir, aims to draw upon a visceral reaction to the knowledge of a woman with multiple sex partners, and she finds ways to telescope Undine's successive marriages into a narrative synchrony that produces the "surprise and repugnance" Herbert Spencer said was the civilized response "on first reading about polyandry." The repugnance is dramatized in Ralph's reaction of "physical nausea" when Elmer Moffatt, upon hearing Ralph's high-handed reference to his divorce from "Mrs. Marvell," announces that he had "been divorced from her myself" (930). For Ralph, the fact that Elmer and his wife were "made one" in a Nebraska ceremony represents horrifying simultaneity of marriages: "he recalled that Moffatt had dined one night in his house, that he and the man who now faced him had sat at the same table, *their wife* between them" (italics added [932]). Wharton here uses one of the very same images that Edward Westermarck employs to illustrate polyandry in his *History of Human Marriage* when he describes the "affront" to the "established custom" of old Vienna "if you invited a woman of quality to dinner, without at the same time inviting her two attendants of lover and husband, between whom she always sits in state with great gravity."[66] From this perspective, Undine's divorces signify only a surface temporizing within an emerging modern polyandry – and even this formal temporizing is removed when Undine undertakes her "honeymoon" with Van Degen before her divorce from Ralph. Ralph's shock at learning of Undine's first marriage, compounded with our shock at Ralph's suicide, returns the force of taboo to Undine's rational, "carefully calculated" transactions in marriage and divorce. Placed under the sign of a sexual taboo, the thrill of agency is formally estranged as a monstrous excess.

An even more damning disavowal of Undine is effected through the figure of nine-year-old Paul. By casting Undine's son as a kind of orphan, with "scattered affections" (1005) and without any sure knowledge of his own father, Wharton echoes the ethnographers who emphasized the scandalous results of the "diffused" paternity under polyandry. "Maternal parenthood alone being concentrated, and paternal parenthood diffused, family bonds are little stronger than those accompanying promiscuity." In the Kulu district of the Punjab, Westermarck writes, "the son calls all the husbands of his mother . . . his fathers." In the Paris mansion of Undine Moffatt

(neé de Chelles, née Marvell, née Moffatt, née Spragg), the son
confuses the multiple fathers variously referred to as his "Papa"
(1006), "his step-father" (1009), and "the gentleman he called his
French father" ("the father he had been most used to and liked
best" but "who had abruptly disappeared from his life" [1003]).
Above and beyond its affective power, the pathos of Paul's story
registers the era's sociological obsession with what Weir called the
problem of "posterity." To many, the "age of luxury" and of the
"new woman" posed grievous dangers to the fertility of the ruling
classes, hence to the health of their families and the strength of the
larger social body. The latter-day polyandry created through American divorce, or through (as Herbert Spencer joked) "an agitation
for the establishment of polyandry in the West" by "the strong-
minded ladies (of America)," was an ethnographic image that distilled anxieties about the control of sexual, and hence social, reproduction. The proof of the danger was in the anthropological record:
"polyandric societies" are doomed, Spencer declared, for "this inferior family-type has yielded to superior family-types; both because
of its inferior fertility, and because of the smaller family-cohesion,
and consequently smaller social cohesion, resulting from it."[67]

Weir and other observers urged that all social innovations should
be judged according to their effects on posterity. The final chapter
of *The Custom of the Country*, by presenting Paul's puzzled and doleful
view of "his mother's marriages" (1007), does just that. Through
Paul's eyes the chapter presents a painful juxtaposition of plural
husbands and a darkly comic simultaneity of marriage and divorce,
conveyed through the newspaper report Paul absorbs of the
Moffatt's "top speed" dash from the Reno divorce court to the Reno
justice of the peace. The effect of this shift in perspective is a sharp,
almost vengeful disengagement from the complex pleasures of narrating Undine's marital machinations. It enlarges upon earlier moments that, taking my cue from Wharton's own vocabulary, I have
called instances of narrative alienation, moments such as Ralph's
confrontation with his wife, when, "as they stood there face to face,
almost touching, she became something immeasurably alien and
far off" (767). Or a parallel episode with another husband (this
time Raymond de Chelles), who "stood looking at her coldly and
curiously, as though she were some alien apparition his eyes had
never before beheld" (981). In these moments Undine is transfixed
by the remote stare of a novelistic ethnography that turns the

American divorcée into a figure of cultural strangeness and menace. The pleasure of divorce – our own pleasure as readers, as well
as Undine's as divorcée – is thus made foreign to us, and Undine
becomes an estranged image of a desire we share but would never
openly imitate.

That Edith Wharton was transacting her own divorce while she
struggled to finish *The Custom of the Country* adds an intriguing ambiguity to the portrait of this her most powerful protagonist. It is
tempting to read the particularly savage representations of Undine
as providing Wharton with a form of self-inoculation. "Whatever
freedoms I may be granting myself by seeking a divorce," Wharton
the satirist seems to be saying, "surely they are not those of this
transatlantic Amazon who traffics in husbands and barters with
her own child." But to my mind there is something more compelling in the fact that Wharton risked such a dazzling embodiment of
desire in creating Undine, that she gave vivid fictional life to the
thrill of agency Undine discovers in divorce and remarriage. Certainly for Edith Wharton there was a greater risk of damage than
promise of protection in writing the story of a rich American divorcée who travels between New York and European capitals and
circulates among a coterie of male companions. As Gilman warned,
"for the woman who dares admit that she wishes further society
than that of her husband we have but one name."[68] But there is the
possibility that Wharton runs this risk in her novel for the same
reason that Undine does: because it is risk that pays. The rewards
of Wharton's novel writing, moreover, are remarkably like those of
Undine's divorces: a new social mobility and economic power. But
there is also a crucial difference between author and protagonist.
Unlike Undine, Wharton did not look upon her divorce as an
instrument with which to exercise a new personal agency, or she did
so only to the extent that divorce gave her a wider field not for
remarriage but for professional novel writing. In the end, Wharton
relies on the boundary between divorce and writing, and between
imitation and productive creation, precisely the boundary that
Wharton's novel by turns anxiously questions and obsessively reas-
serts. In this sense, the uncertainties about divorce are ultimately
productive for Wharton, rather than either damaging or subver-
sive: the mimetic desire of the divorcée can be transformed into the
mimesis of realist novels.

The profit for Wharton in writing about divorce is evident in the last few pages of the novel. It is significant that she shifts the narrative from Paul's point of view to portray once again Undine's own sensations of limitless desire. Undine's divorces have brought her what had once seemed unattainable prizes, including the Chelles tapestries and an intimate proximity to many "brilliant names" (1014) of the best society. But the divorces have also brought one seemingly ineradicable, inalienable desire: precisely because she is a divorcée, Moffatt informs her, Undine can never be the wife of an ambassador. The novel thus ends with a strategic uncertainty. Divorce may be the one effective and immovable obstacle to Undine's mimetic desire; it seems there is finally one self-transformation closed to her. But Wharton also clearly signals that for Undine it is precisely obstacles that generate desire. Learning that there "was something she could never get" incites her strongest longing yet: "it was the one part she was really made for." The previous forty-five chapters have taught us that nothing makes Undine more powerful than desire. In this sense, the one part she was "made for" – and the part that made her – is the role of divorcée, because divorce is a self-perpetuating and self-producing incitement, an unending form of mimetic desire. This final wavering image of unfixed energies of desire and the social power they portend closes the novel with a memorable emblem of an atavistic woman. A figure both exhilarating and alarming, the atavistic woman produces a counter-desire for the continuing supervision provided by realists through a proliferation of representations in novels, ethnographies, journal articles, political tracts, and museums. "The condition of women in society," as Broca put it, "must be most carefully studied." As long as the divorcée remained an alien, she would be an incitement to expert observation and authorship.

In Wharton's life, then, authorship seems to have required the alienation of the divorcée and her powerful marital transactions. Wharton's novel ends with the possibility of Undine's perpetual marriages – like the female "Paramount Chief" of the tribes of the Sierra Leone, she appears able to acquire "as many men as she pleases."[69] But the novel, which appeared in *Scribner's* in serial form from January through November 1913, could be said to end as well with the ending of Wharton's marriage: her divorce was granted April 16 of that year, and, like the angels in heaven, who neither marry nor are given in marriage, Wharton from that time on contracted marriages only in her fiction. Her divorce secured, Wharton renounced marriage and embraced authorship. Though she was playfully referred to by friends as an "Angel of Devastation," her power was never the atavistic specter of an excess of marriage; instead her international recognition and influence were acquired through a growing list of her fictions rather than a roster of husbands.[70] A single divorce, together with her professional novel writing, made Wharton one of the most formidable women of her time, a free economic agent who became powerful through the form of mimesis known as the realist novel.

Notes

CHAPTER I. THE EQUIVOCATION OF CULTURE

1. *Henry James Letters*, vol. 1, ed. Leon Edel (Cambridge, Mass.: Harvard University Press, 1974), p. 484; Bronislaw Malinowski, A *Diary in the Strict Sense of the Term* (1967; rpt. Stanford: Stanford University Press, 1989), p. 236. All further references to passages in the *Diary* will be indicated in the text.

2. A classic description of the liberal authority associated with both the ethnographer and the novelist can be found in Susan Sontag's essay, "The Anthropologist as Hero," in *Claude Lévi-Strauss: The Anthropologist as Hero*, ed. Nelson Hayes and Tanya Hayes (Cambridge, Mass.: MIT Press, 1970), pp. 184–96. Levi-Strauss rather than Malinowski is Sontag's central example, but her introduction presents the then standard view – a view since seriously challenged – that anthropologists, like the artists who live "in self-imposed exile and in compulsive travel," practice a holistic occupation of "spiritual commitment." Like certain artists, the anthropologist seeks a cure for modern "homelessness" and does so in his or her role as the "custodian" of primitive culture (185). The professional calling is politically innocent: "He cannot seek power, he can only be a critical dissenting voice" (189).

3. Clifford Geertz, *The Interpretation of Culture* (New York: Basic Books, 1973), p. 5.

4. Edward Said, "Representing the Colonized: Anthropology's Interlocutors," *Critical Inquiry* 15 (Winter 1989): 205–25; James Clifford, *The Predicament of Culture: Twentieth-Century Ethnography, Literature, and Art* (Cambridge, Mass.: Harvard University Press, 1988), p. 10.

5. Edward B. Tylor, *Primitive Culture*, vol. 1 (1871; rpt. New York: Putnam's Sons, 1920), p. 1; Raymond Williams, *Culture and Society, 1780–1950* (New York: Columbia University Press, 1983), p. 233.

6. Clifford refers to the culture concept as a "serious fiction" employed by both novelists and ethnographers (*Predicament of Culture*, p. 10). The literature on the "epistomological ennui" (the phrase appears in John Comaroff and Jean Comaroff, *Ethnography and the Historical Imagination* [Boulder, Colo.: Westview Press, 1992], p. ix) that is plaguing anthropology and its paradigm of culture has become large. Said has summarized the literature on this "malaise," a condition which is perhaps "now true of every field in the human sciences" but "is especially true of anthropology" ("Representing the Colonized," p. 208). He

discusses the different scholarly responses to the "crippling attacks on ethnographic authority" (p. 211), including the response by proponents of postmodern anthropology and by pragmatists who emphasize practice. For an analysis of the vestiges of imperial ideology in anthropological thought, see Johannes Fabian, *Times and the Other: How Anthropology Makes Its Object* (New York: Columbia University Press, 1983), and Talal Asad, ed., *Anthropology and the Colonial Encounter* (London: Ithaca Press, 1973). Christopher Herbert's *Culture and Anomie: Ethnographic Imagination in the Nineteenth Century* (Chicago: University of Chicago Press, 1991) presents a detailed historical and theoretical analysis of the culture concept and its problematic circularity. For a recent study of ethnographic writing, see Arnold Krupat, *Ethnocriticism: Ethnography, History, Literature* (Berkeley and Los Angeles: University of California Press, 1992).

7. Bronislaw Malinowski, *Argonauts of the Western Pacific* (1922; rpt. Prospect Heights, Ill.: Waveland Press, 1984), p. 6; Henry James, *The Complete Notebooks of Henry James*, ed. Leon Edel and Lyall H. Powers (New York: Oxford University Press, 1987), p. 127.

8. See Comaroff and Comaroff, *Ethnography*, p. ix.

9. Concentrating on *The Marble Faun*, Richard Brodhead chronicles the formation of an American canon around Hawthorne's career, a formation accomplished through interlocking institutions of education, publishing, and editorial promotion. James and Wharton's receptions of Hawthorne, Brodhead argues, show that Hawthorne's canonical authority was nourished as much by strategic critique as by adulation. *The School of Hawthorne* (New York: Oxford University Press, 1986). In *The Office of the Scarlet Letter* (Baltimore: Johns Hopkins University Press, 1991), Sacvan Bercovitch analyzes the cultural context and function of the "ideological mimesis" in *The Scarlet Letter*, the novel that "began the institutionalization of an American literary tradition" (p. xix).

10. Pierre Bourdieu, *Outline of a Theory of Practice*, trans. Richard Nice (Cambridge: Cambridge University Press, 1977), pp. 94–5

11. See, for example, Mark Seltzer, *Henry James and the Art of Power* (Ithaca: Cornell University Press, 1984); Susan Mizruchi, "Reproducing Women in *The Awkward Age*," *Representations* 38 (1992): 101–30; Lynn Wardley, "Woman's Voice, Democracy's Body, and *The Bostonians*," *ELH* 56 (1989): 639–65; Ross Posnock, *The Trial of Curiosity: Henry James, William James, and the Challenge of Modernity* (New York: Oxford University Press, 1991); Jonathan Freedman, *Professions of Taste: Henry James, British Aestheticism, and Commodity Culture* (Stanford: Stanford University Press, 1990); Jean-Christophe Agnew, "The Consuming Vision of Henry James," in *The Culture of Consumption*, ed. Richard Wightman Fox and T. J. Jackson Lears (New York: Pantheon Books, 1983), pp. 65–100; Kenneth Warren, *Black and White Strangers: Race and American Literary Realism* (Chicago: University of Chicago Press, 1993); and Joseph Litvak, *Caught in the Act: Theatricality in the Nineteenth-Century English Novel* (Berkeley and Los Angeles: University of California Press, 1992).

12. Seltzer, in *Henry James and the Art of Power*, presents James's fiction as an

apparatus of surveillance, whereas Posnock's *Trial of Curiosity* sees in the late texts a power of radical critique.

13. Michel de Certeau, *The Practice of Everyday Life,* trans. Steven R. Rendall (Berkeley and Los Angeles: University of California Press, 1984), p. 62.

14. Sigmund Freud, *Totem and Taboo* (1913; rpt. New York: Knopf, 1946), p. 125. For an extended study of Freud's use of anthropology, see Edwin R. Wallace, *Freud and Anthropology* (New York: International Universities Press, 1983).

15. See Philip Fisher, "Appearing and Disappearing in Public: Social Space in Late-Nineteenth-Century Literature and Culture," in *Reconstructing American Literary History,* ed. Sacvan Bercovitch (Cambridge, Mass.: Harvard University Press, 1986), pp. 155–88.

16. Henry James; quoted in *Critical Essays on Henry James: The Late Novels,* ed. James W. Gargano (Boston: Hall, 1987), p. 9.

17. Henry James, *The Sacred Fount* (New York: Scribner, 1901), pp. 28–9, 23, 214, 149, 167, 29. Further references to the novel will be indicated by page numbers in the text.

18. "War as Moral Medicine," *Atlantic Monthly* 86 (December 1900): 735–8.

19. James Weir, Jr., "The Methods of the Rioting Striker as Evidence of Degeneration," *Century* 48 (October 1894): 952–3.

20. See, for instance, Henry Childs Merwin, "On Being Civilized Too Much," *Atlantic Monthly* 79 (June 1897): 838–46. An important treatment of late nineteenth-century ideas of degeneration in the United States appears in T. J. Jackson Lears, *No Place of Grace: Antimodernism and the Transformation of American Culture, 1880–1920* (New York: Pantheon Books, 1981).

21. Harry T. Peck, "*The Sacred Fount:* Analysis of Analysis," and anonymous review, "*The Sacred Fount:* Subtlety Somewhat Overdone," in Gargano, *Critical Essays,* pp. 44–6, 9.

22. Mark Seltzer, *Bodies and Machines* (New York: Routledge, 1992), p. 21.

23. Marcel Mauss, *The Gift: Forms and Functions of Exchange in Archaic Societies,* trans. Ian Cunnison (1925; rpt. New York: Norton, 1967), p. 81.

24. William Graham Sumner, *Folkways* (1907; rpt. New York: Arno Press, 1979), pp. 36, 38. Sumner argues that "the folkways are the widest, most fundamental, and most important operation by which the interests of men in groups are served" (p. 34), preceding law, philosophy and ethics, which "are never original and creative; they are secondary and derived" (p. 38). Sumner also links folkways with coercive force: "There is always a large element of force in the folkways" (p. 64). Disguised as self-discipline and ritual, social coercion "is always present, and brutal, cruel force has entered largely into the development of all our mores, even those we think most noble and excellent" (p. 65).

25. Malinowski, *Argonauts,* p. 9. The rest of Malinowski's description of the achievements of early ethnology could stand as a manifesto of the social results scholars hoped to foster – both at home and in colonial outposts – through their discipline and through the other emergent social sciences: "It has transformed for us the sensational, wild and unaccountable world of 'savages' into a

number of well-ordered communities, governed by law, behaving and thinking according to consistent principles."

26. A. H. Pitt Rivers, quoted in George W. Stocking, *Victorian Anthropology* (New York: Free Press, 1987), p. 232.

27. Thorstein Veblen, *The Theory of the Leisure Class* (1899; rpt. New York: Viking, 1983), pp. 1–21.

28. Sumner, *Folkways*, pp. 198–9. Writing in the same period, American sociologist E. A. Ross provided a description of suspect schools of art, citing "naturalism in fiction, 'decadence' in poetry, realism in art, tragedy in music, skepticism in religion, cynicism in politics, and pessimism in philosophy." Ross is quoted in Robert Bannister, *Social Darwinism: Science and Myth in Anglo-American Social Thought* (Philadelphia: Temple University Press, 1970), p. 140.

29. Patrick Geddes and J. Arthur Thomson, *The Evolution of Sex* (New York: Scribner, 1890), p. 26. Cynthia Eagle Russett discusses Geddes and other contemporary theorists of a sexual economy in *Sexual Science: The Victorian Construction of Womanhood* (Cambridge, Mass.: Harvard University Press, 1989), pp. 89–92.

30. On the holism of culture, see, for instance, Herbert, *Culture and Anomie*, pp. 1–28. Lévi-Strauss quoted on p. 5.

31. Seltzer, *Henry James*, pp. 25–58. Peter Brooks's description of the narrator's gaze could be just as aptly applied to Malinowski's in this case: "it searches for the indices that will allow him to figure [others] as naked, both as defenseless and as erotically engaged in a sphere of privacy" or of culture "that he would lay bare." *Body Work: Objects of Desire in Modern Narrative* (Cambridge, Mass.: Harvard University Press, 1993), p. 107.

32. In order to track the shifting and almost indecipherable pairings in the narrator's theory, Peter Brooks even includes graphs. See Brooks, *Body Work*, pp. 109, 113. What destabilizes these speculative relations even further, as Brooks notes, is the narrator's recognition that he may be a participant in the very affective and erotic calculus that he is trying to unveil. The range of possible permutations, I would argue, includes his erotic alignment with May Server, at one moment, and with Gilbert Long at another. Joseph Litvak alerted me to the homoerotic energies in the novel.

33. Anonymous review cited in Gargano, *Critical Essays*, p. 10.

34. Brodhead, *School of Hawthorne*, pp. 104–22.

35. Edwin Ardener links classical cultural anthropology with literary modernism, situating both movements within a broad postcolonial history: a "'stretching' of Western language by the rapid territorial expansion that took place in the age of discovery. It is characteristic of our present situation that the 'deconstruction' of those 'stretched' (but still Western) concepts should be necessary to accommodate the hitherto unaccommodated cultural representations of the muted majority of the world." "Social Anthropology and the Decline of Modernism," in *Social Anthropology and Language*, ed. Edwin Ardener (New York: Tavistock, 1971), p. 65. Also see Said, "Representing the Colonized," who

argues that the "fundamental historical problem of modernism" was the "suddenly achieved disruptive articulation" of the subaltern (p. 223).

36. Posnock, *Trial of Curiosity*, p. 4.

37. Edward Said, *Culture and Imperialism* (New York: Knopf, 1993). Eric Cheyfitz also traces the links between aesthetic expression and colonial politics in *The Poetics of Imperialism: Translation and Colonization from The Tempest to Tarzan* (New York: Oxford University Press, 1991).

38. On the "link between internal and external colonization" and "between domestic racial oppression and imperialism," see Hazel W. Carby, "'On the Threshold of Woman's Era': Lynching, Empire and Sexuality in Black Feminist Theory," *Critical Inquiry* 12 (Autumn 1985): 265.

39. Richard Godden, *Fictions of Capital: The American Novel from James to Mailer* (Cambridge: Cambridge University Press, 1990), pp. 30, 20, 37; Posnock, *Trial of Curiosity*, p. 5.

CHAPTER 2. NATHANIEL HAWTHORNE AND THE FETISH
OF RACE

1. Nathaniel Hawthorne, "Chiefly about War Matters," in *The Writings of Nathaniel Hawthorne*, vol. 17 (Boston: Houghton Mifflin, 1876), pp. 386, 361, 362.

2. Nathaniel Hawthorne, *The French and Italian Notebooks*, ed. Thomas Woodson, vol. 14 of the Centenary Edition (Columbus, Ohio: Ohio State University Press, 1980), pp. 173–4.

3. The category of woman by itself was associated with the primitive. In *Sexual Science: The Victorian Construction of Womanhood* (Cambridge, Mass.: Harvard University Press, 1989), Cynthia Eagle Russett demonstrates that in nineteenth-century science "woman was a developmental anomaly": "Like the Negro, woman stopped growing too soon." Interestingly, although the beard on the woman in Hawthorne's description seems to link her with the orang-utan, the usual lack of a beard was one more sign of woman's primitive development: "The female, failing to develop to the full the characteristic of the race, was 'an arrested male.' For the human race, then, 'possession of a beard must be regarded as a general characteristic of our race . . . when a female, from disease or mutilation or old age, assumes a resemblance to the male, the change is an advance'" (74–5). Russett also quotes Henry Maudsley on the "scientific" linkage between a "brute brain" and "an orang's brain" (67). T. Walter Herbert (who notes that Hawthorne transforms Praxiteles' Resting Satyr into a faun, "so as to remove the implication of brutish lust") argues for an association between Hawthorne's notebook description of the faun-woman and Margaret Fuller, in *Dearest Beloved: The Hawthornes and the Making of the Middle-Class Family* (Berkeley and Los Angeles: University of California Press, 1993), pp. 225–6.

4. Nathaniel Hawthorne, *The Marble Faun*, in *Nathaniel Hawthorne: Novels*, ed. Milli-

cent Bell (New York: Library of America, 1983), p. 1239. All further references will be indicated by page numbers in the text.

5. Hayden White discusses this "suppressed function" in "The Noble Savage: Theme as Fetish," in *First Images of America: The Impact of the New World on the Old*, vol. 1, ed. Fredi Chiappelli (Berkeley and Los Angeles: University of California Press, 1976), pp. 121–35. My essay draws from White's suggestions about the fetishistic nature of early images of primitivism.

6. Harriet Beecher Stowe, "Introductory Note" to *Agnes of Sorrento* (Boston: Houghton Mifflin), p. ix; Herman Melville, *Pierre; or, The Ambiguities*, in *Melville: Novels*, ed. Harrison Hayford (New York: Library of America, 1984), p. 322.

7. Shelley, quoted in R. S. Pine-Coffin, *Bibliography of British and American Travel in Italy to 1860* (Florence: Olschki, 1974), p. 39.

8. Samuel Topliff, quoted in Paul R. Baker, *The Fortunate Pilgrims: Americans in Italy, 1800–1860* (Cambridge, Mass.: Harvard University Press, 1964), p. 202.

9. Michel de Certeau, "Montaigne's 'Of Cannibals': The Savage 'I,'" in *Heterologies: Discourse on the Other*, trans. Brian Massumi (Minneapolis: University of Minneapolis Press, 1986), p. 86. For a different analysis of Montaigne and "the writing of savagery," see Eric Cheyfitz, *The Poetics of Imperialism* (New York: Oxford University Press, 1991).

10. Sebastian Muenster, "Cosmosgraphia," in Margaret T. Hodgen, *Early Anthropology in the Sixteenth and Seventeenth Centuries* (Philadelphia: University of Pennsylvania Press, 1964), p. 179. See chapters 2–5.

11. Herbert Spencer and Edward C. Hayes, quoted in George W. Stocking, *Race, Culture, and Evolution: Essays in the History of Anthropology* (Chicago: University of Chicago Press, 1982), pp. 242, 245.

12. On the contribution of Herder and other Romantic writers to the anthropological idea of culture, see Stocking, *Race, Culture, and Evolution*, pp. 65–6.

13. Ibid., p. 65.

14. Herbert Spencer, *Principles of Psychology*, 2nd ed., 2 vols. (London, Williams & Norgate, 1870), 1:422. On the importance of Lamarckian ideas of transmission in anthropology and other social thought, see Stocking, *Race, Culture, and Evolution*, pp. 234–69.

15. Richard Brodhead, *The School of Hawthorne* (New York: Oxford University Press, 1986), p. 77; Myra Jehlen, *American Incarnation: The Individual, the Nation, and the Continent* (Cambridge, Mass.: Harvard University Press, 1986), p. 173.

16. Frederick Douglass, *Narrative of the Life of Frederick Douglass, An American Slave, Written By Himself* (1845; rpt. New York: Penguin Books, 1986), p. 107.

17. Charles Ellwood, "The Theory of Imitation in Social Psychology," *American Journal of Sociology* 6 (1901): 731–6.

18. Quoted in Otto Olsen, *The Thin Disguise: Plessy v. Ferguson, A Documentary Presentation* (New York: Humanities Press, 1967), pp. 108–9.

19. Robert Park, "Racial Assimilation in Secondary Groups," *American Journal of Sociology* 12 (1906): 232; Ulysses S. Weatherly, "Race and Marriage," *American Journal of Sociology* 9 (1904): 435.

20. Olsen, *Thin Disguise*, pp. 111–12; see Eric Sundquist, "Mark Twain and Homer Plessy," in *The New American Studies: Essays from Representations*, ed. Philip Fisher (Berkeley and Los Angeles: University of California Press), pp. 112–38. Sundquist's essay analyzes Twain's *Pudd'nhead Wilson* for the novel's extraordinary representation of legal and racial theories that supported Reconstruction.

21. Richard H. Millington, *Practicing Romance: Narrative Form and Cultural Engagement in Hawthorne's Fiction* (Princeton: Princeton University Press, 1992), p. 178; Jehlen, *American Incarnation*, p. 173.

22. For a related analysis of Hawthorne's strategies of irresolution, see Jonathan Arac, "The Politics of *The Scarlet Letter*," in *Ideology and Classic American Literature*, ed. Sacvan Bercovitch and Myra Jehlen (Cambridge, Mass.: Harvard University Press, 1986), pp. 247–66.

23. Olsen, *Thin Disguise*, p. 109.

24. Alfred Kroeber, "Eighteen Professions," *American Anthropologist* 17 (1915): 285; Kroeber, *Nature of Culture* (Chicago: University of Chicago Press, 1952), p. 22.

25. Edward B. Tylor, *Primitive Culture*, 2 vols. (1871; rpt. New York: Putnam, 1920), 1:1, 27; Stocking, *Race, Culture, and Evolution*, p. 265.

26. Frederick Douglass, quoted in Sundquist, "Mark Twain and Homer Plessy," p. 119.

27. William Thomas, "The Scope of Folk Psychology," *American Journal of Sociology* 1 (1895): 439; Frederick Jackson Turner, "The Significance of the Frontier in American History," reprinted in Turner, *The Frontier in American History* (New York: Holt, 1920), pp. 22–3.

28. John W. Burgess, "The Ideal of an American Commonwealth," *Political Science Quarterly* 10 (1895): 407; Burgess, "Germany, Great Britain, and the United States," *Political Science Quarterly* 19 (1904): 2; Woodrow Wilson, "The Ideals of America," *Atlantic Monthly* 90 (1902): 730.

29. William Z. Ripley, "Acclimatization," *Political Science Quarterly* 48 (1896): 662–75, 779–93; Daniel Brinton, *Races and Peoples: Lectures on the Science of Ethnography* (Philadelphia: McKay, 1901), pp. 278–83. For a discussion of the influence of racial thinking on U.S. policies, see John Higham, *Strangers in the Land: Patterns of American Nativism, 1860–1925*, 2nd ed. (New Brunswick, N.J.: Rutgers University Press, 1988).

30. Nathaniel Hawthorne, *Life of Franklin Pierce* (Boston: Ticknor, 1852), pp. 111–12; Hawthorne, quoted in James R. Mellow, *Nathaniel Hawthorne in His Times* (Boston: Houghton Mifflin, 1980), pp. 562, 536; Hawthorne, quoted in Arlin Turner, *Nathaniel Hawthorne, A Biography* (New York: Oxford University Press, 1980), p. 370.

31. Hawthorne, quoted in Mellow, *Hawthorne*, p. 549; Henry James, *Nathaniel Hawthorne*, in *Henry James: Literary Criticism*, vol. 2, ed. Leon Edel (New York: Library of America, 1984), p. 425. Hawthorne, quoted in Mellow, *Hawthorne*, pp. 502–3.

32. Tylor, *Primitive Culture*, 1:19, 24, 158. Recent scholarship has examined the history of British and American anthropology in light of a range of ideological

pressures in the later nineteenth century, including the perceived dangers from emergent feminism and from a threat of mass democracy that produced anxious responses in the mostly liberal anthropologists. The "seething problems" most often mentioned by anthropologists were the threats from below. Important studies of the ideological pressures on anthropology include J. W. Burrow, *Evolution and Society: A Study in Victorian Social Theory* (Cambridge: Cambridge University Press, 1966): Curtis Hinsley, *Savages and Scientists: The Smithsonian Institution and the Development of American Anthropology, 1846–1910* (Washington, D.C.: Smithsonian Institution Press, 1981); and George W. Stocking, Jr., *Victorian Anthropology* (New York: Free Press, 1987).

33. Tylor, *Primitive Culture*, 1:25.

34. See Stocking, chapter 6, "Victorian Cultural Ideology and the Image of Savagery (1780–1870)," in *Victorian Anthropology*, pp. 186–237; Herbert Spencer, *The Principles of Sociology*, 3 vols. (1876; rpt., New York: Appleton, 1923), 1:73, 61, 73, 68, 77, 79, 59.

35. Stocking, *Victorian Anthropology*, pp. 53–6.

36. William John Thomas, quoted in Stocking, *Victorian Anthropology*, p. 56; Tylor, *Primitive Culture*, 2:227; Alfred Russel Wallace, *A Narrative of Travels on the Amazon and Rio Negro*, 3rd ed. (New York: Ward, Lock, 1890), pp. 83, 180.

37. Stocking, *Victorian Anthropology*, p. 36; Wallace, *Travels on the Amazon*, pp. 261, 231–2.

38. Thomas Farnham, quoted in Roy Harvey Pearce, *Savagism and Civilization* (1953; rev. ed., Berkeley and Los Angeles: University of California Press, 1988), p. 65; Washington Irving, *The Sketch Book of Geoffry Crayon, Gent.*, in *Washington Irving: History, Tales and Sketches*, ed. James W. Tuttleton (New York: Library of America, 1983), pp. 1011–12.

39. J. F. McLennan, *Primitive Marriage* (1965; rpt. Chicago: University of Chicago Press, 1970), p. 9.

40. See F. S. Schwarzbach, "'Terra Incognita' – An Image of the City in English Literature, 1820–1855," in *The Art of Travel: Essays on Travel Writing*, ed. Philip Dodd (London: Cass, 1982), pp. 61–84. In *The Manufacturing Population of England* (1833), Peter Gaskell drew upon anthropological researches in Africa to argue that the high temperatures and promiscuous intermingling in factories were changing the moral and physical constitution of mill children. He claimed adult workers exhibited short stature and broad noses and lips.

41. Lewis Henry Morgan, *Ancient Society* (New York: Holt, Rinehart & Winston, 1877; rpt. Tucson: University of Arizona Press, 1985).

42. *Eclectic Review*, quoted in Schwarzbach, "*Terra Incognita*," p. 75.

43. Bayard J. Taylor, *Views A-Foot* (1848; rpt. Philadelphia: McKay, 1979), p. 171.

44. Tylor, *Primitive Culture*, 1:16.

45. Johann Bachofen, quoted in George Stocking, "Some Problems in the Understanding of Nineteenth-Century Cultural Evolutionism," in *Readings in the History of Anthropology*, ed. Regna Darnell (New York: Harper & Row, 1974), p. 423.

46. Hawthorne, "War Matters," p. 319.

47. Sacvan Bercovitch, *The Office of the Scarlet Letter* (Baltimore: John Hopkins University Press, 1991).

48. Henry Summer Maine, *Ancient Law* (1861; rpt. Tucson: University of Arizona Press, 1986), p. ix; Sigmund Freud, *Totem and Taboo* (1918; rpt. New York: Knopf, 1946), pp. 320–34. Comparisons between savage law and Kantian ethics also appear in the writings of Tylor, Frazer, McLennan, and Malinowski.

49. Millington, *Practicing Romance*, p. 178. Millington's recent analysis of an "unresolvable opposition" in Hawthorne's novel is representative in this respect: "In the territory that constitutes *The Marble Faun*, a plot of redemption confronts a plot of condemnation; maturation confronts regression; freedom confronts restriction; a cynical, cosmopolitan narrator confronts a pious, sentimental one; plot confronts travelogue; an aesthetic of originality confronts an aesthetic of imitation; moral complexity confronts moral absolutism" (p. 178).

50. Mellow notes (*Hawthorne*, p. 468) that the practice of stationing soldiers along the Corso had been established in 1848 in response to the republican revolution. French troops under Napoleon III had been called in to put down the revolt.

51. One of Hawthorne's notebook entries imagines the response of the American populace if the Roman Carnival were transplanted to U.S. soil: "the whole street would go mad in earnest, and come to blows and bloodshed, were the population to let themselves loose to the extent we see here." *French and Italian Notebooks*, p. 502. Robert S. Levine reads the Carnival scene in the context of antebellum American discourse on Catholicism, in "'Antebellum Rome' in *The Marble Faun*," *American Literary History* 2 (Spring 1990): 19–38.

52. Stocking summarizes the telescoping of pagan and Catholic belief by British folklorists: "In general, 'popular antiquities' represented the continuity of error and superstition in an enlightened age, and were explained in terms of the impact of Roman Catholicism on prior pagan belief." *Victorian Anthropology*, pp. 54–5.

53. See Bercovitch, *Office of the Scarlet Letter*, and Arac, "Politics of *The Scarlet Letter*." I am indebted to Bercovitch's analysis of the aesthetics of liberal compromise in Hawthorne.

54. Tylor, *Primitive Culture*, 1:494.

55. Analyzing the importance of painting and sculpture in Hawthorne's romance, Wendy Steiner explores the way *The Marble Faun* represents categories of aesthetic culture. Steiner calls the novel "one of the great imaginative works of aesthetic theory." *Pictures of Romance: Form against Context in Painting and Literature* (Chicago: University of Chicago Press, 1988), p. 92.

56. Quoted in Alan Tractenberg, *The Incorporation of America: Culture and Society in the Gilded Age* (New York: Hill & Wang, 1982), p. 150.

57. Patrick Buchanan, ABC Television Network, *This Week with David Brinkley*, December 8, 1991, quoted in "In Buchanan's Words," *Washington Post* (February 29, 1992): 9.

CHAPTER 3. THE DISCIPLINE OF MANNERS

1. Patrick Brantlinger discusses the fiction he calls "imperial gothic" in *Rule of Darkness: British Literature and Imperialism, 1830–1914* (Ithaca: Cornell University Press, 1988), pp. 227–54.
2. The 1902 *Bookman* review, by F. M. Colby, appears in James W. Gargano, *Critical Essays on Henry James: The Late Novels* (Boston: Hall, 1987), pp. 47–8.
3. Thorstein Veblen, *The Theory of the Leisure Class* (1899; rpt. New York: Penguin Books, 1983), pp. 213, 243, 47.
4. Henry James, "Matthew Arnold," in *Henry James: Literary Criticism*, vol 2, ed. Leon Edel (New York: Library of America, 1984), p. 730.
5. Edward Burnett Tylor, *Primitive Culture*, vol. 1 (1871; rpt. New York: Putnam, 1920), pp. 25, 26, 32; Matthew Arnold, *Culture and Anarchy* (1869; rpt. Cambridge: Cambridge University Press, 1988), p. 49. George Stocking argues that Tylor chose his title in the context of Arnold's popular polemic on culture. See "Matthew Arnold, E. B. Tylor, and the Uses of Invention," in *Race, Culture, and Evolution* (Chicago: University of Chicago Press, 1968).
6. Tylor, *Primitive Culture*, 1:1, 8, 12.
7. Arnold, *Culture and Anarchy*, pp. 49, 52.
8. Michel de Certeau, *The Practice of Everyday Life*, trans. Steven F. Rendall (Berkeley and Los Angeles: University of California Press, 1984), p. 62.
9. Tylor, *Primitive Culture*, 1:7; Arnold, *Culture and Anarchy*, p. 105. For a discussion of the loss of the earlier civic notion of "society" in nineteenth-century America, see Thomas Bender, "The Erosion of Public Culture: Cities, Discourses, and Professional Disciplines," in *The Authority of Experts*, ed. Thomas L. Haskell (Bloomington: Indiana University Press, 1984), pp. 84–106.
10. Norbert Elias, *The Civilizing Process*, 2 vols.: vol. 1, trans. Edmund Jephcott (1939; rpt. New York: Pantheon Books, 1982). See chapter 1, "The Sociogenesis of the Difference between *Kultur* and *Zivilization*," pp. 1–49. With colonialism, Elias argues, the "civilization" newly claimed by the middle classes becomes "the upper class to the non-European world" (p. 49).
11. Johannes Fabian, *Time and the Other: How Anthropology Makes Its Object* (New York: Columbia University Press, 1983), p. 46.
12. Ibid, pp. 45–51.
13. Henry Mayhew, *London Labour and the London Poor*, vol. 1 (1861; rpt. New York, 1968), pp. 1, 5. For a discussion of the "anthropological imagination" in Mayhew's study, see Christopher Herbert, *Culture and Anomie: Ethnographic Imagination in the Nineteenth Century* (Chicago: University of Chicago Press, 1991), pp. 204–52. Josiah Strong, *Our Country:Its Possible Future and Its Present Crisis* (New York: American Home Missionary Society, 1885), p. 129.
14. James, "Matthew Arnold," p. 728; Veblen, *Theory of the Leisure Class*, pp. 66, 392.
15. Thomas L. Haskell discusses the "hunger for expert guidance" in *The Emergence of Professional Social Science* (Urbana: University of Illinois Press, 1977).

16. Mayhew, *London Labour*, p. 1; Thackeray quoted in F. S. Schwarzbach, *"Terra Incognita* – An Image of the City in English Literature, 1820–1855," in *The Art of Travel*, ed. Philip Dodd (London: Cass, 1982), p. 68; John F. McLennan, *Primitive Marriage* (1865; rpt. Chicago: University of Chicago Press, 1970), p. 69; Arnold, *Culture and Anarchy*, p. 161–2.

17. Pierre Bourdieu, *Outline of a Theory of Practice*, trans. Richard Nice (Cambridge: Cambridge University Press, 1977), pp. 169, 233. Lionel Trilling's phrase for manners, "a culture's hum and buzz of implication," is in "Manners, Morals, and the Novel," in *The Liberal Imagination* (New York: Scribner, 1950), p. 206.

18. T. J. Jackson Lears, *No Place of Grace: Antimodernism and the Transformation of American Culture, 1880–1920* (New York: Pantheon Books, 1981); Lears, "From Salvation to Self-Realization," in *The Culture of Consumption*, ed. Richard Wight Fox and T. J. Jackson Lears (New York: Pantheon Books, 1983), p. 6.

19. Bourdieu, *Outline of a Theory of Practice*, p. 233.

20. Tylor, *Primitive Culture*, 1:19, 24.

21. Ibid., 1:17.

22. See Leonardo Benevolo, *History of Modern Architecture*, trans. H. J. Landry (Cambridge, Mass.: MIT Press, 1971), vol. 1, and Siegfried Giedion, *Mechanization Takes Command* (New York: Norton, 1969).

23. Brooks Adams, *The Law of Civilization and Decay* (New York: Macmillan, 1896), p. 383: Giedion, *Mechanization Takes Command*, p. 339.

24. Edith Wharton, *The Custom of the Country*, in *Edith Wharton: Novels*, ed. R. W. B. Lewis (1913; rpt. New York: Library of America, 1985), p. 669.

25. See Benevolo, *History of Modern Architecture*, 1:160–3.

26. Edith Wharton and Ogden Codman, Jr., *The Decoration of Houses* (1897; rpt. New York: Norton, 1978); Certeau, *Practice of Everyday Life*, p. 63.

27. Edmund Wilson, "Justice to Edith Wharton," in *Edith Wharton: A Collection of Critical Essays*, ed. Irving Howe (Englewood Cliffs, N.J.: Prentice-Hall, 1962), p. 23; Mary Douglas and Baron Isherwood, *The World of Goods: Towards an Anthropology of Consumption* (London: Penguin Books, 1978), pp. 10, 5.

28. Henry James, *The Awkward Age*, vol. 9 of the New York Edition (New York: Scribner, 1908), p. 239; Edith Wharton, *The Age of Innocence*, in *Edith Wharton: Novels*, p. 1282; anonymous review, quoted in Gargano, *Critical Essays*, p. 46.

29. Anonymous review, in Gargano, *Critical Essays*, 46; ibid, p. 40.

30. Bronislaw Malinowski, *Crime and Custom in Savage Society* (1926; rpt. Totowa, N.J.: Rowman & Allanheld, 1985), p. 2; Robert Lowie, *Primitive Society* (1920; rpt. New York: Harper & Row, 1961), p. 387.

31. James, *Awkward Age*, pp. 51–2.

32. See, for instance, Karen Haltunnen, "Gothic Imagination and Social Reform: The Haunted Houses of Lyman Beecher, Henry Ward Beecher, and Harriet Beecher Stowe," in *New Essays on Uncle Tom's Cabin*, ed. Eric J. Sundquist (Cambridge: Cambridge University Press, 1986), pp. 107–34.

33. Eric Hobsbawm, "Mass-producing Traditions: Europe, 1870–1914," in *The Invention of Tradition*, ed. Eric Hobsbawm and Terence Ranger (Cambridge: Cambridge University Press, 1983), p. 269.

34. Malinowski, *Crime and Custom in Savage Society,* p. 1.
35. James G. Frazer, *The Golden Bough: A Study in Magic and Religion* (1890–1915; rpt. 1 vol., abridged ed., New York: Collier, 1963), p. 1.
36. McLennan, *Primitive Marriage,* pp. 121–2.
37. Ibid., p. 69; Tylor, *Primitive Culture,* 1:155; Frazer, *Golden Bough,* p. 64.
38. Tylor, *Primitive Culture,* 1:31.
39. Tylor, in fact, drew an analogy between ethnographic "relics" and urban statistics as parallel evidence about culture. Anthropology is possible because of the great "regularity in the composition of societies of men": the "general level of art and knowledge" of any culture is as regular as the "recurrence, year after year, of such obscure and seemingly incalculable products of national life as the numbers of murders and suicides," the "proportion of the very weapons of crime," and "the annual regularity of persons accidentally killed in London streets." *Primitive Culture,* 1:10–11.
40. Ibid., p. 11; Hobsbawm, "Mass-producing Traditions," p. 268.
41. Lears, *No Place of Grace,* p. 137. Lears also describes efforts among the American elite to harness the perceived vitality of primitive culture for a weakening human stock. Psychologist G. Stanley Hall, for instance, writing that "civilization is at root morbific and sure to end in reaction and decay," urged a program of development for children in which they would "repeat the experiences and emotions of their primitive ancestors" (pp. 146–7).
42. See Hobsbawm's introduction to *Invention of Tradition,* pp. 1–14. He notes that "Anthropology may help to elucidate the differences, if any, between invented and old traditional practices" (p. 10). Yet the ability of anthropology to identify the traditional made it one of the disciplines through which middle-class observers attempted to determine the role of "the irrational" in the regulation of the social order. See "Mass-producing Traditions," p. 268.
43. Emile Durkheim, *The Elementary Forms of The Religious Life* (1912; rpt. New York: Free Press, 1965), p. 43; Veblen, *Theory of the Leisure Class,* pp. 235–6; Sigmund Freud, *Totem and Taboo* (1913; rpt. New York: Vintage Books, 1946), p. 125. For an extended study of Freud's use of anthropology, see Edwin R. Wallace, *Freud and Anthropology* (New York: International Universities Press, 1983).
44. Fred G. See, for instance, describes a structure of "possession" in James's late discourse in which power is generated through the "violent exclusion of a ritual victim." "Henry James and the Art of Possession," in *Literary Realism: New Essays,* ed. Eric J. Sundquist (Baltimore: Johns Hopkins University Press, 1982), p. 121. See's essay links James's fiction – in particular, *The Spoils of Poynton* – to Rene Girard's arguments about ritual violence and the "theoretical geography of Culture" that such violence puts in place.
45. Peter Brooks argues that James's novels constitute a fiction of melodrama, in *The Melodramatic Imagination: Balzac, Henry James, Melodrama, and the Mode of Excess* (New York: Columbia University Press, 1985). Brooks's analysis of the mode of melodrama discovers persuasive affiliations between Gothic fiction, early anthropology, and James's excessive imagery. I do not agree, however,

that James's fiction, like melodrama, is designed to "strip the facade of manners" so as "to discover the primal sources of being" (pp. 3, 197) and argue instead that manners themselves constitute the essential or "primal" category for James's imagination.

46. Henry James, *The Golden Bowl*, vols. 23 and 24 of the New York Edition (New York: Scribner, 1909), 2:234.
47. Mark Seltzer, *Henry James and the Art of Power* (Ithaca: Cornell University Press, 1984), p. 89.
48. James, *Golden Bowl*, 2:38.
49. Seltzer, *Henry James*, p. 61.
50. Edith Wharton, *The House of Mirth*, in *Edith Wharton: Novels*, p. 109.
51. Ibid., pp. 239, 227–8.
52. Malinowski, *Crime and Punishment in Savage Society*, pp. 72, 100.
53. Lears, *No Place of Grace*, p. 137.
54. Bourdieu, *Outline of a Theory of Practice*, p. 171.
55. Ludwig Wittgenstein, *Remarks on Frazer's "Golden Bough,"* trans. A. C. Miles, ed. Rush Rhees (Retford, U.K.: Brynmill Press, 1979), pp. 2–3.
56. Ibid., pp. 17, 13, 8, 16.
57. Ibid., p. 16.
58. "In other words, one might begin a book on anthropology this way: When we watch the life and behavior of men all over the earth we see that apart from what we might call animal activities, taking food &c., &c., men also carry out actions that bear a peculiar character and might be called ritualistic." Ibid., p. 7.
59. James, *Golden Bowl*, 2:229–300.
60. Tylor, *Primitive Culture*, 1:10. Malinowski's phrase appears in manuscript materials held at the London School of Economics. George Stocking quotes from the manuscript in his article "Malinowski's Encounter with Freudian Psychoanalysis," in *Malinowski, Rivers, Benedict and Others: Essays on Culture and Personality*, ed. George W. Stocking, Jr. (Madison: University of Wisconsin Press, 1986), pp. 13–49. Introducing the notebook passage, Stocking writes, "His goal – as suggested in some undated early notes toward his never realized theoretical book on kinship – was to solve 'the fundamental Mystery of the Social': 'When we understand how this system [kinship] comes into being, how it imposes the prototype values of future social morals: respect for authority, personal loyalty, subordination of impulses to feelings – when we discover that, we have really answered (in a concrete instance, but one which allows of a simple generalization by extension) the main question: how does society impress its norms on the individual?' "
61. William Graham Sumner, *Folkways* (1907; rpt. New York: Arno Press, 1979), p. 418.
62. Malinowski, *Argonauts of the Western Pacific* (1922; rpt. Prospect Heights, Ill.: Waveland Press, 1984), p. lxix. James Boon argues Malinowski introduced literary realism into ethnography. Unlike Frazer's massive collection of rites from all parts of the globe, "Malinowski's prose accounts adopt mechanistic

models and conventions of space-time isolates that are associated with realist and naturalist novels (and literary theories)." *Other Tribes, Other Scribes* (Cambridge: Cambridge University Press, 1982), p. 11.

63. Elias, *Power and Civilization*, 2:275–6.

64. Sumner, *Folkways*, p. 34.

65. Claude Lévi-Strauss, "The Anthropologist and the Human Condition," in *The View from Afar*, trans. Joachim Neugroschel (New York: Basic Books, 1985), p. 34. Dewey's remarks, from his *Human Nature and Conduct*, are cited in an epigraph to Malinowski's *Sex and Repression in Savage Society* (1927; rpt. Chicago: University of Chicago Press, 1985).

66. Sumner, *Folkways*, pp. 36, 38, 52.

67. William James, *The Principles of Psychology* (1890; rpt. New York: Dover, 1950), 1:121–2.

68. James, *Golden Bowl*, 2:292.

69. Ruth Benedict, quoted in Margaret M. Caffrey, *Ruth Benedict: Stranger in This Land* (Austin: University of Texas Press, 1989), p. 161; Ruth Benedict, "The Science of Custom: The Bearing of Anthropology on Contemporary Thought," *Century Magazine* 117 (April 1929): 641–9.

70. On Wharton's reading, see R. W. B. Lewis, *Edith Wharton: A Biography* (New York: Fromm, 1985), pp. 56, 108, 230. Wharton's description of Malinowski's work and her comment on the "inward relation to reality" appear in *The Letters of Edith Wharton*, ed. R. W. B. Lewis and Nancy Lewis (New York: Simon & Schuster, 1988), pp. 546, 102. The quotation from Durkheim is taken from Emile Durkheim, *Selected Writings*, trans. Anthony Giddens (Cambridge: Cambridge University Press, 1972), p. 232.

71. Franz Boas, "Psychological Problems in Anthropology," in *A Franz Boas Reader*, ed. George W. Stocking (Chicago: University of Chicago Press, 1974), pp. 252–3.

72. Robert Lowie, *Are We Civilized?: Human Culture in Perspective* (New York: Harcourt, Brace, 1929), p. 48; Claude Lévi-Strauss, *Tristes Tropiques*, trans. John Weightman and Doreen Weightman (New York: Atheneum, 1984), p. 85.

73. Malinowski, *Argonauts of the Western Pacific*, p. 156.

74. Ibid., pp. 106, 397.

75. Ibid., p. 22.

76. Trilling, "Manners, Morals, and the Novel," p. 212.

77. Wharton, *Age of Innocence*, p. 1021. Further references will be indicated by page numbers in the text.

78. Malinowski, *Sexual Lives of Savages* (1929; rpt. Boston: Beacon Press, 1987), p. 13.

79. Valéry quoted in Philip Fisher, *Making and Effacing Art: Modern American Art in a Culture of Museums* (New York: Oxford University Press, 1991), pp. 10–11. I have drawn from Fisher's discussion of the authenticity invested in museum objects from "alien societal, religious, and artistic communities" (p. 20). Alan Tractenberg discusses the establishment of American museums during this period in *The Incorporation of America: Culture and Society in the Gilded Age* (New

York: Hill & Wang, 1982). On the socializing function of museums as "civic temples," see Pierre Bourdieu, "Artistic Taste and Cultural Capital," in *Culture and Society: Contemporary Debates*, ed. Jeffrey C. Alexander and Steven Seidman (Cambridge: Cambridge University Press, 1990), pp. 205–15.

80. Fisher, *Making and Effacing Art*, p. 29.
81. Edith Wharton, *A Backward Glance*, in *Edith Wharton: Novellas and Other Writings*, ed. Cynthia Griffin Wolff (New York: Library of America, 1990), p. 781.
82. "Symbolic violence is that form of domination which, transcending the opposition usually drawn between sense relations and power relations, communication and domination, is only exerted *through* the communication in which it is disguised." Bourdieu, *Outline of a Theory of Practice*, p. 237.
83. Malinowski, *Crime and Custom in Savage Society*, p. 55. Malinowski discusses conditional curses in chapter 12, "Specific Legal Arrangements," pp. 60–2, and in *Sexual Lives*, chapter 11, "The Magic of Love and Beauty," pp. 290–318.
84. Malinowski, *Crime and Custom in Savage Society*, pp. 72, 9, 73, 11.
85. Malinowski, *Sexual Lives of Savages*, p. 323.
86. Though I do not classify James and Wharton unreservedly with Lears's antimodernists, I do claim that the enterprise of writing about manners as they practiced it was revitalized and redefined for a modern order that both writers faced with real reservations. Lears argues that "American antimodernism unknowingly provided part of the psychological foundation for a streamlined liberal culture appropriate to twentieth-century consumer capitalism." *No Place of Grace*, p. 6.

CHAPTER 4. HENRY JAMES AND MAGICAL PROPERTY

1. Edith Wharton, *A Backward Glance*, in *Edith Wharton: Novellas and Other Writings*, ed. Cynthia Griffen Wolff (New York: Library of America, 1990), p. 949.
2. John Carlos Rowe, *The Theoretical Dimensions of Henry James* (Madison: University of Wisconsin Press, 1984), p. 89; David Lodge, introduction to Henry James, *The Spoils of Poynton* (New York: Penguin Books, 1987), p. 16.
3. Anonymous review in the *Edinburgh Review* (January 1903), reprinted in James W. Gargano, ed., *Critical Essays on Henry James: The Late Novels* (Boston: Hall, 1987), p. 31.
4. Jackson Lears describes the enthusiasts who believed that "premodern art promised spiritual comfort and therapeutic restoration." *No Place of Grace* (New York: Pantheon Books, 1981), p. 190. Also see Thomas Richards, who locates the beginnings of a new belief in "the transformative power of interior decoration" in the Crystal Palace exhibition. *The Commodity Culture of Victorian England* (Stanford: Stanford University Press, 1990), p. 29.
5. "Sociologically, Society can be seen as a system of quasi-kinship relationships which was used to 'place' mobile individuals during the period of structural differentiation fostered by industrialization and urbanization." Leonore

Davidoff, *The Best Circles: Society Etiquette and the Season* (London: Croom Helm, 1973), p. 15.

6. Emile Durkheim, *Suicide: A Study in Sociology* (1897; New York: Free Press, 1951), pp. 252–3.

7. Asa Briggs lifts this phrase from Thomas Hardy's diary, from a passage in which Hardy records a conversation with a friend about comparative culture. *Victorian Things* (Chicago: University of Chicago Press, 1988), p. 18. Hardy adds that "this barbaric idea . . . is, by the way, also common to the highest imaginative genius – that of the poet," an idea that many anthropologists themselves advanced about the nature of poetry.

8. Max Weber, "Class, Status, Party," in *From Max Weber: Essays in Sociology*, trans. and ed. H. H. Gerth and C. Wright Mills (New York: Oxford University Press, 1946), pp. 187–9.

9. Thorstein Veblen, *The Theory of the Leisure Class* (1899; rpt. New York: Penguin Books, 1983), p. 12.

10. Edith Wharton, *The Age of Innocence*, ed. R. W. B. Lewis (New York: Library of America, 1985), pp. 1018, 1051, 1069.

11. Henry James, *The American Scene* (Bloomington: Indiana University Press, 1968), p. 279; James, *The Spoils of Poynton*, vol. 10 of the New York Edition (New York: Scribner 1908), pp. xiii, 79. All further references will be indicated by page numbers in the text.

12. Henry James, quoted in F. O. Matthiessen, *The James Family: Including Selections from the Writings of Henry James, Senior, William, Henry, and Alice James* (New York: Knopf, 1947), pp. 331, 330.

13. Bronislaw Malinowski, *The Sexual Lives of Savages* (1929; rpt. Boston: Beacon Press, 1987), p. 14.

14. Henry James, *The Complete Notebooks of Henry James*, ed. Leon Edel and Lyall H. Powers (New York: Oxford University Press, 1987), p. 215.

15. Lewis Henry Morgan argued that the "growth of property" led to the discrimination of "degrees of consanguinity," in *Systems of Consanguinity and Affinity of the Human Family* (Washington, D. C.: Smithsonian Institution, 1870), p. 14. Countless controversies over kinship have followed since Morgan, but modern definitions still describe it as a system that "has to do with the allocation of rights and their transmission from one generation to the next." See Rodney Needham, "Remarks on the Analysis of Kinship and Marriage," in *Rethinking Kinship and Marriage*, ed. Rodney Needham (London: Tavistock, 1971), p. 3.

16. Max Beerbohm, "1880," *Yellow Book* 4 (January 1895): 275–83.

17. William Graham Sumner, *Folkways* (1906: rpt. New York: Arno Press, 1979), p. 189; Veblen, *Theory of the Leisure Class*, p. 66.

18. Lawrence Stone, *An Open Elite? England, 1540–1880* (Oxford: Clarendon Press, 1984), p. 404.

19. Veblen, *Theory of the Leisure Class*, p. 153; Sumner, *Folkways*, p. 47; Charlotte Perkins Gilman, *Women and Economics* (1898; rpt. Harper & Row, 1966), p. 204.

20. Mark Seltzer, *Bodies and Machines* (New York: Routledge, 1992), p. 48.

21. Durkheim, *Suicide*, p. 255; Gilman, *Women and Economics*, p. 204.

22. Jean Baudrillard establishes this argument theoretically. Rather than repro-
    ducing a "moral and rationalistic connotation" for commodity fetishism, an
    effective critique must "reconstitute the *process of fetishization*" in terms of a
    logic of cultural differentiation and social power. *For a Critique of the Political
    Economy of the Sign*, trans. Charles Levin (Telos Press, 1981), pp. 88, 90.
23. Seltzer notes that a domestic animism finds its way into a novel like *Uncle Tom's
    Cabin*, but he shows Stowe's anxious exorcism of the idea of "living property,"
    in *Bodies and Machines*, pp. 47–8. For a different view of this problem in *Uncle
    Tom's Cabin*, see Gillian Brown, *Domestic Individualism: Imagining Self in
    Nineteenth-Century America* (Berkeley and Los Angeles: University of California
    Press, 1990).
24. Nancy Armstrong, *Desire and Domestic Fiction* (New York: Oxford University
    Press, 1987), pp. 6, 8.
25. Walter Bagehot, *Economic Studies*, ed. Richard Holt Hutton (London: Long-
    mans, 1880), p. 81.
26. Quoted in Briggs, *Victorian Things*, p. 15.
27. Ibid., p. 13.
28. On the Pitt Rivers Museum, see ibid., pp. 29–31, and W. R. Chapman,
    "Arranging Ethnology: A. H. L. F. Pitt Rivers and the Typological Tradi-
    tion," in *Objects and Others: Essays on Museums and Material Culture*, ed. George
    Stocking (Madison: University of Wisconsin Press, 1985). On the develop-
    ment of ethnological collections and museums in the United States, see Curtis
    Hinsley, Jr., *Savages and Scientists: The Smithsonian Institution and the Development of
    American Anthropology, 1846–1910* (Washington D.C., Smithsonian Institution
    Press, 1981).
29. Marcel Mauss, *The Gift: Forms and Functions of Exchange in Archaic Societies*, trans.
    Ian Cunnison (1925; rpt. New York: Norton, 1967), p. 43.
30. On the interchangeable social functions of homes and museums, see Lynn
    Wardley, "Woman's Voice, Democracy's Body, and *The Bostonians*," *ELH 56*
    (1989): 658.
31. Veblen, *Theory of the Leisure Class*, pp. xiii, 160, 65, 56, 67.
32. James Frazer, *Totemism and Exogamy*, vol. 1 (1887; rpt. London: Dawsons,
    1968), p. 3; Mauss, *Gift*, p. 48, 42–3.
33. Frazer, *Totemism and Exogamy*, 4:62–3; Freud, *Totem and Taboo: Resemblances
    between the Psychic Lives of Savages and Neurotics*, trans. A. A. Brill (1818; rpt. New
    York: Vintage Books, 1946), p. 153.
34. One of the exceptions to this tendency to repeat rather than analyze the
    fetishistic desire is Fred G. See, "Henry James and the Art of Possession," in
    American Realism: New Essays, ed. Eric J. Sundquist (Baltimore: Johns Hopkins
    University Press, 1982), pp. 119–37. See's analysis of the "space of possession"
    in *The Spoils of Poynton* is insightful about the multidimensional nature of
    ownership in the novel, a possession "sometimes erotic, sometimes materialis-
    tic, sometimes demonic, but always the dramatic struggle of one will to cir-
    cumscribe and use another" (p. 120). See's semiotic treatment of the theme,
    however, tends to overlook the historical dimension of possession and its pow-

ers, leaving out a clear sense of the particular power relations and the context of consumption that structure the novel's economy of desire.

35. On the economic meanings of James's "appreciation," see Jean-Christophe Agnew, "The Consuming Vision of Henry James," in *The Culture of Consumption: Critical Essays in American History, 1880–1980,* ed. Richard Wightman Fox and T. J. Jackson Lears (New York: Pantheon Books, 1983), p. 93.

36. Christopher Herbert, *Culture and Anomie* (Chicago: University of Chicago Press, 1990), pp. 42, 60, 29.

37. For a study of the way contemporary social-scientific debates on women and reproduction also recast the bourgeois family in James's fiction, see Susan L. Mizruchi, "Reproducing Women in *The Awkward Age,*" *Representations 38* (1992): 101–30.

38. James, *Complete Notebooks,* p. 215.

39. This is the title of one of Morgan's monographs (Chicago: University of Chicago Press, 1965).

40. Anonymous reviews, collected in Gargano, *Critical Essays on James,* pp. 29–31.

41. Mauss, *Gift,* p. 11.

42. James, *Complete Notebooks,* pp. 121, 216, 217.

43. Malinowski, *Sexual Lives of Savages,* pp. 6, 11.

44. Pierre Bourdieu, *Outline of a Theory of Practice,* trans. Richard Nice (Cambridge: Cambridge University Press, 1977), p. 237.

45. Tylor, "A Method of Investigating the Development of Institutions: Applied to Laws of Marriage and Descent," in *Readings in Kinship and Social Science,* ed. Nelson Graburn (New York: Harper & Row, 1971), p. 20.

46. Freud, *Totem and Taboo,* p. 21, 20; Karen Haltunnen, *Confidence Men and Painted Women: A Study of Middle-Class Culture in America, 1830–1870* (New Haven: Yale University Press, 1982), p. 160.

47. Malinowski, *Sexual Lives,* pp. 38–9; Bourdieu, *Outline of a Theory of Practice,* p. 41.

48. Malinowski, *Sexual Lives,* p. 39.

49. David Lodge describes Mrs. Gereth as "a kind of bawd or female pander" to Fleda in his introduction to the Penguin edition, p. 9.

50. Jack Goody, *Property, Death, and the Ancestors* (London: Tavistock, 1962), p. 354.

51. Quoted in Haltunnen, *Confidence Men,* p. 111.

52. Veblen, *Theory of the Leisure Class,* pp. 131, 24.

53. Ibid., pp. 64, 289, 64, 134.

54. George Simmel, "Fashion," in *On Individual and Social Forms,* ed. Donald N. Levine (Chicago: University of Chicago Press, 1971), pp. 298–301.

55. Stone, *An Open Elite?,* p. 72; Simmel, "Fashion," p. 301.

56. Simmel, "Fashion," p. 306.

57. Mauss, *Gift,* p. 73.

58. Ibid., pp. 3, 11–12.

59. Ibid., pp. 64, 74, 8.

60. Ibid., pp. 72, 41, 35.

61. This is the tradition of Lewis Hyde's *The Gift: Imagination and the Erotic Life of Property* (New York: Vintage Books, 1979).

62. Mauss, *Gift*, pp. 4, 80.
63. Bourdieu, *Outline of a Theory of Practice*, p. 192.
64. See Mauss, *Gift*, p. 7.
65. Ibid., p. 79.
66. For feminist analysis of the contemporary anthropological literature on the purchase and bartering of wives, see Gayle Rubin, "The Traffic in Women: Notes on the Political Economy of Sex," in *Toward an Anthropology of Women*, ed. Rayna Reiter (New York: Monthly Review Press, 1975), pp. 157–210, and Nanneke Redclift, "Rights in Women: Kinship, Culture and Materialism," in *Engels Revisited: New Feminist Essays*, ed. Janet Sayers, Mary Evans, and Nanneke Redclift (London: Tavistock, 1987), pp. 113–44. For analysis of marriage and the marketplace in fiction from this period, see Walter Benn Michaels, "The Contracted Heart," *New Literary History* 21 (Spring 1990): 495–531; Margit Stange, "Personal Property: Exchange Value and the Female Self in *The Awakening*," *Genders* 5 (Summer 1989): 106–19; and Mizruchi, "Reproducing Women in *The Awkward Age*."
67. Mauss, *Gift*, p. 42.
68. See Lodge, introduction to Penguin edition, p. 5.
69. Mauss, *Gift*, p. 54
70. James, *Complete Notebooks*, pp. 217, 218.
71. Ibid., pp. 134, 127.
72. Mauss, *Gift*, pp. 35, 14.
73. See Richard Brodhead, *The School of Hawthorne* (New York: Oxford University Press, 1989).
74. Bourdieu, *Outline of a Theory of Production*, p. 197.
75. For interpretations of the place and implications of primitivism within modernism, see Marianna Torgovnick, *Gone Primitive: Savage Intellects, Modern Lives* (Chicago: University of Chicago Press, 1990), and James Clifford, *The Predicament of Culture: Twentieth-Century Ethnography, Literature, and Art* (Cambridge, Mass.: Harvard University Press, 1988).

CHAPTER 5. EDITH WHARTON AND THE ALIENATION OF DIVORCE

1. Edith Wharton, *The Custom of the Country*, in *Edith Wharton:Novels*, ed. R. W. B. Lewis (New York: Library of America, 1985), p. 805. All further references will be indicated by page numbers in the text.
2. Elaine Tyler May, *Great Expectations: Marriage and Divorce in Post-Victorian America* (Chicago: University of Chicago Press, 1980), p. 2; William L. O'Neill, *Divorce in the Progressive Era* (New Haven: Yale University Press, 1967), pp. 20–5.
3. May, *Great Expectations*, p. 7; Greely quoted in Glenda Riley, *Divorce: An American Tradition* (New York: Oxford University Press, 1991), p. 62.
4. "Broca on Anthropology." *Anthropological Review* 6 (1868): 46.
5. James Weir, Jr., "The Effect of Female Suffrage on Posterity," *American Naturalist* 29 (1895): 825.

6. Elsie Clews Parsons, *The Old-fashioned Woman* (New York: Putnam, 1913), pp. v–vi.
7. Charlotte Perkins Gilman, *Women and Economics*, ed. Carl N. Degler (1898; rpt. New Yorker: Harper & Row, 1966), p. 49.
8. On ethnographic and anatomical waxworks and other exhibitions (including Peale's and Reimer's), see Richard D. Altick; *The Shows of London* (Cambridge, Mass.: Belknap, 1978), pp. 333–49, and Barbara Kirshenblatt-Gimblett, "Objects of Ethnography," in *Exhibiting Cultures: The Poetics and Politics of Museum Display*, ed. Ivan Karp and Steven D. Lavine (Washington, D.C.: Smithsonian Institution Press, 1991), especially pp. 397–407. Donna Haraway analyzes the representational techniques of the American Museum of Natural History in "Teddy Bear Patriarchy: Taxidermy in the Garden of Eden, New York City, 1908–1936," *Social Text* 11 (Winter 1984–5): 20–64.
9. Cuvier quoted in Sander L. Gilman, "Black Bodies, White Bodies: Toward an Iconography of Female Sexuality in Late Nineteenth-Century Art, Medicine, and Literature," in *"Race," Writing, and Difference*, ed. Henry Louis Gates, Jr. (Chicago: University of Chicago Press, 1985), pp. 23–35. Gilman claims that "Sarah Bartmann's sexual parts, her genitalia and her buttocks, serve as the central image for the black female throughout the nineteenth century. And the model of de Blainville's and Cuvier's descriptions, which center on the detailed presentation of the sexual parts of the black, dominates all medical description of the black during the nineteenth century. To an extent, this reflects the general nineteenth-century understanding of female sexuality as pathological: the female genitalia were of interest partly as examples of the various pathologies which could befall them but also because the female genitalia come to define the female for the nineteenth century" (p. 235).
10. Gilman notes that, in contrast to the autopsy reports of Hottentot women, which focused on supposed anomalies of the labia and hymen, in "autopsies of black males from approximately the same period, the absence of any discussion of the male genitalia whatsoever is striking"; "Black Bodies, White Bodies," pp. 236–7. On wax "Venuses," see Altick, *Shows of London*, pp. 338–42; and Kirshenblatt-Gimblett, "Objects of Ethnography, pp. 398–401. Kirshenblatt–Gimblett discusses "group life" installations, as does Ira Jacknis in "Franz Boas and Exhibits," in *Objects and Others: Essays on Museums and Material Culture*, ed. George W. Stocking, Jr. (Madison: University of Wisconsin Press, 1985), pp. 75–111.
11. Mark Seltzer, *Bodies and Machines* (New York: Routledge, 1992), p. 90; Haraway, "Teddy Bear Patriarchy," p. 21.
12. "For women," Simmel writes, "species characteristics and personal characteristics coincide more. If women are indeed closer to the dark, primitive forces of nature, then their most essential and personal characteristics are more strongly rooted in the most natural, most universal, and most biologically important functions. And it further follows that this unity of womankind in which there is less distinction between universal and individual elements than among men must be reflected in the greater homogeneity of each wom-

an's nature." "Prostitution," in *George Simmel: On Individuality and Social Forms,* ed. Donald N. Levine (Chicago: University of Chicago Press, 1971), p. 123.

13. Altick, *Shows of London,* p. 339; Jacknis, "Franz Boas," p. 401; James Boon, "Why museums make me sad," in Karp and Lavine, *Exhibiting Cultures,* pp. 255–77.

14. Jacknis, "Franz Boas," pp. 102–3; Kirshenblatt-Gimblett, "Objects of Ethnography," p. 398.

15. Peter Stallybrass and Allon White, *The Politics and Poetics of Transgression* (Ithaca: Cornell University Press, 1986), p. 171.

16. Jacknis, "Franz Boas," p. 92. Haraway discusses the American Museum as an "ideal incarnation" of the ethos of a new class of American capitalists ("Teddy Bear Patriarchy," 54). For analysis of the department store mannequin, see Stuart Culver, "What Manikins Want: *The Wonderful Wizard of Oz* and *The Art of Decorating Dry Goods Windows,*" *Representations* 21 (Winter 1988): 97–116, and Rachel Bowlby, *Just Looking: Consumer Culture in Dreiser, Gissing, and Zola* (New York: Columbia University Press, 1981).

17. Jacknis, "Franz Boas," pp. 100, 93.

18. Quoted in Altick, *Shows of London,* p. 496.

19. Bronislaw Malinowski, *Argonauts of the Western Pacific* (1922; rpt. Prospect Heights, Ill.: Waveland Press, 1984), p. 18.

20. Pierre Bourdieu analyzes the theoretical gap that constitutes this kind of anthropological vision: "The anthropologist's particular relation to the object of his study contains the makings of a theoretical distortion inasmuch as his situation as an observer, excluded from the real play of social activities by the fact that he has no place (except by choice or by way of a game) in the system observed and has no need to make a place for himself there, inclines him to a hermeneutic representation of practices, leading him to reduce all social relations to communicative relations and, more precisely, to decoding operations . . . . And exaltation of the virtues of the distance secured by externality simply transmutes into an epistemological choice the anthropologist's objective situation, that of the 'impartial spectator', as Husserl puts it, condemned to see all practice as spectacle." *Outline of a Theory of Practice,* trans. Richard Nice (Cambridge: Cambridge University Press, 1977), p. 1.

21. Havelock Ellis, *Man and Woman: A Study of Human Secondary Sexual Characteristics* (London: Walter Scott, 1894), p. 371; W. K. Brooks, *The Law of Heredity* (Baltimore: John Murphy, 1883), p. 257. Cynthia Eagle Russet discusses these theories of male variability and female species identity in *Sexual Science: The Victorian Construction of Womanhood* (Cambridge, Mass.: Harvard University Press, 1989), pp. 78–103.

22. Cynthia Griffin Wolff, *A Feast of Words: The Triumph of Edith Wharton* (New York: Oxford University Press, 1977), pp. 251–3. Also see Elizabeth Ammons, *Edith Wharton's Argument with America* (Athens: University of Georgia Press, 1980).

23. Gillian Brown analyzes the "transcendental femininity" of nineteenth-century sentimentalism in *Domestic Individualism: Imagining Self in Nineteenth-Century America* (Berkeley and Los Angeles: University of California Press, 1990),

pp. 64–5. The feminist argument for a female agency "seeing, judging, and directing" social forces is expressed by Mary Ritter Beard, quoted in Nancy F. Cott, *The Grounding of Modern Feminism* (New Haven: Yale University Press, 1987), p. 37.

24. Ammons, *Edith Wharton's Argument*, p. 119; Peter Conn, *The Divided Mind: Ideology and Imagination in America, 1898–1917* (Cambridge: Cambridge University Press, 1983), p. 190.

25. James George Frazer, *The Golden Bough* (New York: Macmillan, 1922), pp. 12–16.

26. Charles Darwin, *Charles Darwin's Diary of the Voyage of H.M.S. "Beagle,"* ed. Nora Barow (Cambridge: Cambridge University Press, 1934), pp. 118–19; Darwin, *Journal of Researches* . . . (New York: Appleton, 1896), p. 206; C. Gilman, *Women and Economics*, pp. 120, 119. Jean Baudrillard critiques the "romanticism of productivity" in Western thought, its theoretical underpinnings in anthropology and its implications for Marxist and progressive analyses of production. The enlightenment myth of *homo economicus* naturalized the market and its forms, Baudrillard argues, yet even the critique of the market employed a similar naturalization of production and of "man's predestination for the object transformation of the world," a "simulation model bound to *code* all human material in terms of value, finality, and production" (p. 19). This naturalization of production results in a "critical imperialism" over tribal societies that matches economic and political imperialisms, since the practices of "all other cultures were entered in its museum as vestiges of its own image" (pp. 88–9).

27. C. Gilman, *Women and Economics*, p. 120.

28. Seltzer, *Bodies and Machines*, p. 95.

29. Wolff, *Feast of Words*, p. 245.

30. Edith Wharton, *The Letters of Edith Wharton*, ed. R. W. B. Lewis and Nancy Lewis (New York: Simon & Schuster, 1988), p. 547.

31. Emile Durkheim, *The Elementary Forms of Religious Life,* trans. L. W. Swain (New York: Free Press, 1965), p. 395.

32. Edith Wharton, "George Eliot," *Bookman* (May 1902): 247.

33. Renato Rosaldo, *Culture and Truth: The Remaking of Social Analysis* (Boston: Beacon Press, 1989), p. 69.

34. Stephen Greenblatt, *Shakespearian Negotiations: The Circulation of Social Energy in Renaissance England* (Berkeley and Los Angeles: University of California Press, 1988), p. 16.

35. Amy Kaplan examines the issues of spectatorship and publicity that inform class relations in Wharton's *House of Mirth* and shape the conditions of Wharton's own authorship, in *The Social Construction of American Realism* (Chicago: University of Chicago Press, 1988), pp. 65–103. More broadly, Philip Fisher discusses the new conditions of public visibility and performance in American culture during this era, in "Appearing and Disappearing in Public," in *Reconstructing American Literary History*, ed. Sacvan Bercovitch (Cambridge, Mass.: Harvard University Press, 1986), pp. 155–88.

36. Edith Wharton, *A Backward Glance*, in *Novellas and Other Writings,* ed. Cynthia Griffin Wolff (New York: Library of America, 1990), p. 781.

37. See, for instance, Seltzer's *Bodies and Machines* for an analysis of the way "relations of power in the realist text are insistently articulated along lines of sight" and of how the "erotization of power and of the power of making-visible" function in fiction (p. 96).

38. Seltzer, *Bodies and Machines*, p. 96.

39. Bronislaw Malinowski, *The Sexual Lives of Savages* (1929; rpt. Boston: Beacon Press, 1929), p. lxxxiii; Malinowski, *Argonauts of the Western Pacific*, p. 6.

40. Bonislaw Malinowski, *A Diary in the Strict Sense of the Word* (Stanford: Stanford University Press, 1989), p. 130; Raymond Firth calls the diary an "obsessional document" and discusses the reception of the book by leading anthropologists in his introduction to this edition.

41. See, for instance, May, *Great Expectations*, p. 3.

42. C. Gilman, *Women and Economics*, p. 227.

43. For a provocative discussion of the anxious exploration of the uncertain boundaries between marriage, prostitution, and free love in the literature of this era, see Walter Benn Michaels, "The Contracted Heart," *New Literary History* 21 (Spring 1990): 495–531. On the figure of the actress as a model for selfhood, see Philip Fisher, *Hard Facts: Setting and Form in the American Novel* (New York: Oxford University Press, 1987), pp. 162–9.

44. Edith Wharton, *The House of Mirth*, in *Edith Wharton: Novels*, p. 142. All further references will be indicated by page numbers in the text.

45. On Wharton's analysis in this novel of the marketplace values that structure social life, see Wai-chee Dimock, "Debasing Exchange: Edith Wharton's *The House of Mirth*," *PMLA* 100 (October 1985): 783-92.

46. This is the opposition Wharton asserts in her memoir *A Backward Glance* (in *Wharton: Novellas and Other Writings*) when she writes that "a frivolous society can acquire dramatic significance only through what its frivolity destroys. Its tragic implication lies in its power of debasing people and ideals" (p. 940).

47. Haraway, "Teddy Bear Patriarchy," 53, 42.

48. It is important to note that Moffatt's "dead sure thing" is a reference to a Wall Street deal involving speculation on water rights and that it signifies certainty only in relation to the conditions of risk and speculative investment of the marketplace. Similarly, Walter Benn Michaels analyzes Lily's death as a speculative action that Lily takes only to capitalize on a valuable uncertainty about her intentions. Taking the drug is Lily's final gamble: "To 'rouse speculation' *in* herself, she must, as it were, speculate *on* herself," for "only speculative acts can guarantee" a restoration of interest in Lily. *The Gold Standard and the Logic of Naturalism* (Berkeley and Los Angeles: University of California Press, 1987), p. 233. In my brief reading of *The House of Mirth*, I stress Wharton's attraction to the certainty of a taxonomic order of identity as a counter-force to the exciting but unsettling insights of what Michaels calls "Wharton's extraordinary market psychology" and argue that *The Custom of the Country* is the novel in which Wharton presents a freer expression of (as well as a stronger resistance to) a speculative or market-based model of the self.

49. Margaret Higonnet, "Speaking Silences: Women's Suicide," in *The Female Body in Western Culture: Contemporary Perspectives*, ed. Susan Rubin Suleiman (Cam-

bridge, Mass.: Harvard University Press, 1986), p. 78; Strindberg quoted in Higonnet, p. 78.

50. C. Gilman, *Women and Economics*, pp. 153, 262, 97, 63, 186, 168, 72, 23.
51. Elaine Showalter, "The Death of the Lady (Novelist)," in *The New American Studies*, ed. Philip Fisher (Berkeley and Los Angeles: University of California Press, 1991), p. 37.
52. For a discussion of the cult of the "beautiful corpse," see Higonnet, "Speaking Silences," pp. 74–6.
53. Walter Benjamin discusses the polarities of "cult value" and "exhibition value" in his well-known essay "The Work of Art in the Age of Mechanical Reproduction," in *Illuminations*, trans. Harry Zohn (New York: Schocken Books, 1968), pp. 217–52.
54. Stephen Greenblatt, *Marvelous Possessions: The Wonder of the New World* (Chicago: University of Chicago Press, 1991), p. 6.
55. Higonnet, "Speaking Silences," p. 72.
56. Weir, "Effect of Female Suffrage," 824.
57. C. Gilman, *Women and Economics*, p. 259; Weir, "Effect of Female Suffrage," 818.
58. Weir, "Effect of Female Suffrage," 817.
59. Lewis Morgan, *Ancient Society* (1877; rpt. Tucson: University of Arizona Press, 1985), p. 505.
60. Weir, "Effect of Female Suffrage," 824.
61. See Edith Wharton, *A Backward Glance*, in *Edith Wharton: Novellas*, p. 856.
62. C. Gilman, *Women and Economics*, p. 63.
63. Ibid., p. 208.
64. For instance, this is May's explanation, in *Great Expectations*, of why Americans "were more eager to marry . . . and more willing to divorce" (p. 11).
65. Weir, "Effect of Female Suffrage," 823; Simmel, "Prostitution," p. 124.
66. Herbert Spencer, *The Principles of Sociology*, 3rd ed., vol. 1 (London: Williams & Norgate, 1897), p. 652; Edward Westermarck, *The History of Human Marriage*, vol. 3 (London: Macmillan, 1921), p. 145.
67. Spencer, *Principles of Sociology*, p. 645; Westermarck, *History of Human Marriage*, p. 119; Spencer, *Principles*, pp. 648, 651. On the anxieties about the fertility and health of the "better" classes, see for instance, Russett, *Sexual Science*, pp. 118–25.
68. C. Gilman, *Women and Economics*, p. 303.
69. Westermarck, *History of Human Marriage*, p. 153.
70. On Wharton's divorce and possibilities for remarriage, see R. W. B. Lewis, *Edith Wharton: A Biography* (New York: Fromm International, 1975), pp. 332–45. Lewis discusses the mock-heroic epithet "Angel of Devastation" on page 247.

Index

Adams, Henry, 12, 81
Agnew, Jan-Christophe, 214 n11, 230 n35
Altick, Richard, 232 n8
Ammons, Elizabeth, 233 n22
animism, 120, 127, 131, 143, 168; *see also* fetishism; totemism
anthropology, 7, 75–8, 158, 168; and anthropologists, 10, 16, 84, 213 n2, 233 n20; science of, 17, 19, 99–100, 126, 131–2, 152, 164, 201, 224 n42; and women, 163–70, 192–3
Appadurai, Arjun, 114
Arac, Jonathan, 219 n22
Ardener, Edwin, 216 n35
Armstrong, Nancy, 124
Arnold, Matthew, *Culture and Anarchy*, 5, 71–7, 144, 155
art, 6, 42–5, 180–1; as high culture, 6, 28–9; and primitivism, 65–6, 80–1; as symbolic capital, 148, 157–9
Asad, Talal, 214 n6
assimilation, 26, 48, 66–7
atavism, 63, 69, 168, 172–6, 199, 201

Bachofen, Johann, 56–7
Bartmann, Sarah, 165–6, 232 n9
Baudrillard, Jean, 229 n22, 234 n26
Beerbohm, Max, 119
Bender, Thomas, 222 n9

Benedict, Ruth, 102
Benjamin, Walter, 197
Bentham, Jeremy, 145
Bercovitch, Sacvan, 59, 214 n9, 221 n53
Boas, Franz, 103, 149, 167–9, 170, 198
Boon, James, 167, 225 n62
Bourdieu, Pierre: on the epistemology of anthropologists, 233 n20; on manners, 7, 78–9; on social crisis and discourse, 95–6, 112; on symbolic capital, 149, 158; on symbolic violence, 110–11, 137; on museums, 227 n79
Bowlby, Rachel, 233 n16
Brantlinger, Patrick, 222 n1
Briggs, Asa, 126, 228 n7
Brinton, Daniel, 48
Broca, Paul, 163
Brodhead, Richard, 214 n9, 218 n15, 231 n73
Brooks, Peter, 216 n31, 224 n73
Brown, Gillian, 229 n23, 233 n23
Buchanan, Patrick, 66
Burrow, J. W., 220 n32

capitalism, 22, 163, 182–4, 191
Carby, Hazel, 217 n38
Certeau, Michel de, 9–10, 32–3, 73, 83
Chapman, W. R., 229 n28
Cheyfitz, Eric, 217 n37, 218 n9